Part One

DON'T FORGET YOUR GASMASK

Part Two

DON'T FORGET YOUR PAYBOOK

To,

Ted,

With best wishes

from

Rex Wellard

Rex A Wellard

To my wife Joan

And
For my children
And grandchildren

Part One

DON'T FORGET YOUR GASMASK

Recollections of my life as an evacuee in the war –
And before.

A few months prior to world war two, preparation was made for the mass evacuation of children from London, and so it was that they went to school one morning at the beginning of September 1939 completely unaware that they would not be coming home later that day, and furthermore, would not be coming home for many more days, months, or years to come.

Trams, buses, and trains, were commandeered to take them to far-away places deemed to be safe from aerial bombardment where they were entrusted into the care of complete strangers.

I was one of those children and this is my story.

Part Two

DON'T FORGET YOUR PAYBOOK

Recollections of my experiences and escapades in the Royal Navy.

Following the war, conscription into the armed services for men aged eighteen continued until late into the 1960s. The period of service was for two years and at the beginning of 1948 I became eligible.

I always had a fancy to be a sailor, and rather than wait to be called up and detailed into the army, which was the most likely event, I volunteered for the Royal Navy and signed up for seven years.

It was never my intention to gain promotion, or make a career of it, just a determination to enjoy the experience. This is a light - hearted account of that colourful part of my life.

I picked up a small brown case which was lying on the kitchen table, together with a paper bag containing a few sandwiches, and called out, "I'm going now mum."

"You Rexy, don't forget your gasmask!" She cried out, emerging from the scullery wiping her hands on a tea-towel.

'Why does she keep calling me Rexy, it's babyish, why can't she call me Rex,' I thought, as I shouldered the gas-mask. I said, "I've got it mum. Ta-ta."

"Aren't you going to give your mum a big kiss then?"

She had been fussing over me all morning.

"Hurry up then or I'll be late, the second bell's gone."

From our house in Glenister Road, Greenwich, the hand-held bell which was being rung in the playground of Calvert Road Junior School by the duty teacher could be clearly heard letting me know that I should be ready to file into the main hall for assembly. The bell had been rung five minutes earlier to allow us to be in the playground in a state of preparedness and I knew from experience that if I left now I could file into the hall for morning assembly with the last of the stragglers.

Mum hugged me into her apron which she always wore over her dress like most women in our street, although unlike many her apron was always clean and stiffly starched. However clean it was it could not hide the smell of sisal, and hemp, from the onerous job she had in a nearby rope factory. Poor mum, hands like leather but still not tough enough to stop the splinters of rope piercing through the skin into the flesh, nor was she hard enough to stop the tears flowing as she hugged me close into her body. She had been dreading this moment for a week now since she and my father had attended a meeting at the school concerning the impending war and the evacuation of children to a safe area. No firm date had been set at the meeting, but the parents who had volunteered their children for evacuation had been told that they should prepare for the event on the 29th of August, or soon after.

The headmistress, in addressing a meeting of the parents, knew that they were aware of the likelihood of war with Germany even though at that time peace was still being brokered by the Prime Minister, Neville Chamberlain. Newspapers had been warning of the possibility of war for the past year with some minor level of evacuation having already begun - air-raid shelters had been constructed, or were under construction, and gas masks issued. She outlined to them the reasons and advantages of sending their children away from London until such time that it was safe for them to return, and concluded by saying, "The teachers will tell your children the reasons for evacuation and explain to them that it is for their safety that they are going away for a while. You will also do your best to prepare them for this undertaking and have them attend school each day ready to go with a small case, or bag, holding a change of clothing and a set of pyjamas. On the actual day that they do depart the procedure will be the same as the preceding days and hopefully be less upsetting for them."

It was the 2nd day of September 1939 and the last time I answered the call-bell for Calvert Road School. I arrived in the playground and joined the tail-end of the line of children funnelling through the double doors leading into the assembly hall. Nothing unusual, except that it was Saturday which had led to rumours that this was to be 'the' day.

Morning assembly was carried out as usual, after which, we followed procedures that we had been practicing since the previous Tuesday. I joined my teacher, Mr Roberts, and a pre-arranged group of classmates, in a corner of the hall, and we were marched in an orderly fashion to the Infants playground at the front of the school which flanked the Old Woolwich Road. Other teachers with similar groups were already there, and further teachers with their groups followed until all the children being evacuated were assembled. Previous practice runs had ended there, after which we were led back into the school for a normal day's activity, but today, a small gate leading onto The Old Woolwich Road was opened, which hitherto had always remained shut, and group by group we were marched through it. .

Trams numbered 36, and 38, ran along the Old Woolwich Road from Plumstead to the Embankment, and I was surprised to see that four of them were lined up directly outside of the gate completely empty, with the driver and conductor of each drawn together in a huddle discussing the likely destination with some of the parents.

"Somewhere in Kent I should think. We're taking them to New Cross Gate Station and they're getting a train from there."

We were ushered onto the trams in as orderly fashion as could possibly be maintained under the circumstances which ensued, for the parents of the children had got word and were gathered on the pavements and in the road to see us go, hoping to say their last-minute goodbyes. The trams ran on metal tracks in the centre of the road and in crossing from the school gate, across the pavement and part of the road, some children had broke away from there groups crying, and running to their mothers. At the same time some mothers were pushing through to their children in an effort to embrace them and make last minute goodbyes. A few had a change of mind at the last minute and took their children home, much to the disappointment of the teachers who were trying to maintain a semblance of order.

I caught a glimpse of my mother, still wearing the clean starched floral pinafore over a cotton dress, trying to attract my attention with nervous and frantic waving of her hand. At the time, I was boarding the tram and managed a quick wave in return. Thinking afterwards of that moment, I had pangs of guilt, for I was high on the excitement of this new adventure and more intent on running up the stairs to gain one of the front seats at the rounded end of the tram, which I was able to do, together with the most boisterous and noisy members of my class. If I had not been engaged in horseplay when the tram moved off, and looked back to wave goodbye, I would have seen my mother shedding a tear. I would also have seen my dad, who had arrived late after taking time off from work to bid me goodbye, comforting my mum with his arm around her shoulder.

At New Cross Gate Station we were paraded onto one of the platforms where after a few minutes a steam train puffed in and stopped alongside. All the doors clattered noisily as they were flung open and along with most of the other children I jostled to remain with my friends as we were bundled onto the train. My closest friend was a boy in my class named Stephen Wright, who was inseparable from his uncle Brian, a year younger than him. This was a fact difficult to grasp, even by the enlightened who knew that Brian had a sister some twenty years older than himself, others just refused to believe it. Window seats were a premium and neither Stephen, Brian, nor I managed to get one, we did however share the same compartment which was very smartly furnished with red plush seats.

Many of the children had never been on a train before and to each and every one of us it was a journey into the unknown, even so, had it had no significance at all it would still have been high adventure. However, high adventure turned to boredom long before the train reached its destination, after about fifteen minutes to be more precise, and by then there were children arguing, pushing, and pulling, in the corridor, with teachers unable to give control other than by the occasional raucous shout. This was due to the fact that they were giving solace, and sympathetic attention, to the numerous children who were now crying and appealing to be taken home.

The train completed its journey and our destination became evident by the large signs on the platform. HASTINGS. The excitement grew with intensity when it was realised that this was a seaside town. (A short time into the war all station names were removed, together with most other signs indicating towns, or strategic locations, to make things difficult for the enemy should they invade).

In 1938, a new underground car park had been built in Hastings for one thousand cars, and it was to there that we were taken by coaches (at that time known by us as charabancs) where we joined hundreds of children who had also arrived from other London schools, and elsewhere. This was used as a distribution centre from where the various schools being evacuated were taken to the numerous schools dotted in and around Hastings which were to accommodate them.

We were each given a bag containing a bar of chocolate, a packet of biscuits, and a bottle of lemon-squash, and after a short wait, in which time, like most of the other children I ate my chocolate and some of my biscuits, we were ferried to Lower

Street School in St Leonards which was to be our new edifice of learning.

The main hall in the school was buzzing with excitement. Canvassing had previously been undertaken in all areas local to the school for families to provide homes for us, so apart from the teachers, councillors, billeting officers, and we evacuees, the crowd in the hall also included dozens of would-be foster parents. Some could take just a single child, others could take several depending on the number of spare bedrooms they had available, the conditions being that a single evacuee must have his own room; boys billeted together could share a room, and this also applied to girls, but boys and girls billeted together had to have separate rooms.

The allocation of children to homes then began in alphabetical order, an arrangement which penalises the Yates, and the Youngs, the Wilsons, and the Wellards; my first experience of the drawback in having a name near the end of the alphabet.

At six-o-clock that evening I was still awaiting my turn to be found a foster home, having listened to over a hundred names being called out, and billeting arrangements made for each. Some foster parents were making it difficult by trying to pick children which they found more appealing, or reject children that had been allocated to them. Eventually, only five evacuees remained in the hall. Apart from myself, Stephen Wright and his uncle Brian, there were two brothers, Arthur and Gordon Younghusband, neither of whom I knew very well. I was hoping to be billeted with Stephen and Brian, but they were dealt with out of sequence and went off with foster parents who could only take two.

Finally, Arthur, Gordon, and I, were called to the table where the billeting arrangements were being made, and after checking off our names on the register the billeting officer told us that we were going to be taken to our new home and that we must report back to the school at ten-o-clock the next morning; she then escorted us there. This was about a five minute walk from Lower Street School and turned out to be in Bohemia Road, a busy thoroughfare which channelled traffic directly to the seafront at St. Leonards-on-Sea. To our surprise the billeting officer led us into the police station at No 20, which was the address she had been given, but fortunately the desk sergeant directed us to a side door which was the entrance to the flat above.

In response to the billeting officer's knock, the door was opened by a very tall elderly woman in a cotton dress whose angular frame filled the doorway. Her lined face was dominated by a large bony nose, which seemed to become more prominent as she gave us a welcoming smile.

"Mrs Banks?" The billeting officer enquired.

Mrs Banks nodded, and said, "Yes."

"You indicated a willingness to take three evacuees?"

We, the three evacuees in question, Arthur, Gordon, and myself, by now tired and hungry, stood behind the billeting officer as she made arrangements with Mrs Banks, our gasmasks and scant belongings arranged on the many concrete steps which led up to her front door.

I looked past Mrs Banks to a carpeted staircase, a luxury that I never enjoyed at 43, Glenister Road, and one doubtless not enjoyed by the Younghusbands, which indicated to me that the flat above would be a nice place to stay.

Mrs Banks invited us in and we all trooped up the stairs at the top of which we turned right through a door which opened into a large living room with windows that looked out onto Bohemia Road. Muffled street noises gave company to the loneliness of the room which was well furnished in an austere manner.

"I won't stop, Mrs Banks, I've still got a lot of things to see to. I'll let the children do their own introductions." She handed Mrs Banks a pad. "If you will just sign here I'll be on my way, and don't forget, if there are any problems, or further information you require, pop into the office at any time."

When Mrs Banks came back into the room after seeing the billeting officer to the door, Arthur was sitting on one of two armchairs in the room, and I was sitting on the other, with Gordon perched on the front edge of Arthur's chair.

"You must be worn out," Mrs Banks remarked sympathetically. "How long have you been travelling?"

Arthur answered, as the eldest he took it upon himself to be the spokesman. "Since this morning. We went to school at our usual time."

She looked at a sheet of paper in her hand that had been given to her by the billeting officer which obviously held our names and ages, and probably guidelines on dealing with the guardianship of evacuees. Then looking towards Arthur, she said, "You're Arthur I take it, and this must be your brother Gordon?"

Arthur and Gordon both nodded.

Mrs Banks turned to me. "Then you must be Rex."

Like Arthur and Gordon I nodded too.

"I think the cat's got your tongues," Mrs Banks quipped, bending down and looking at Gordon closely. "Have you had anything to eat?"

Arthur spoke again. "We had some sandwiches on the train this morning."

"And nothing since?" Mrs Banks seemed surprised. "Didn't they give you anything when you arrived at the school?"

"They gave us this when we first got down here," said Arthur, looking at me and Gordon who were content that he should continue the dialogue with Mrs Banks.

She took the paper bag proffered by Arthur and withdrew the bottle of lemon quash and what remained of the packet of biscuits; like us, Arthur had eaten the bar of chocolate. Gordon and I held out our bags and Mrs Banks put the items on the table.

"Well, it's too late now for me to prepare you a meal. I'll run you a bath and before you go to bed you can have some of the biscuits and a glass of lemon squash. Bring your things and I'll show you to your bedroom."

Mrs Banks led us through a door adjacent to the one we had entered which opened onto a large bedroom with three single beds, two to the right of the door, and one to the left. Gordon and Arthur were allocated each of the pair, and I was given the other. She then told us to unpack our cases, and get into our pyjamas while she ran a bath.

The spacious bathroom had a large white enamel bath with plumbed-in hot and cold water and a soft rug on the floor which looked most inviting, but inviting as it looked I told Mrs Banks that I did not need a bath as I had had one the night before.

"Well it won't do you any harm to have another," Mrs Banks said, as she ran hot and cold water into the bath and ushered

Gordon and me into it. This was a luxury strange to us, especially with the bath emptied and refilled with fresh water for Arthur, a far cry from my bath the night before. The plumbing arrangement in our house certainly never catered for such luxury, which was no more than mains water to the cistern in the outside toilet, and a single tap serving a shallow butler sink in the scullery. (The scullery was a single story extension to the rear of the kitchen).

Bath night at home involved a procession of us all through the same water. My mother would take a large cast iron saucepan, fill it with water from the sink, and pour it into a copper which was brick-built into a corner of the scullery. The copper had a grate beneath it into which a coal-fire was laid and lit. When the water was hot she would take down an oval galvanised bath which hung from a nail on the scullery wall, place it on the floor and add water; hot from the copper, and cold from the tap. I would bathe first in a minimal amount of warm water followed by my sister Jean, with a little more hot water added to maintain the temperature. My mother followed with a little more hot water, and finally, my father enjoyed his bath, albeit the dirtiest, with the remainder of the hot water.

After biscuits and lemon squash it was bedtime. Mrs Banks instructed us to join her in kneeling by one of the beds where she led us in simple prayers which we followed line-by-line asking God's blessings for us and our families. Praying by the bedside was unfamiliar territory to us which we found amusing. Afterwards, although exhausted by the long and eventful day, it was difficult to sleep and Arthur, Gordon, and I, lay in the dark discussing all that had happened and the current situation we were in, including our impression of Mrs Banks.

"She's a bit like our granny," Arthur said. An opinion I could not concur with, having never seen their granny, she was certainly nothing like mine.

Arthur had just turned eleven. He was nearly two years older than me, tall for his age, lean and streetwise; I had noticed him in the playground where he cut a figure telling dirty jokes. Gordon was a year younger and contrastingly different to Arthur, even allowing for the three year age difference. He was chubby with a round rosy bucolic face not befitting a Londoner of the time, and with his gentle and naive manner he soon became a favourite with Mrs Banks.

The following morning we were up early and to our surprise introduced to Mrs Banks' son, Ernest. He was partly dressed in the uniform of a policeman (shirtsleeve order) tucking into a fried breakfast, his tunic hanging on the back of his chair. When he stood up to greet us he was enormous, a heavily built man well over six feet tall in his big black boots, and although smiling it belied fearsomeness.

After breakfast Mrs Banks directed Arthur to Lower Street School and we headed off there. Assembled in the main hall, everyone shared a mixture of anticipation, and insecurity, but each of us was pleased to be with familiar faces. The kind matronly figure of our headmistress, Mrs Thompson, stood gently smiling on a dais at the end of the hall, whilst we were all seated on the floor. She had been accompanied to Hastings by Mr Clothier, Mr Roberts, and Mr Munday, (the latter two, both Welshmen), and Miss Thomas, who was not much more than a teenager herself. Mr Gill, the deputy headmaster, had stayed behind with a few other teachers to maintain a programme of teaching for the children who had remained at home.

I was glad that Mr Roberts had not stayed behind, unlike the other two male teachers, who I found boring, his classes were fun, and often exciting. He was in his mid-twenties and it was obvious that he liked children, often swinging them around in the playground, or carrying them on his shoulders. His chalk throwing at misbehaving or inattentive pupils kept the class on it's toes, he was a dead shot and rarely missed, although now and again he did, and on one occasion he aimed at a boy and caught another in the eye, only it was not a piece of chalk, it was a tennis ball which he had confiscated earlier and was laying on his desk alongside another confiscated item - a bag of sweets. He picked up the bag of sweets and took them to the boy who had started sobbing, more through shock than pain, saying, "Sorry Manners," Manners being the boy's name, "You should have ducked, now keep awake." Handing him the sweets, he said. "Take these they'll help you forget about it." I remembered the incident well because the sweets had been mine, and at the end of the lesson

Mr Roberts stopped me as I was leaving the classroom and gave me tup'pence for some more. With unusual honesty regarding such a situation, I said, ""They were only ha'pence, Sir." "Well get some for me," he replied.

Alongside Mrs Thompson stood a man whom she introduced as Mr Baker, the headmaster of Lower Street School. "Mr Baker has kindly agreed to us sharing his school, and hopefully it will not be for too long," she said.

In return Mr Baker welcomed us and hoped that we would enjoy our stay.

There was no merger between the two schools, each retaining its own identity. Lower Street School had, like our own, both 'Infants' and 'Juniors', each having its own set of classrooms and playgrounds. This caused overcrowding, so frequent walking excursions, and nature rambles, were held to relieve the pressure that an over-crowded school engendered, especially on the teachers. A lot of the excursions were thus of an informal nature; games in the park or on the beach; a visit to the famous castle of Hastings; the caves and the cliffs; and in that respect September, October, and November of 1939 were not an educational burden for me, although hanging on to my gasmask was.

"Don't forget your gasmask!" became a bye-word. This reminder was given to us every time we left a location, or a building. It was drummed into us, with the added advice, "It might save your life one day." Nevertheless, I lost mine. Unfortunately, I left it on the beach and it was washed out to sea, then, unbeknown to me, washed back the next day, ruined. I never even missed it until I was leaving for school the following morning.

After school I was told to report to a police station in Hastings where I was given a dressing down by the duty officer and handed the soggy cardboard box holding my gasmask which was still inside the torn and now useless Rexene cover that my mum had carefully made for it. The ticking off was nothing to the rollicking I received from my mum when next I saw her because a few days after losing my gasmask I left my overcoat on the beach. "You must think I'm made of money - and where am I going to get clothing coupons for a new one - you'd lose your head if it wasn't screwed on."

Nevertheless, I did get a new overcoat and a shop-bought cover for the new gas mask I was issued with.

Soon after we were evacuated arrangements were made between our parents, the school, and a coach company, to run an excursion from Greenwich to Hastings each Sunday. My mum and dad took advantage of this to pop down to see me frequently, albeit for a few hours each time. I looked forward to this and showed them all my haunts and places of interest that I had been to on school trips. They always brought a bag of goodies with them; comics, sweets, and sometimes one of my toys; on one occasion it was my wooden fort and lead soldiers. Whether they visited or not, each Monday morning, together with the rest of my class, I wrote a letter home. This procedure had started on the first Monday at Lower Street School when we were instructed to compose a letter and advise our parents of our safe arrival. Also to tell them that we were happy in our new homes, the address of which we printed clearly in the top right hand corner.

Living with Mrs Banks and her son was serious stuff, especially at meal times. I was a very fussy eater, 'didn't like this' and 'wouldn't eat that'. I would retch at a hard piece of potato in the mash, or a lumpy bit in the porridge, I was a nightmare. It was not new, I had given my mother problems for years and she had tried everything to make me eat the food she put in front of me, the ultimate being an incident when I was in the last year of the Infant School.

I had gone home for lunch and my mother had prepared a meal of meat, potatoes, and peas, which she placed before me. After poking the meal about, and hardly eating any of it, I moaned, "I don't want any more."

"You haven't eaten anything!" A declaration my mother had made countless times in the past.

"Yes I have, anyway a fly's been on it." An excuse I had used frequently before.

"Well you're not leaving the table until you've eaten it," said my mum, resorting to blackmail, hoping that the thought of being deprived of play during my dinner -time break would do the trick.

No chance. I sat sullenly at the table in front of the dinner until the school bell rang without eating another morsel. At the second bell my mum said, "Go on off you go, and don't go thinking that's the last of it."

Sitting in class a short time later that afternoon the door opened and Mrs Churchill, the headmistress, entered. After a word with my teacher I was called to the front of the class and told to go with her, which I did, following her into the main hall where my mother was standing holding a china plate with an enamel plate upside down on top. I knew immediately what was under the enamel plate; as the same arrangement was used too keep my father's dinner warm in the oven when he was late home from work.

"I am very disappointed with you Rex," Mrs Churchill said in a stern voice. "Your mother tells me that she cooks you a nice meal each day and you refuse to eat it; this dinner has hardly been touched." She went on about the starving children all over the world who would like to have it, a line which I had heard countless times before and which I would have gladly complied with if it had been at all possible. "Now you're going to sit on that form over there," pointing to a bench at the side of the hall, "and you will not move until you have eaten the very last bit. I will be keeping a special eye on you." Taking the dinner plate from my mother, who kept hold of the enamel plate, Mrs Churchill bade my mother goodbye and told her, in a voice loud enough for me to hear, to let her know if things did not improve.

I was left alone in the hall nibbling at the food which I eventually ate, but although I improved sufficiently for my mother not to repeat her trip to the school with my dinner I was still very finicky.

Mrs Banks was not the sort of women to suffer such a problem readily. The first main meal she put in front of me had swede as an accompanying vegetable and after tasting it I left it on the plate.

"I don't like that," I said.

"Like it or not you are going to eat it up," Came back her sharp reply.

The taste of swede was alien to me, it had never formed part of the vegetable accompaniments with dinners at home, and those that were, such as cabbage, brussel sprouts and spring greens, I never liked, but this was the worst of all. I took one more mouthful and immediately heaved.

"Don't be such a baby!" Mrs Banks said.

I heaved again on the next mouthful.

"Control yourself, and don't be so silly," barked Ernest.

I mashed the swede into the potato with my fork and managed with some difficulty to eat what was considered to be an acceptable amount.

For desert Mrs Banks produced boiled rice. I had never eaten boiled rice as a desert or otherwise. At home, rice had always been made with milk; sweet, creamy, and cooked in the oven, which I enjoyed. The brown burnt skin on top was always eaten with relish by my father.

The rice pudding, moulded in the shape of the basin it was cooked in, was set on a plate in the middle of the table. Mrs Banks poured a tablespoon of golden-syrup over the top and cut it into portions as you would a cake, or a golden sponge, (how I wish it had been). My portion was put in front of me and on trying a mouthful I immediately showed my dislike for it, even though I was trying not to. There was no added sugar, it was lumpy, and the amount of golden syrup was not enough to sweeten the taste, apart from which it absorbed all the moisture from my mouth making it impossible to swallow; wallpaper paste was probably tastier. Although I must admit, Gordon and Arthur were not encountering the same problem.

"Now what's wrong with that?" Mrs Banks asked sharply.

"I don't like it," I replied.

"Don't be silly, there's nothing to dislike about it," Mrs Banks retorted.

"It makes me feel sick," I moaned.

"Don't be such a baby, eat it up," Ernest blasted.

I took another tentative mouthful, immediately retched, and spit the rice back onto the plate.

At this point, having been irritated by my antics throughout the meal, Ernest lost his temper with me and rising from his chair he shouted, "You stupid boy," whilst at the same time swinging his hand in an arc which was intended to connect with the back of my head. Unfortunately for him, and more so for his mother, I saw it coming and ducked the blow which caught her on the shoulder causing her to topple from her chair.

"Ernest!" she screamed, "What are you doing?" Ernest was already out of his chair and helping her up.

Turning to me she said, "You can go to your bedroom, I'll deal with you later."

I got no biscuits and lemonade that night, which had become our evening titbit before turning in, but instead received a good dressing down. I also warranted a mention when she took bedtime prayers. Apart from the usual blessings for us and our families, a plea was made for me...."and please make Rex enjoy the good food that you have helped me provide."

I was not happy with my behaviour and felt miserable, and sorry for myself. I cried that night for the first time since coming away, wishing that I was home in my own bed without all the anguish that evacuation was bringing me. I also acknowledged to myself that I had acted like a baby. Arthur and Gordon had both ate their food without any fuss, in fact they seemed to enjoy it, and this sunk home to me, and for all the years of evacuation which followed I never repeated such an incident and ate almost anything which was put in front of me.

Mrs Banks must have had a generosity and kindness which escaped me at the time for she took Arthur and Gordon out and bought them new clothes. They came from a large family with a baby and several younger children under school age still at home. Even though the clothes they had brought away with them were the best they could muster, they were old, poor in quality, and way past their best. She kitted them out in grey. Grey shirt, grey flannel short trousers, grey pullover, with grey socks and tie to match, and dressed in their new attire Mrs Banks paraded them in the parlour. Gordon with his red face glowing was as proud as Punch, and Arthur, although reluctant, bore his with an air of satisfaction. I watched in envy even though I had no reason to. My own clothes, which my mother always kept clean and tidy, were invariably dark in colour and by contrast those now worn by Arthur and Gordon, to my mind, looked smarter in a casual sporty manner. I appreciated their need for new clothes but found it difficult to comprehend why Mrs Banks had bought them new clothes and not me. Not that it did Arthur much good, for soon after, he was climbing a fence around the periphery of the Police Station when he slipped and one of the metal spikes adorning the top of the fence went up and through his trouser leg. It could have been very nasty, but fortunately for him he suffered nothing worse, but the incident was enough to cause Mrs Banks extreme concern, not only at the thought of him coming to a nasty end, but at the ruination of his trousers, and she certainly let him know it. This was enough for Mrs Banks, the last straw, Arthur had to go. In her words, "He's been keeping bad company and become a bit of a handful." A new billet was found for him, but he never took it up, returning to London and his family. I found out later that he never returned to school and although barely twelve was found a job.

Three evacuees were really too much for Mrs Banks, even two, for soon after Arthur got his 'marching orders' she made a complaint about me to the billeting officer and I was re-housed. She was not completely without justification; serving the Police Station was a huge coal bunker and one afternoon after a delivery, when the coal was mountainously high, along with a couple of like-minded boys living close by I found it great fun scrambling up to the top and sliding down on an old tea tray. The expression on Mrs Bank's face on seeing me when she returned from a spot of shopping said it all. The thunderous look, and the verbal blast that followed, directed me post-haste to the bathroom. This proved too much for Mrs Banks and a few days later saw me, with my belongings, taking a long walk with the billeting officer to a new home on a council estate located in East Hastings: I had been with Mrs Banks for no more than ten weeks.

My new foster parents were Mr and Mrs Joliffe, and I was to remain with them for the rest of my time in Hastings. They had three children, Patricia, John, and Iris. Patricia was thirteen and the eldest, John was going on twelve. Both were tall for their age, slimly built, and with large round wire-rimmed glasses they looked 'brainy', which in fact they were, both attending Grammar School, and rightfully so. Their younger sister was only seven and on the tubby side; she became my best friend in the house.

The house had three bedrooms and as regulations demanded I was given a room of my own, a small box room which overlooked the back garden. This had been John's room. Consequently, John had to sleep in the front room downstairs on a divan which doubled as a settee during the day, although nobody used the room except on high days, and holidays, that is, with the exception of Mrs Joliffe who taught piano, and the students who came to learn. John resented the loss of his bedroom which was apparent from the start as he made a huge fuss about it, so to mollify him he had his pocket money upped by sixpence a week.

A payment of ten shillings and sixpence per week was made to foster parents for housing one evacuee and eight shillings and sixpence for each additional child. This was to help with their keep and not to be considered as an inducement; the inducement in this case was made to John for the sacrifice of his bedroom. (Parents of evacuees made a payment towards it of six shillings for each child).

The house was in sharp contrast to Mrs Banks' flat where her routine was strictly formal with living conditions pristine, and austere; the Joliffe's lived in a free and easy manner, bordering on squalor.

Although Mrs Joliffe was an intelligent, good looking woman, with a pleasant disposition, who encouraged her children in artistic and studious pursuits, household chores never figured high on her list of priorities. Mr Joliffe, who looked in permanent need of a shave, was at home in such surroundings. He was a weedy looking man, a window cleaner by trade who never seemed to be cleaning any windows, certainly not in his own house, and usually to be found in the living- room at the rear of the house slumped in an old armchair when he was not down the pub. Both Mr and Mrs Joliffe were in their mid-thirties.

Meal times were not a problem where Mrs Joliffe was concerned, she provided and cooked the sort of food that children liked, and if you left it, so what, someone else finished it, or it was fed to the cat. It suited me.

Although I had my own room, it was mine only to sleep in as far as John was concerned. At any other time he would monopolise it for whatever purpose he wanted it for, homework or play. Both he and his elder sister kept very much to themselves and when I tried to join them in their games I was given a cool reception, as was their younger sister, obviously due to our lack of acumen and competitiveness.

Apart from mealtimes, and late evening, I was hardly in the house. There were a lot of children living on the housing estate, a few of them evacuees in my class including Stephen Wright and Brian. My mum always used to call me a street-raker and billeted with the Joliffe's I had more freedom to roam or just play outdoors than I had ever previously been allowed. There were two parks close by which were good for the various games we played, but I was mostly to be found at or near the sea front.

I would spend hours scaling the white chalk cliffs laying beneath Hastings castle into which over the years a myriad of channels, crevices, ledges, and footholds, had been cut, or worn away, presenting a challenge to an adventure seeking lad like me to climb, or descend, the many routes from top to bottom. The routes varied from easy, to extremely difficult, and the number of times that I nearly fell are too numerous to mention.

The pier was closed for the duration of the war, but the narrow lanes of old Hastings, with their mysterious history, and the many curiosity shops, held a fascination for me, as did the fishermen on the East beach with their fishing boats, and the unusual two storey huts used for drying and mending their nets.

Nearby was the ancient Harbour Arm (now almost disintegrated) projecting about sixty feet into the sea and from which anglers pursued their activity. I was drawn to this, not just to watch the men cast their lines and make their catch, but to face the challenge of getting on there and be thrilled by the dangers it presented. It was a stone built structure about ten feet wide, and about the same height above average sea level, purported to be the remains of a wall which formed part of the medieval harbour of Hastings. There were no guard rails, and at high tide with a strong wind the waves broke over the end, and high up the sides.

Although the top was flat it was jagged, and uneven, and considered hazardous to venture upon; a sign on the beach warned of this with the heading 'DANGER' in very big red letters. Getting on to the main part projecting out to sea was the most difficult, for although the wall started level with the beach at the promenade by the time it reached the shoreline it was its full ten feet high and at that very point the continuity of the wall was broken by a gap just under a yard wide. Men found this easy to jump, no more than a large stride, but it confronted me with a dilemma. Could I jump it? Would I jump it? I withdrew to the prom and with a piece of chalk off the beach I drew two lines about the same distance as the width of the gap and with a standing jump cleared it with a little to spare. Doing this a few more times and proving to myself that it was within my capability I went back onto the Harbour Arm to leap the gap. I braced myself with one foot on the edge, rocked back and forward to give myself some momentum for the jump, but my nerve failed me: I bottled it.

A few days later I went back again after having practiced a standing long jump with the confidence that this time I would definitely succeed in doing it. I went to the edge of the gap, looked down at the jagged rocks in the sea at the bottom, steadied myself, and --- bottled it again. I never did jump that gap unaided.

Fortunately, a man going onto the Arm saw me standing there in 'my attempting to jump mode' and asked me if I wanted help to cross. "Yes please!" I blurted out, and from the other side he easily reached across to take hold of my hand, saying, "Jump," which I did. With him pulling at the same time I cleared it easily and got back in a similar manner.

From that day on, whenever I went onto the Harbour Arm, I waited at the edge of the gap until a man going on was willing to give me a tug.

I went Home for the Christmas holidays, as did most of the evacuees, for although we had been away for over three months no bombs had dropped – our reason for being sent away.

Entering the small kitchen warmed by the fire in the grate of the range, shining black where my mother had applied Zebo oven cleaner to the door and the surround, I felt so glad, so pleased to be home. As I looked around that tiny kitchen the pleasing picture taken in by my eyes etched itself into my memory for ever. The dresser, with plates and saucers neatly aligned on the shelves which had hooks on their edges holding cups, and the space at the lower level neatly curtained off which I knew would still be accommodating my toys. The larder in the corner of the room holding basic needs, nothing fancy, just good wholesome food. A scrubbed table, with four chairs, set against the wall under a window that looked out onto a six-foot high fence within touching distance. Two well-worn mis-matching armchairs flanking the fireplace, one of which folded out in an elaborate arrangement of slats and rods to form a bed that was made up for my sister or me when we were ill. And finally, a bright coconut mat which covered a large part of the floor weaved in an array of colours to form a symmetrical pattern. Kneeling on that mat left indentations of the weave etched in my knee; although colourful it was not exactly Wilton. My father lived in that house himself as a boy and apart from the mat and the curtains I doubt whether much had changed.

In the New Year I reluctantly returned to the Joliffe household in Hastings to continue my life as I had left it. The dangers that I had been sent away for had not materialised; in fact, for months after the outbreak of the war the expected swarms of German bombers of the mighty Luftwaffe failed to appear over British cities, this edgy period came to be known as the 'phoney war' and lasted until the late summer of 1940. It was not surprising therefore that following Christmas, and into the spring, evacuees were returning in droves, and so it was that by mid-April I was back home.

With Germany now occupying France it was strongly anticipated that the phoney war would soon be coming to an end and that London, without doubt, would be heavily bombed, thus a second wave of evacuation was planned. My cousin Sylvia went to the Park Modern Central School in Barking where such arrangements were being made, and she, with her brother George, were going with it. It was thought a good idea if I was to go with them, but to be eligible I had to be residing in their house at the time of registration so I was despatched poste-haste to 49, Davington Road, Dagenham, to make my home with them.

Their mother, my aunt Violet, was my mother's younger sister, so living with her, and her husband George, presented me with no problems as our families had a close relationship and had been visiting with each other for as long as I could remember. I however, presented an immediate problem to them as I was seriously infected with scabies, discovered when I was itching profusely and a rash observed all over my body. A visit to the doctors resulted in this diagnosis which is a contagious skin complaint caused by a mite associated with living in unclean conditions. The remedy at that time was not very pleasant. I was put into their bath filled with water as hot as I could bear it, and after a good soaking I was made to stand in the steaming water while my aunt Vi took a nail brush and scrubbed the tops off all the spots, of which there were hundreds from my head to my toes. This was most debilitating and I fainted early into the procedure from whereon I had to be held up by my uncle George so that my aunt could complete the treatment which ended after she had rubbed sulphur ointment all over my body. Fortunately, I only needed the treatment once more, to a lesser degree, and more fortunately still Sylvia and George never caught it.

It was lucky that my Uncle George was there as he was away more often than not; he worked as an asphalter, and at that time was working on military installations all around the country, coming home only at weekends.

Although registered for evacuation with Sylvia's school I was required in the meantime to attend the same school as George, this spanned a period of about eight weeks. Sylvia was a year older than me, a lovely fair haired girl with a pleasing nature, and George, whilst a year younger, and much smaller, was just as streetwise, so we all got along well together.

My recollection is of a warm and pleasant summer that year and my time living in Dagenham sped by. Barking Lido had not long been built and it saw us there every weekend. What a swimming pool, people on Li-Los in and out of the water, high diving boards, and the tallest and steepest chute that I had ever seen; it bordered on being dangerous. There were parks nearby and a short ride to Hainault Forest provided us with all the outdoor fun we needed; indoors, we played 'Monopoly' incessantly. The game was new to me, and I think it was new on the market.

The day of evacuation came and we were out of the house by seven-o-clock that morning with our gas masks slung over our shoulders and lugging our packed cases on a long walk through Parsloes Park to Sylvia's school where we were to pick up a coach at eight. Many students of the school, ranging from eleven to fifteen years of age, were already there together with younger siblings and their parents, with more still arriving. It was a journey into the unknown for most of them and a mixture of emotions -- some sad; some apprehensive; and some excited, seeing it as an adventure. It became known that I had already been evacuated and I was sought after to share my experience regarding the routine to be expected and found some enjoyment in my new found advisory status.

Coaches took us all to Barking Underground Station and from there we went by tube to Paddington, the premium station of The Great Western Railway - its vastness took my breath away. A corridor train was waiting for us at a platform which had more carriages than I could have imagined, unlike the small trains I had been on to Southend-on-Sea, or Margate; or the one that took me to Hastings. We were martialled onto it and the same scramble for seats ensued as I had previously encountered on my Hastings experience where everyone was trying to remain with their friends.

We were not the only school taking the train, children being evacuated from other areas of London were already on board, and others were still to follow. It seemed an interminable wait before the train was full and left the station bound for a destination then unknown, which turned out to be Taunton; we reached it four days later. (It was actually about four hours, it just seemed that long). The excitement and high spirits at the beginning of the journey soon palled and quickly turned to boredom which the teachers tried to relieve by arranging singing rounds, spelling bees, and telling stories, but this used such little time up, as did eating the packed lunches that we had brought. The train made several stops along the way, each time gorging out children who had reached their destination, and each time giving us false hopes that it was ours, but we were destined to go the whole distance.

On reaching Taunton we found out that we had still not arrived at our final destination, but arrangements had been made for us to have a hot drink, and some sandwiches, before boarding another train. Taunton is the major city of Somerset and its station was a terminus of the Great Western Railway, which apart from main lines to and from major cities had small branch lines to outlying towns and villages, and it was to a platform serving one of these that we were then taken. This particular branch line served all stations to Barnstaple.

The train we boarded usually had no more than three carriages, but on this day extra carriages had been added for our benefit. It stopped at numerous stations before it reached Dulverton which we had been informed a little earlier was to be our final destination. It might just well have been Timbuktu because none of us had ever heard of it.

Dulverton station was actually located in the village of Brushford, about two miles from the town of Dulverton, and when we arrived there several coaches were lined up to take us to Dulverton Town Hall where billeting arrangements were being made.

Dulverton is a small historic town in North Somerset and lies in the lush Barle valley, overshadowed by the hills around it, with Exmoor close by. It featured prominently in the classic story of Lorna Doone. The River Barle runs through Dulverton, and then Brushford, before joining the River Exe at Exeford. The road from Brushford runs alongside the River Barle and it was along this road that we travelled on the final leg of our journey.

We piled off the buses and were directed into the town hall by local officials where we were fed hot soup before any billeting arrangements were carried out.

The routine for housing us was similar to that which I had experienced at Hastings except that because many billets were a fair distance from the town, some of them miles away, more of the would-be foster parents were not there to receive their wards. For this a car ferrying service was arranged using volunteer car owners. Again it was done in alphabetical order but this time I was mid-way down the list being grouped on the register with my cousins whose surname was Old. This was comforting to me when I saw other children being taken off on their own to some remote destination without having anyone to share their fears. Fortunately, these were children without siblings who were eleven or over.

Before any of us had left the Town Hall, Mr Searle, our headmaster, informed us that we were all to assemble back there again the following morning.

When our names were called, Sylvia, George, and I, were handed over to an elderly lady introduced to us as Lady Herbert who led us from the hall with our cases. She chatted away to us in a very posh accent, which she habitually impregnated with, "What, what," and ushered us into a large American Dodge saloon car, the three of us only taking up half of the back seat. It was a new experience for me, I had never ridden in a car before, that alone one of this magnificence.

The journey took about ten minutes along country lanes, a large part of it up a long gravel drive after passing through a huge white gate and rumbling over a cattle grid.

We stopped at a group of three adjoining cottages, by which time it was early evening, and told by our custodian that we had arrived at our new home, or homes as it turned out to be. She knocked at the door of the first cottage and a thin mean-looking old woman came to the door.

"Ah, Minnie," she said. "I've brought you an evacuee, her name is Sylvia."

"I don't want her, I don't want her. I've got enough to look after with mother," She screamed. Upon which a very old woman

29

shuffled through the door and said in a high pitched squeaky voice, "Minnie, who's that at the door Minnie?"

Lady Herbert adopted a most authoritative manner. "Now don't be silly Minnie, she's not going anywhere else, and she's staying with you."

"No! No she's not! Mother's more than I can handle." But to no avail, she was ushered back through her door together with her mother and Sylvia, who looked shocked and extremely concerned.

We later learned that Minnie had never been married, spending her entire adult life in the service of the Herbert family, and looking after her elderly parents. Her father, when he was alive, also worked on the Herbert estate.

George and I were shocked too. For Sylvia to be split from us, and to be greeted in such a manner, took us completely by surprise. Both of us worried about what was to become of her, and wondered what lay in wait for us.

Lady Herbert led George and me, clutching our cases, around the corner and through a large pair of gates into a large cobbled yard where we were met by a stocky built man of medium height. He had a friendly weather-beaten face and was clad in riding breeches with leather gaiters, a collarless shirt, and a cap, with several dogs milling around him. He touched his cap and greeted Lady Herbert.

"Um, Pike, I have two young chaps for you, George, and Rex. What! What! They're from London."

I wondered if Lady Herbert realised how often she said, "What! What!" All the time I was in Dulverton whenever I heard her in conversation with somebody she peppered it with this expletive?

"Thank you Ma'am, we'll make them welcome, you can be sure of that."

This cordial reception was in sharp contrast to that received by Sylvia and immediately put us at ease.

Mr Pike led us through an archway formed into a building at the rear of the yard, within which, let into the left hand wall, was the front door to his house. On the right was a much larger door which was open and through which we could see a number of stables, we learned later that they were capable of housing five horses. He took us into his house where we met his wife who was waiting for us in the parlour; she would have been observing our arrival from one of her windows which looked out onto the yard.

Mrs Pike, a refined looking woman in her fifties with hair prematurely silver, looked us over as we entered the room and said, "What have we got here then?"

"This is George, and this is Rex," Mr Pike said, pointing to each of us in turn. "They're from London."

"You've come a long way then," Mrs Pike observed. "Now take off your hats, and your coats, and make yourself comfortable."

A friendly interrogation then took place. How old were we? What part of London did we come from? What was our relationship to each other? Any brothers or sisters?....and so on, following which Mrs Pike took us upstairs to show us our bedroom. It was a small room with a single bed placed against one wall and included drawers and cupboards for our clothes. She left us there to unpack.

When we returned downstairs Mrs Pike was in the kitchen preparing some food and she beckoned us in. A doorway within the kitchen opened onto a small courtyard. This door was open and Sylvia could be seen standing in the middle of the area looking very lonely and weeping. George and I joined her to find that the kitchen doors of both houses had access to this yard.

"They don't want me," Sylvia said.

We were trying to console her when Mrs Pike came out, put an arm around Sylvia, and ushered us all into her kitchen.

Sylvia blurted out about the reception she had received, and Mrs Pike after comforting her some more said, "She'll come around to it, (meaning Minnie), things will be much better tomorrow, you'll see."

Things did become a little better after a few days, and as further days passed Sylvia's presence in Minnie's household became more welcome as she helped with the housework and other little chores.

The following morning we were up early, and after breakfast we set off for school following directions given to us by Mr Pike, of the shortest route into town. This was by of way of a well

31

trodden footpath through fields in which dozens of bullocks were grazing. They could have been cows, or bulls, as far as we were concerned, but we were informed later that they were bullocks. Anyway, it was the first time that any of us had seen such creatures other than in cowboy films at the cinema on a Saturday morning featuring Tom Mix, or Hoppalong Cassidy, and so it was with trepidation that we ventured through the gate into the first field. As the bullocks seemed to be more interested in what they where doing, rather than what we were doing, we tentatively ventured through the gate and made our way across the field keeping close together but still feeling extremely vulnerable. There were three grazing fields linked together, none of which had gates to separate them from each other, and by the time we were halfway across the second field we were feeling quite confident of getting through unscathed and broke into a trot.

The opening in the hedge between the second and third field was about ten feet wide with a brook running across it. At one end of the opening the brook was bridged by a huge stone about three feet wide upon which we stepped before being brought to a sudden halt. This third and last field was very small, and triangular in shape, with the gate which we required to exit from at the narrow end blocked by at least a dozen bullocks. We stood there for a moment not knowing what to do next before deciding to work our way around keeping close to the hedge, but as soon as we moved they saw us as a threat and charged towards us - well that was our perception of the situation. In actual fact they made for their only avenue of escape, which was the gap that we were now standing in. But twenty bullocks stampeding in our direction frightened the living daylights out of us and I immediately gained the legs of an Olympic runner and ran for cover back into the field we had just left with George close on my heels, but Sylvia remained transfixed, her hands covering her face and screaming.

George and I found refuge behind a tree with Sylvia not in our sights. Was she dead? Badly trampled? We imagined the worst, but amazingly, apart from being petrified she was untouched, none of the bullocks attempted to run over the slab of stone on which she stood, all running through the brook.

It was plain sailing after that, and fifteen minutes later we were standing outside Dulverton Town Hall milling with all the other evacuees waiting to be let in.

Once inside we found out that the town hall was indeed to be our school. We were dumbstruck, it was such a small area, nobody could believe it, but we had to believe it, it was true. Everyone had to assist in bringing trestle tables, and folding chairs, from a store-room below the stage and set them up on the floor of the hall. Tables were arranged side-by-side in pairs with a gap between each pair, and arrayed in such a way over the entire floor area, each pair constituting a 'classroom'. Five or six classrooms were formed this way and a junior class was set out on the stage.

The headmaster had an office on the ground floor, where there was also a staff room. Also on the ground floor there was a kitchen, and dining room, with a large pair of glass panelled doors leading directly onto the High Street under an arch formed by dual steps leading to the main entrance door of the hall above.

The Park Modern Central School had near grammar school status with the students having passed an eleven-plus examination; it now had to cater for additional children a lot younger and with various degrees of ability, siblings of the students, such as George. He was one of the youngest and in the junior class on the stage. The class I was in was located in the hall just below the stage and taught by a Miss Evans, a young lady in her twenties.

The early days of schooling in that hall were bedlam, with incessant noise from chairs, and tables, continually being scraped on the floor, together with the cacophony of sounds from one hundred and fifty students and teachers. Eventually, screens were erected which gave the semblance at least of individual classes, and slightly muffled the noise.

It was during this early chaotic period that I made a memorable contribution to this clamour. There were twelve of us around a trestle table, five on each side plus one at each end, and I had managed to acquire one of these choice end seats where I was able to put my feet on the horizontal bar of the trestle supporting the table top. Unfortunately, the pressure of my feet on the bar caused it to fold inwards little by little until all of a sudden it collapsed and the table top crashed to the floor with an almighty clatter sending writing paper, pencils, and other paraphernalia, in all directions. (Fortunately, no pens or ink were supplied, obviously such an incident being anticipated). Everybody in the hall stood up to see who, or what it was, that caused the rumpus, while at the same time giving a rousing cheer.

It seemed to embarrass Miss Evans more than it did me and she gave me a stiff talking to. I wish it had been a bit more effective, because within a short time I had inadvertently pushed the trestle flat again, and the same raucous response was repeated. This time it was my misfortune that Mr Searle, the headmaster, was carrying out one of his frequent tours of the hall and was passing close to our table.

Of course, Miss Evans immediately shouted, "Rex! There's no excuse for it this time, you're doing it on purpose."

I was not of course. Even if I had known then the kind of kudos this action was to bring me I was not that brave, for I was not unaware of what the consequence was likely to be.

Mr Searle strode up to Miss Evans and had a word with her, both of them looking in my direction. He then roared, "Wellard! When you've helped tidy up this mess, and put the table back together, report to my study."

I knew that I was in for the cane, and what to expect. A caning given by a teacher in the classroom was invariably across the hand, but when administered by the headmaster it was across the seat of your pants, and much more painful.

This was not the first time that I had received this level of punishment. A couple of years earlier, when I was in Calvert Road Junior School I landed myself in a similar situation. It occurred during morning assembly. I was sitting cross-legged on the floor of the main hall listening to a longer than usual preamble before prayers, and bored with the proceedings, as were all the other children, fished in my pocket and found a small white bone-handled penknife which I showed to the boy sitting next to me.

Mr Gill, the assistant headmaster who was boring us all from the stage, spotted me, and shouted.

"You!" I looked up. "Yes! You boy! What are you doing?"

"Nothing Sir," I said.

"Well, I don't want to see you doing nothing again, pay attention."

I went back to being bored and stupidly got the knife out again and got as far as opening the two blades. This impressed the boys sitting either side of me but also drew the attention of a teacher standing at the side of the hall who hauled me out.

This time Mr Gill was not so tolerant and I was called onto the stage and given a bawling out in front of the whole assembly. But worse was to come, he sent for the cane, and punishment book, and there on the stage I was made to bend over while he gave me three very hard strokes. The humiliation I felt, as I returned to my place in the hall, was more to do with crying than the disgrace which having the cane was supposed to engender.

Bearing in mind this earlier experience, as I made my way to Mr Searle's study I stuffed my school cap down the back of my trousers to reduce the sting of the cane. Mr Searle was a lean man over six feet tall and invariably wore a dark grey suit, he had jet black hair and a long thin face which sported a large round mole, like the tip of a snooker cue, on his left cheek. He was a man known to stand no nonsense, so when I knocked on the door of his study it was not without fear.

When I entered he already had the cane in his hand, obviously eager to apply it while he was still steaming, and in a very severe voice, he said, "Right Wellard, bend over and touch your toes."

I bent over and he immediately spotted the lumpy bulge in the seat of my trousers. He pulled back my waistband and pulled out my cap. "Are you stupid boy, or do you think I am?" He then administered four stinging strokes, one more than the standard number usually applied, which I assumed was for trying it on with the cap.

I told myself before I went in that this time I would not cry, but tears just seem to follow pain when you're young no matter how hard you try to stop them, well it did with me, and I hung about until I had stopped sobbing, but even so, when I rejoined my class, even though I mustered a weak grin in a show of bravado, my red eyes gave me away.

George and I quickly adapted to the lifestyle of Mr and Mrs Pike, who themselves had had a lifestyle change thrust upon them. They had no children of their own and now found themselves with two lively boys from a completely different background who had already developed their own individuality. Mr Pike was a groom in the service of Lady Herbert and responsible for the well-being of her eight riding horses, many of which were rode out almost daily by the various members of her family, often to 'The Hunt', which surprisingly continued throughout the course of the war.

'The Stables', our new home, had a magnificent view across the countryside. It was about one hundred and fifty yards from a large mansion called Pixton House and in a setting of immense beauty.

Pixton House was the seat of The Honourable Lady Herbert (to give her full title) who resided there with her unmarried son Aubrey. Two married daughters and their children were also living there for the duration of the war.

The large house with some forty rooms was in its own grounds surrounded by expansive and carefully kept lawns, flower gardens, and trees; with a walled kitchen garden and laundry on the periphery. This formed the centrepiece of Pixton Park, an area of grassland, and forest, which covered an area of about four square miles. Her estate further extended over a vast area which included, and went beyond the village of Bury, some two miles away. Most of the farms on her land were leased, and run by tenant farmers, except Weir Farm, bordering on Pixton Park, which was controlled by a manager.

Mr Pike soon had us mucking out the stables, and laying down sawdust, or straw bedding. Also, grooming the horses with a curry-comb and dandy-brush; and cutting hay into chaff, -- this was done by a manually operated cutting device installed in a large loft above the stables. Hay was also fed from the loft through trapdoors to the feeding baskets located high on the stable walls below; this became another of our jobs.

On wet days we would also help Mr Pike in the harness room polishing the leather saddles, and reins, as well as burnishing the brass-work on the bridle equipment. We were willing servants as we enjoyed the tasks which were usually carried out when giving assistance to Mr Pike whilst he was undertaking his normal duties.

At first, grooming the horses was quite daunting, they towered above us and pushed us off the box we stood on to brush their backs, or comb their manes, but we soon learned that with all their strength they were gentle creatures and warmed to the task, although on one occasion, a large horse named Gold-digger stood on my foot. I was wearing wellington boots at the time, fortunately a little too big, for I was able to draw my toes back such that he trapped the empty toe part of the boot with his hoof. He stood there without budging, even though I was pushing him, and trying to lift his leg, (some hope), but he just looked at me with a twinkle in his eye enjoying the situation.

After a time Mr Pike taught us to ride the horses using a bridle only, and with him on the leading horse we would help him take them to more remote pastures for grazing. To our dismay, we never rode out on the horses in a proper manner, with saddle, stirrups, and bridle, and come to that I only ever saw Mr Pike ride out on one or two occasions, even though he was an expert horseman having spent many years in the cavalry during the First World War, many of them in Mesopotamia. I can only presume that he was not allowed to use the horses for his own purposes, or he chose not to do so.

In a field close by a very small white Shetland pony called Puffin was kept for the pleasure of the Herbert children, although George and I spent more time with him, and received greater pleasure from him, than they ever did. We would attract him to the gate with a handful of oats and pull him close to the bars, where one of us would straddle his back and ride him until being thrown off. This was invariably quite soon, as he was a strong and lively little fellow and preferred us off his back rather than on it. It was not exactly up to rodeo standard but it did have an element of danger; on one occasion he gave me a nasty kick when I leap-frogged him from behind and slipped off his back. That was out of character, and probably because I surprised him, for he was always very friendly with us, and rightly so, as he was a favourite of ours, keeping him well groomed and supplied with plenty of oats.

Apart from the horses, Mr Pike looked after numerous dogs, none of which were his own, all belonging to various members of the Herbert family. George and I benefited from this arrangement, as we enjoyed their company and they seemed to enjoy ours, for wherever we went they followed. They were a motley ensemble. There was a red-setter, and a golden retriever, aptly named Red and Daffodil; two dachshunds Fiddle, and Sticks; and a boisterous Ikey who could not be categorised. He was the most fun of them all, and when Mr Pike shaved all of his body except his head, which he did during the summer months, he also looked the oddest. The Herbert's liked their dogs, but as with their horses, they never undertook any of the tedious tasks that went with their well-being.

Anne and Polly, the granddaughters of Lady Herbert, also had a pet lamb answering to the name of Tommy which followed them around like a dog. George and I would join them on the park and we became quite fond of him ourselves, but were saddened when one day in the following spring we were looking over the gate into a field where 'last years' lambs were held before being taken to market (on their way to the butchers) and wondered if Tommy was amongst them. We called his name, not really expecting him to be there, and was shocked when he came trotting across to see us. Naively, we thought that being a pet Tommy would have been kept on the park, possibly becoming one of the few rams used to sire the ewes.

The long walk to Dulverton, and school, soon became second nature to us, and we quickly learned that the bullocks, which we first feared, were more fearful of us than we were of them. The distance to school meant that we never returned until late afternoon; the first few weeks enjoying a packed lunch, but later, when kitchen arrangements were finalised, suffering school dinners.

There was no playground to kick our heels in, and so playtimes were spent milling around in the High Street, or on the steps of the Town Hall. Climbing up the steps on the wrong side of the railings which overlooked the road was a popular and challenging activity, and on one occasion whilst endeavouring to do this, traversing from the bottom step on one side to the bottom step on the other, I lost my grip whilst crossing the top landing and fell. Fortunately for me, in the road below a group of senior boys were chin-wagging and my fall was broken when I landed full across the shoulders of a boy named Charlie (Chas) Monk, an athletic sort who was a regular in the school football team. He pulled me up from the ground by my shirt and was on the point of giving me a good hiding when one of his friends took hold of him and pointed out that he had just saved me from breaking my neck. It was a wonder that I never broke his neck, but its funny how things work out because he became friendly disposed to me after that, helped by the fact that he recognised me as the boy that had given them all a good laugh when I caused the table to collapse.

He was amongst a group of half-a-dozen boys who were billeted in the Rock House Inn, one of the public houses in Dulverton (incidentally, the place where my mum and dad stayed when they came down to visit me) and all of us who listened to the tales they told were in envy of their good fortune in landing such digs. They were all boys of fourteen, and fifteen, and on Friday and Saturday nights they would be up late enjoying the pleasantries, and ribaldry, that surrounded them in this popular place of such merriment, having the odd glass of the very potent rough cider, and no doubt a few fags. The Rock House Inn was almost opposite the Rectory, so it inevitably became only a matter of time before religious do-gooders made an issue of it whence it was brought up before the local council with the recommendation that they all be found new billets. The up-shot of it was that none of them were willing to be re-housed and they all returned to their homes in East London. Perhaps with hindsight those responsible may have realised that there was less harm from living in the pub than dodging the bombs back there.

At dinner times we would wander in and around Dulverton. It was a small town with a dozen or more shops, most of them being in the High Street, opposite or adjacent to the Town Hall. The most important to me was Mr Harding's sweetshop where I got my weekly sweet ration and the bakers shop on the corner where

I was able to buy a cake, or a sticky bun, even though the old woman in there always took the rise out of me. "Don't talk through your nose," she would say, mimicking the way I spoke.

Other shops were intermittently scattered the length of Fore Street which ran downhill from The Rock House Inn to the bridge spanning the River Barle.

A narrow road leading from a point close to the Rock House Inn, and opposite the Rectory, led to Dulverton Church. The lane then skirted the church and rose steeply upward to Dulverton School which overlooked the town. The small school built to accommodate local children was full beyond its expected capacity having already shared its classrooms and facilities with a wave of evacuees who had been received at the very start of the war, although by the time we arrived the pressure had eased as many who were evacuated then had returned home.

The children attending Dulverton School called us 'vaccies', and in those early days skirmishes between us was not uncommon. Nothing serious that I can recall, but there was an ongoing battle for some time where we fired paper pellets at each other. A pellet was made by folding a piece of stiff paper, such as a strip from a cigarette packet, into a vee shape which was catapulted from an elastic band fastened to thumb and index finger. It certainly stung when you were hit in the face from close range.

The church was typical of most country churches which were built in years gone by; a strongly built edifice complete with bell-tower, cold and forbidding inside. From the first Sunday, after settling in, all the pupils from Park Modern had to attend morning service, except those who lived exceptional distances away; I envied them. Dressed in our best clothes, and with the headmaster's beady eyes upon us, we pretended to listen to boring sermons, or chapters read from the bible, by a vicar who droned on for an interminable length of time in a deep monotone voice. It was purgatory, worse than being at school. It was probably this that put me off of religion for ever.

I had never been to church before I was evacuated. For a period, my mum and dad packed my sister and me off to Sunday school held in the afternoon at a nearby church hall, probably

40

more for their benefit than ours as they had always been 'up for a lie down' when we returned home. It must have been worth the penny each they gave us, ha'penny for the collection box, and ha'penny to spend on sweets. I did try on one occasion to avoid putting my ha'penny into the collection box by just tapping the top of the box with it, but the Sunday school teacher was obviously awake to such practices and after I had passed the box she asked me to open up my hand. Seeing two ha-pennies in it she made me put them both in, which taught me a sharp lesson; to keep one ha-penny in my pocket.

When putting our money in the collection box we were required to walk around the hall in single file and as we passed the box put our coins in the slot on the top. Whilst we were parading in single file for this purpose we were required to chant:-

"Hear the pennies dropping,
Listen while they fall,
Every one is going,
To Jesus Christ our Lord."

This puzzled me greatly. I wondered how, or when, Jesus came down from heaven to collect the money.

The bridge at the bottom of Fore Street crossed the River Barle and led to a recreation ground (The Rec) on the other side, flanking the river. The river was a favourite spot for us all and a constant source of entertainment. Trout could always be seen from the bridge, but catching the Tiddlers and Tommy-Battle-heads (Sticklebacks and Bullheads), was more fun; this required gently removing the stone they were under without disturbing them. The main challenge however, was crossing the river on protruding rocks and stones without falling in, or getting your feet wet, the degree of difficulty being dependant on the depth of the water. The times that we went back to school in the afternoon wearing wet socks was too many to count, although our drying process of smacking the wet sock on a warm stone, or the wall of the shelter in the 'Rec', helped to varying degrees depending on how sunny the day was.

The Rec was also used by our school for various sports - football, cricket, rounders, wall-ball, etc.

On one occasion, following a football match involving senior boys, along with a lad named Bolton, I went into the dilapidated hut used as a changing room while the players were getting their strip off, and chided them at losing by a large margin to a local team. We were both grabbed and bundled into a large wooden chest housing their kit, which was immediately latched. We waited awhile for someone to let us out, but whoever locked us in had no intention of doing so, at least, not until they had made us suffer. Inside the box it was dark, hot, and cramped, and very claustrophobic, so of course we raised Cain, hollering and shouting to be released, but this only invited further harassment. This came in the form of someone kicking the side of the chest, followed by sticks being poked through cracks in the lid. This was most alarming as we could not avoid them and they were digging into our face, neck, and shoulders, until the inevitable happened, a stick penetrated one of Bolton's eyes. The blood curdling scream that he gave out caused our tormentors to flee, fortunately not before releasing the latch and enabling us to clamber free from our incarceration. Bolton's eye was red with blood and he was quickly rushed to the doctor's surgery - lucky for him he never suffered any loss of sight.

Mr Pike seemed to like the company of George and me even though we were sometimes into mischief, on one occasion by his own prompting.

From the back yard by the kitchen some steep steps rose to a level of about fifteen feet onto a path leading to a back gate which was used to avoid the main drive which served the 'big house'. (Using the drive was not encouraged). The path passed by and above a large yard at the rear of the stables which housed a compound in which all the dung-impregnated straw from the stables was deposited. Mr Pike told us, with a twinkle in his eye, that his nephew had jumped from the path into this, which we took to be a challenge, and seeing how soft the landing would be we made the same leap, tentative at first, but many more times with greater enthusiasm. Mr Pike was falling about with laughter as we fell and rolled in the straw, albeit laced with horse manure, which I must admit we never gave too much consideration to, but

Mrs Pike did, and wasn't at all pleased when we indoors smelling to high heaven with clothes in urgent need of washing.

Mr Pike never got really upset, even when we cracked the plaster of the ceiling in the harness room; a room filled with saddles, harnessing, and other associated paraphernalia. A room which was his pride and joy, for adorning the walls was dozens of rosettes which had been won at various horse shows over the years by the many horses that he had entered. Hanging from the centre of the ceiling was a rod which terminated about six feet from the floor with four upturned hooks shaped like umbrella handles. The purpose of the hooks was to allow reins, stirrups, and other items of harness to be hung from them to facilitate cleaning. The rod had a universal joint at the top such that it could be swivelled and positioned for convenience, but George and I found a more exiting use for it. If we got on top of one of the many cabinets, or tables around the room we could swing from one to the other. A good rainy day sport until the plaster let us down.

On another occasion we took some small planks of wood for the purpose of building a tree house, and having constructed a platform about three feet square in a suitable tree about half-a-mile from the house, we were told to stop by Lord Aubrey (Lady Herbert's son) who happened to be passing. He reported this to Mr Pike who then told us off, but we had the feeling that he was more upset with Lord Aubrey than with us for being such a spoilsport. Still, George, Sylvia, and I, had a great deal of fun with that small square wooden platform; we would build walls and a roof with foliage and bracken, which we would hang from the surrounding branches allowing just enough room for us to squeeze in.

I could understand Mr Pike's dilemma as a short time before he had received a complaint from the 'big house' concerning damage that we had done to the thatch on the roof of a small summer-house alongside the tennis-court. We had been sliding down it. The summer-house was old and in disrepair, as was the tennis-court, but obviously using its thatch as a slide had done nothing to improve it. Climbing along the branch of a tree close by, we had been able to drop onto the peak of the roof, and with grass cuttings piled up to provide a soft landing it was quite exciting and a lot of fun, the more you slid down the softer the landing became as each slide we made brought a little bit more thatch with it.

Mr Pike was an amiable man who easily made allowances for such transgressions, I had the feeling from some of the stories he told us that he had been no angel in his own childhood and early youth, but we did rock his equilibrium with one of our misdemeanours. It was on a warm, still, late-summer's day, when he was having a nap in an old armchair he kept for this purpose in the harness room. It was following lunch and after he had smoked a pipe, which Mrs Pipe did not like him doing in the house. He had left a box of matches outside the stables on the concrete mounting block where he had lit his pipe, and on seeing it there George and I thought it a good idea to light a small bonfire a little way from the house.

It would have been a better idea to have chosen to light it a long way from the house and in a place where it was safe to do so. We lit it however, in a spot barely hidden from the stables, and close to the perimeter fence around the inner grounds of Pixton House. It was following a dry spell of weather and the paper and sticks we used to start the fire were soon ablaze, unfortunately so was the grass all around it, and within minutes the fire had ignited the brush close by which spread to embrace some dead branches of a nearby fir tree. The fir tree was some thirty feet high and there was nothing we could do to stop the flames climbing up through the small dry branches that fir trees seem to have growing from the lower part of their trunks. Before we could raise the alarm, or make ourselves scarce, which probably passed through our minds, it was observed by Mr Pike, who had finished his nap, and by some gardeners who were working in the grounds. Fortunately, they were quick to form a bucket-chain from the stables where there was an outside tap sited over a half-barrel filled with water from which the horses drank. They threw water, not onto the flames which had now taken a very strong hold, but onto the surrounding grass and bushes to stop it spreading. The fir tree stood crackling like a giant Roman candle, the flames spluttering and rising high into the sky, fortunately in isolation from other trees, with only the now wet bushes and grass around it. George and I stood back watching in amazement, feeling guilty, foolish, and very frightened; wondering our fate.

Mr Pike was summoned to the 'big house' to give an account of the events, and following this, things got a bit tough for us. Not his attitude, he was still very friendly towards us, although middle-aged he was young at heart and being associated with young spirits the pattern of his life had been changed and he seemed to be enjoying it. No, a decision had been made to keep us busy, and so, out of trouble, and that's how the next day found George and me carrying out a task of extreme tediousness. The yard in front of Mr Pike's house and stables was rectangular in shape, measuring about twenty-five by sixty feet, and covered in cobbles, each one being roughly two inches wide and four inches long - over twenty thousand cobbles with moss and small weeds growing between each one. Armed with a small hook each, and pads made out of an old horse blanket to kneel on, we were made to scrape out the dirt between each cobble, a mission of hard labour which was to take us several weeks.

Further jobs followed, usually assisting Mr Pike, some interesting, some hard work, but none as onerous as de-weeding the cobbles. One of these concerned his allotment which demanded a lot of attention and his method of preparing the soil was most arduous but did yield results second to none resulting in a variety of magnificent vegetables. He called it trenching, which required a trench to be dug about a foot wide and six inches deep across the end of each vegetable patch, of which there were two about the size of the cobbled yard we had recently come to know so well. The earth from the trench was then taken to the other end of the vegetable patch and horse manure brought from the stables (fortunately not by us, but by horse and cart) was put into the trench. A second trench was then dug and the earth put over the horse manure in the first trench and so on until the end of the patch was reached where the earth from the first trench previously piled there was put into it. Every year the earth in the vegetable patch moved forward by one foot.

Gathering and storing wood for the fire was another task. There was always a fallen tree somewhere close by and off the three of us would go armed with a huge five foot long cross-cut saw, an axe, and an array of wedges; again, very hard work for two puny city boys. Mr Pike would be on one end of the saw, and George or I would be on the other end. Of course, there was a knack in it and Mr Pike made it clear from the start, "Don't push, only pull. Let the saw do the work." Pushing caused the thin wide blade of the saw to bend and hindered the smooth passage of the blade through the timber. We bent the saw a few times but soon got the hang of it. The thing was that the saw didn't do all the work, after pulling it through a tree trunk thirty inches across our arms felt like they had done some work too, and the thing was that our collective effort was equal to that of Mr Pikes and his arms were almost as thick as the branches of the tree we were cutting. Mind you, his efforts did not end there, he would then split the trunk with the wedges, driving them in along the grain with the back of the axe until it tore apart, repeating the process until the trunk was in numerous handy sized lengths which we could barrow back to the stables where sawing again reduced them to handy sized logs for the fire.

Coal or coke was never used. How different from home where the coal merchant would deliver our coal in sacks each week, but then again, how handy. On occasions my mum could not afford to pay for the minimal amount of a delivery, which was a one hundredweight sackful, and she would send me to a coal merchant down the end of our street who traded in selling it loose in small amounts and also loaned his barrow to bring it home on.

When the weather grew colder Mr Pike arranged for George and me to work in Pixton House chopping logs into firewood which we undertook each Saturday morning, not without some enthusiasm as we each received six-pence for this from the head maid. There was no central heating in this mansion and with the many rooms having a fireplace to be lit by maids at the crack of dawn, the amount of firewood required filled nearly two tea-chests, which took us all morning.

This activity took place in one of the rooms in the cellar which had a hatch through which the logs were tipped, having been cut and delivered from the saw mills at Weir Farm. We would both choose a large log to sit on, and a larger one upon which we

46

would place the log we were cutting up into firewood, for this purpose we were each given a very sharp billhook. The procedure was to select a nice straight log free from any large knots and cut it into thin slices about half-inch thick, these slices we then cut into sticks which would readily catch light when the maids lit the paper on which they were arranged in the fireplace.

Another little job for our sixpence was grinding coffee beans. The coffee grinder was sited in the very large kitchen which pleasantly smelt of food being either prepared or cooked. The smell of the coffee beans mingled and added to this aroma. We were further rewarded before we left with a couple of the cook's homemade cakes, or a piece of tart, washed down with her fruit drink of the day.

On Sunday evenings Mr Pike was in the habit of taking a long walk, and of course George and I accompanied him. On these occasions he always carried a walking-stick, not that he needed one to support him, but he showed us how it came in handy to clear a path through nettles, or brambles; consequently, we wanted one, so Mr Pike provided us each with a cut down version of his own. The walks would take us over the fringes of heather-laden Exmoor, or Haddon Hill, invariably coming back through Dulverton, where he would stop for a pint, or two, of ale, and a chat with some of the locals, buying George and me a glass of lemonade. Mrs Pike never joined us as she did not enjoy the best of health.

Although my life now had a variety of new interests, activities, and adventures, there were times that I longed to be home with my mum and dad, and my sister Jean. Having Sylvia and George with me helped, but on the odd occasion when I was alone I would have moments of despondency, I would think of life as it was before the war and wonder if I would ever see that life again. The loving care and security given to me by my parents, which I once took for granted, I now valued and missed so much. My optimism was such that I never feared that they would not survive the war, and that one day I would be back with them again, but it seemed such a long way off, and I knew things would never be the same.

It was probably, with times like this in mind, the 'Evacuee Song' was written:-

> Goodnight children everywhere,
> Your mummy thinks of you tonight,
> Lay your head upon your pillow,
> Don't be a kid or a weeping willow,
> Close your eyes and say a little prayer,
> And surely you can find a kiss to spare,
> Although you're far away,
> She's with you night and day,
> Goodnight children everywhere.

Although Mrs Pike provided us with a home and to all sense of purposes the care and security which was expected, her sufferance of us was far less. This was first brought home to me when I had the misfortune to wet the bed. I dreamt that it was a warm sunny day, and with my swimming costume on I was paddling in a stream with the water rippling around my ankles. This stimulated my need to urinate and it seemed most natural to do it there and then. As I was performing this function I woke up and was surprised to find that I was in bed and alarmed at what I was doing, and worried about the consequences. The sheets were soaked, top and bottom, and George shared the discomfort with me as we laid in them until the morning.

Mrs Pike was none too pleased and told me off. "A boy of your age should be able to control himself." I had never seen her so angry. I apologised and told her about my dream but she was unforgiving which exposed an element in her character of intolerance with regard to childhood problems. I pointed out that I was not in the habit of wetting the bed, and could not even remember having wet the bed before.

I wish that this had been an isolated incident but unfortunately the same thing happened about a week later. I woke up with my pyjamas wet, all down one side, with the sheets soaked as before.

I asked George, "Have you wet the bed?"

He said, "No!" To which I replied, "Well it wasn't me."

When having wet the bed previously I was well aware of doing it and so I was convinced that it could not have been me on this occasion. However George insisted that it was not him and continued to do so when we were confronted by an irate Mrs Pike. I was disappointed in George for not owning up, thinking that he must have known that it was him, but then again, he could have done it without being aware that he had done it, and come to that, maybe I had actually done it this time without knowing. I pointed out that the front of my pyjamas was not wet but it did not cut any ice, having wet the bed before I was deemed to be the guilty party. "I'm disappointed with you Rex," she said. "I can't have you continually wetting the bed, if it happens again you'll end up in The Retreat." Fortunately it never did, although a short time later I did end up in The Retreat.

The Retreat was a large house in Dulverton at the lower part of Fore Street which had been converted into a residential centre for evacuees who had complaints which their foster parents could not, or would not, deal with. I was there with boils. Ugly red boils had broken out profusely on numerous parts of my body; my neck, my arms, my back, my buttocks, and my legs; no part of me seemed to be without a boil. It was 'good living,' or so I was told - fresh air and wholesome food.

It was a terrible place to be in, the rooms were bare, without carpets or curtains, and very poorly furnished. The food was sub-standard, and the dining room was straight out of 'Oliver Twist' with its long scrubbed deal table and benches. We ate off of enamel plates, and drank out of chipped enamel mugs - white with blue edging. There were about ten children in residence at that time, boys and girls of different ages with a variety of complaints; impetigo, scabies, ringworm, boils, and bed-wetters.

In charge of this establishment was a matron who was always to be seen wearing her uniform of white starched linen, and the large white hat that completed a matron's ensemble; a stern looking woman whom we all feared. She was assisted by a few cheerless women who by their appearance were not in the nursing profession and undertook no duties of a medical nature, just routine jobs and keeping the children in order.

The boys all slept dormitory style in one room and the girls in another. Several of the boys were bed-wetters and each morning their beds would be stripped down to a rubber underlay which protected the mattress. The stench of the urine soaked bedding permeated the atmosphere of the room and was ever present. With my recent experience I had some sympathy with these boys, but mine was just a lapse from the norm, so I could not really understand their problem. The bed-wetters lived in The Retreat on a permanent basis, attending school each day and allowed out during the evening.

Amongst the bed-wetters was the oldest and largest boy in the establishment, who was also a bully. Fortunately he rarely turned his attentions to me seeming to concentrate on the long-term inmates who were forced to do his fetch and carrying. Resistance resulted in physical abuse or being locked in the broom cupboard for long frightening periods.

Each morning and evening I had to attend the Treatment Room (known as the Torture Chamber, and I soon found out why) where matron attended to your medical needs; her treatment for boils was to squeeze them. When a boil was large and inflamed, sporting a lurid yellow head, squeezing from the base and pushing towards the tip caused the core of the boil to be ejected leaving a hole up to an eighth of an inch in diameter, and about half-inch deep. When the entire puss was removed a dressing would be applied and the boil would expire leaving a small round scar. The squeezing of a boil is extremely painful, and when I had several to be dealt with in this manner twice a day the very thought of treatment filled me with dread. She would bathe a premature boil with hot water to 'bring it on' and often squeeze such a boil before it was ready, which often resulted in just part of the core being removed. This put the boil's development back and necessitated repeating the treatment at the next session. During treatment I would cry in pain which sometimes caused her to stop, possibly knowing that it would squeeze out better next time.

There were children there worse off than me. One small girl, no more than six had sores and scabs all over her body with one on her head like a skull-cap. Her head had been shorn but new hairs were growing through it. One day she fell asleep on an upright wooden chair and an open wound on the back of her leg, directly behind her knee, wept, and the substance dried to a newly formed scab which stuck to the chair. When she woke up she cried out in pain as she tried to free her leg.

Time passed very slowly as there was nothing to do. The few board games, such as Ludo, Snakes and Ladders, and Draughts, were either damaged or had parts missing.

The Retreat had no garden that I can recall, just a yard which had a tree growing in the middle of it through a hole in the concrete. The tree was without any live growth and white where all the bark had fallen off. The branches, of which there were quite a few, were arrayed in such a manner that made it a natural climbing frame and any fun had in that house of horrors was mostly associated with games played in and around that tree.

A large pair of gates some eight foot high led from the yard into Fore Street, with a small door within one of the gates which was used for pedestrian access. It was to this door that I was directed by the matron one Saturday morning and to my surprise Sylvia and George were standing there. To my further surprise so were my mum and dad, who suddenly appeared from hiding behind the gate.

My mum and dad had travelled down on a quickly arranged week-end visit to see me - what irony and disappointment to find me hospitalised and in such poor condition. They had arrived late on the previous day, booked into the Rock House Inn, and gone to Pixton Stables early the next morning, that was why Sylvia and George were with them. I presume that the matron had a mind to the contagious diseases within the hospice for she would not let them in, and would not let me out, so over that week-end I enjoyed the company of my mum and dad through the door to the yard only, albeit frequently during their short stay. Anyway, it was a much needed break for my mum and dad, and they were able to meet Mr and Mrs Pike and have a look at where I was living, which satisfied them knowing that I was in good hands.

I was in The Retreat for just over three weeks and very pleased when I was able to return to Pixton Stables, but unfortunately it was to be short lived because the boils returned. Firstly to George, who had two erupt on the back of his neck, quickly followed by one on his leg behind the knee, making it painful for him to walk. Mrs Pike dressed them with antiseptic cream and bandages, but when he broke out in more, and I had a major relapse, it was back to The Retreat for me, this time accompanied by George. The same unfortunates were still there wetting the bed, or suffering with the discomfort of their diseases and the miserable conditions. Fortunately, after a further few more weeks spent in there neither George nor I saw the inside of that place again.

While we were in the Retreat, Sylvia was moved from Pixton to the centre of Dulverton to be billeted with a Mrs Gibson in Fore Street. Her new billet, although an improvement to living with Minnie and her mother, turned out worse than she had hoped. It should have been a good move because she shared it with another girl from school and was able to meet up with all her friends in town after school hours, but Mrs Gibson was a disciplinarian, and a woman lacking humour. This was in sharp contrast to Sylvia who was a fun loving girl, full of the joys of life.

About this time, my aunt Violet came to live and work in a house close to the Pixton Estate. She had been in service as a young woman and now, with her husband George working away from home most of the time, she had come to Dulverton and found herself a position as housekeeper to an aged wealthy widow, Mrs Hitchen. It was a large house set in spacious grounds and apart from a gardener aunt Vi was the only servant, and treated like a slave. Although she attended to Mrs Hitchin's every needs; cooking, cleaning, laundering, shopping, and personal care; a warm relationship never developed between them. My aunt was never anything more to her than a skivvy paid to undertake her menial tasks. She was also discouraged from having visitors, nevertheless, with her living close by George and I would pop in and see her quite often on our way home from school. When we paid a visit it would be by the back door which led into the kitchen where Aunt Vi would rustle us up a biscuit and a drink, but she was always on tenterhooks waiting for a call from Mrs Hitchins which invariably came after a short time. Was it done deliberately to get rid of us? We thought so.

It was in Dulverton that I first recall noticing that there were many people like Mrs Hitchens who were a lot richer than others, which was not difficult as the area had more than its fair share of the landed gentry and middle classes. In fact, there was an abundance of well-to-do people living in large houses standing in expansive grounds, invariably with cars in the drive. Many owned horses and rode out with the hounds, having been born into a privileged lifestyle. Their pretentious bearing and haughty manner when speaking to those of a lower order displayed an air of arrogance and superiority. Invariably they addressed them by their surnames, whilst giving deference to their equals using their posh Christian or pet names…..."Saddle up my horse Pike, and attend to Aubrey's mount." There were very few exceptions and the comparison between them and farmhands, or others that served them, stood out a mile.

In Glenister Road, and the neighbouring streets, where I had spent my early childhood before the war, anyone that I was likely to encounter were working class and struggling to make ends meet. Their dwellings were more or less the same, some slightly better furnished than others, some a lot worse. With only two children in the family we seemed to be not too badly off, but in fact there was little between us and our neighbours, I just never knew it, and on one occasion when being asked if we were poor I replied that we were middle class…Little did I know?

In late summertime Aunt Violet's husband George came down for a few days and to my delight was accompanied by my mum and dad. Also with them were my mother's youngest sister Rose and her son Donald. Rose's husband was a Sergeant in the army serving abroad and with the bombing having started she thought it best to leave London; where better than a safe haven like Dulverton with us already there. She managed to find permanent lodgings and remained in Dulverton for about a year.

After the bad time young George and I had had in The Retreat it was a real pleasure to have our families visiting and they enjoyed being with us in the countryside away from the blitz.

We took them to all the interesting places in the area and on one occasion it was to Shaky Bridge -- well, not so much interesting as challenging. This bridge was no more than the trunk of a tall pine tree stripped of its branches and laid across the River Barle which at that point was about twenty feet wide. The upper side was sawn off along its entire length to make a flat surface of roughly nine inches wide narrowing to six inches as the trunk tapered. Nailed to one side were upright lengths of wood to which a single wire was attached, firmly fixed to stout posts at each end; the other side was open to the river.

With the fast flowing river some six feet below, none but the fearless ventured upon Shaky Bridge without some trepidation, and fearless was certainly not a term that I would relate to my mum and her two sisters. They were trembling at the very thought of it, but being weary, having walked a long way up the Brushford Road, and after I told them that it was a short cut and a pleasant walk back to Dulverton along a footpath which ran beside the river on the opposite bank, they gave it some consideration. Mind you, that consideration was nearly short lived when Sylvia, George, and I, went onto the middle of the bridge and bounced it up and down revealing how shaky it really was. Nevertheless, after a lot of persuasion by my dad and Uncle George, with the promise of help across the bridge, they agreed to have a go.

Aunt Vi went first, walking between my dad and Uncle George who each held one of her arms whilst gripping the wire rail with their other hand. In this manner, and with hesitant and tentative steps, they traversed the span of the river. It was hair-raising and the rest of us watched with our hearts in our mouths, giving a loud cheer when she reached the other side.

Aunt Rose, and then Donald, each followed in a similar manner but with a little more confidence having seen how Aunt Vi had done it.

When it came to my mum it was a different kettle of fish entirely. Older, built more portly, and consequently less nimble than her sisters, she was petrified from the start and at first refused to step onto the bridge. However, after many false starts she gingerly edged along the log between my dad and Uncle George until she reached the middle. It was then that her legs turned to jelly, you could see them shaking and she refused to move, gripping firmly to the wire. Fortunately, in the firm grip of my dad and Uncle George, and after several minutes in this position, her legs stopped quivering and she felt secure enough to move her feet little by little until they reached terra-firma on the other side, her face bright red with the heat that the anxiety had brought upon her.

She would not have gone across if she had known that the short cut back to Dulverton that I promised her was part way through a field of cows which scared her witless.

The autumn of 1940 came and went and life with Mr and Mrs Pike had settled into a pleasant routine. The boils had cleared up and the bed-wetting a blip on the calendar. We were still undertaking our Saturday morning jobs in Pixton house, and helping with stable work, and the allotment. Our last major task had been to help lay out hundreds of apples in the loft space above the stables and cover them with straw. This kept them from drying out too fast making them edible over the winter months for the Herbert family and their staff; and of course, us.

The space over the stables was an area where we played on wet days but there was still plenty of room in the covered entrance to the stables, and the Harness Room, which was still in bounds - swinging on the bridle support was not.

During the evenings we played in the living room, which was always kept warm with a big log fire, and often Mr and Mrs Pike joined us in a game of Tip-It, or Put and Take, which they introduced to us.

Tippet was played by two teams, one either side of the table, with George or me pairing up with either Mr or Mrs Pike, the only piece of equipment being a button. Each team had the button in turn and the pair holding it would mix their hands together under the table before bringing them back up with the button clenched in one of them, at the same time keeping a poker face to ensure giving nothing away. The opposite team had to guess which hand held the button and scored points depending on how many guesses it took. It sounds simple, which of course it was, but it was great fun and produced a lot of laughter.

Put and Take was played with a little brass top and an allocation of buttons (used as counters) given to each player. The top had six sides which after spinning would fall with instructions uppermost for the spinner to put or take buttons from or to the kitty. The winner was the one with most buttons at the end of the game.

Christmas came and went; it must have been a quiet affair because I can't remember it. The only thing I can recollect is the pocket watch that I received as a Christmas present from my mum and dad which had a train engraved on the back, but I clearly remember an incident which occurred early in the spring of 1941 which etched itself on my mind for ever. I cannot recall the time of year exactly, but after a long cold winter with heavy falls of snow, daffodils were in full bloom all over Pixton Park – thousands and thousands of them.

George and I were both in need of a haircut and Mr Pike who had taken this task upon himself since we had been with him decided it was time to get the clippers out again. He was a dab hand at trimming the horse's coats with a huge pair of electric clippers and he used the same on us, even though they were nearly as big as our heads, to give us a short back-and-sides. He was also adept with a pair of scissors and told us that he had learnt and honed this skill when he was in the army which had earned him a few bob. The hair cutting was carried out in the harness room but the scissors were kept within a drawer in the living room amongst needles and cotton, and other such items.

George, whose hair was to be cut first, was seated on a high stool when Mr Pike said to me, "Go and ask Mrs Pike for the scissors, would you Rex?"

Off to do his bidding, I ran down the passageway of the house and into the living room saying as I went through the door, "Mrs Pike. Mr Pike wants the scissors to cut our hair."

Mrs Pike was sitting in her armchair beside the fireplace with her back to me and as I entered the room she gave a loud groan. I thought that she was asleep and putting my hand on her shoulder gave a gentle shake, but with this, her head lolled to the left and she gave another groan.

I shook her again and said, "Come on Mrs Pike, don't mess about." It was then that I noticed foam coming from her mouth.

"Are you alright Mrs Pike? Mrs Pike are you alright?" I could see that she was not but I was hopeful of a positive response, instead she just slumped forward with her mouth frothing some more and still groaning.

Knowing that something was seriously wrong with her I ran from the house and into the harness room shouting, "Mr Pike, Mr Pike, something's wrong with Mrs Pike, she's all funny, she won't wake up and she's got foam coming from her mouth."

Mr Pike said, "Oh my God!" and ran from the harness room and into the house with me on his heels, closely followed by George.

Mrs Pike was still slumped in the armchair just as I had left her, except that now she was not moving and had stopped groaning. Mr Pike took her face in his hands for a brief moment before turning around to leave the house, blurting out, "I must get a doctor."

He was no great shakes as a runner but he jogged along as fast as he could, shadowed by George and me, to Pixton House and a phone.

On reaching Pixton House he burst through the side door and trotted down the long passageway, his feet clattering on the flagstones until he was confronted by the head cook, Miss Mackay, who had popped out of the kitchen to see what was causing all the noise, but before she could speak Mr Pike blurted out, "She's gone. It's her heart, I must phone the doctor."

Miss Mackay led Mr Pike to the telephone which was located in the main entrance hall and phoned the doctor for him.

"You go home and wait for the doctor," she said. "I'll take care of the boys."

When Mr Pike had gone Miss Mackay took us into the kitchen and gave us tea and biscuits whilst I related to her the details of what had happened. She then took us to Miss Goss, the housekeeper, who made arrangements for George and me to be temporarily accommodated in Pixton House itself. She found us a small uninviting room in the attic which looked like it had not been used for years. The room was bare except for two small unmade iron bedsteads, a small chest of drawers, and a large framed picture of Queen Victoria on the wall with the glass cracked diagonally from top to bottom. It was probably put into that room because nobody else wanted it and no-one had the will to throw it away, it certainly did nothing to brighten up the room; in fact, we found it rather scary, one of those pictures where the eyes follow you wherever you go.

The room had a small window which was let into the sloping roof above the servant's quarters and overlooked the long drive and the big white gates leading into the gardens which formed the approach to the house.

Miss Goss left us, and whilst we were in the room giving it the once-over two maids, Bridie and Collette, came in with bed linen and made up the beds. Like most of the half-a-dozen maids in the house they had come over from Ireland to work and with our comings and goings to the house we had got to know them all quite well. They were full of fun and often teasing us, but on this occasion they had obviously heard why we were there and offered their sympathy. Miss Mackay followed them up and told us that we would not be able to collect our clothes until the morning and would have to sleep in our underwear that night.

We never went to school the next day. The cook served us breakfast in the kitchen after which we returned to The Stables to fetch our clothes where we were surprised to find a young lady answer the door. She was in her early twenties, tall and slim with jet black hair who introduced herself as Christine, Mr Pike's niece. She knew who we were and told us that she had come to keep house for Mr Pike until he could manage on his own.

Going into the living room we found Mr Pike slumped in his armchair looking tired and careworn, but he put on a brave face when he saw us and stood up. We could see that he was feeling very low and when we said how sorry we were that Mrs Pike had died he put his arms around both of us at the same time and hugged us close. He held us like this for a few minutes without saying a word, then in a choked voice he said something like, "Yes, I've lost her boys, and I'm sorry but it looks like I'm losing you too."

We stayed like this for a few moments until Christine said, "Come on you two, I'll help you pack your things."

As we climbed the stairs with Christine I had it in my mind that Mrs Pike's body would be laid out on her bed, but on passing the open door to her bedroom it was clean and tidy with the bed empty and made up as usual, I realised then that it had been taken away to somewhere else.

I had only ever experienced the death of someone known to me once before and that was a boy who lived directly across the road from me, Bobby Anderson, who had died from tuberculosis and his body laid out in the front room of his house where friends and relatives could view it and pay their last respects. I recalled it quite clearly because I went with a group of older boys who were his friends of the same age, to see him lying in his coffin. I was a couple of years younger but they tolerated me hanging around with them and when Mrs Anderson let them in I latched on to the tail end of the group and followed them through the front door and up the passage, but before I got anywhere near the coffin she turfed me out. "You're too young," she said.

Christine helped us pack our clothes, and other belongings, and apologised for us having to leave so hurriedly, but as she said, there was only two bedrooms and she now needed one of them.

Back in Pixton House our garret looked more welcoming once the bed was made up and we had our clothes and toys to adorn the room, but it was cold comfort compared to what we had just lost.

The format of dinner that evening was a great surprise to me; I certainly did not expect it to be as elegant as it was .This was our first visit to the staff dining room so when we entered I was taken aback on seeing a long table laid out with silverware for about ten places. I could have been forgiven if I thought that I was at the other end of the house about to have dinner with the Herbert's, but Miss Goss was already seated with other members of the staff in their places.

Being the housekeeper, Miss Goss sat at the head of the table (there was no head butler) with the head maid to her right, and Miss Mackay, the head cook, to her left. There was a young lady who looked after a nursery of infant evacuees (about forty of them were housed somewhere in the building), several maids, and a handyman. George and me sat between them and felt very grown-up being served by assistant cooks and helping ourselves to vegetables from the silver tureens placed on the table.

We spent several weeks living with the staff of Pixton House, still chopping the firewood and grinding the coffee, until we were found a new billet.

Our new home was with a Mr and Mrs Rough in Brushwood who ran a garden nursery producing tomatoes. They were a very old couple, at least in their seventies, possibly in their eighties, and not the likeliest of people to be given the responsibility of looking after two young boys like us. Nevertheless, they were kind, the house was warm, and they fed us well, but unfortunately little attention was given to what we wore, or what we were doing, leaving us to arrange our own programme of activities which included getting up in time for school.

The journey to school from Brushford required us to catch 'Danny's Bus'. It was the only bus that ran between Dulverton and Brushwood and made the journey numerous times throughout the day, mainly to collect, or take, passengers arriving or leaving the trains stopping at Dulverton Station. In the morning it was run early enough to get us to school on time, and Danny who owned and ran the bus - a colourful and friendly character - would hold it up if a regular passenger was late, which he did for us quite often. Even so, we frequently missed the bus and had to walk the mile-and-a-half to school arriving cold, wet, and very late.

The teachers at the school soon became aware that our living arrangements were not all they should be, and my mum and dad brought it to a head when they came to Dulverton on a flying visit and found us in snowy weather, admittedly late for the time of the year, wearing skimpy clothes and light shoes. They demanded that we be found more suitable accommodation poste-haste which happened within the next few days.

The reason for my mum and dad's sudden arrival was nothing to do with the unsuitability of our digs but concerned the welfare of my sister Jean. Our house, back home in Glenister Road, Greenwich, had become one of the casualties of the Luftwaffe's bombing campaign which had raged over London for the past six months and Jean was in the house at the time. Fortunately, it was not a direct hit otherwise she would have 'been no more'. At the time she was sheltering under the kitchen table, a stoutly built deal table with strong legs such that when the roof and upper floors caved in and buried her she was dug out of the rubble in one piece, a bit shaken but otherwise unscathed.

She had just turned sixteen and this life threatening experience had not only shaken her up, but it was also a big shock to my mum and dad. They already knew that it was needless of her to be exposed to the ravages of the blitz, now they had to do something about it; unlike them, employed on war-work, she was only working in a shop. Also, still burning in their minds was a recent incident concerning friends of theirs living close-by. Their son, Ronnie, who was a year younger than Jean, was helping his father dig a hole in the back garden for an Anderson shelter. It was after the 'All Clear' had gone following an air-raid, and to all sense and purposes safe to be doing so, when a late stray bomber dropped it's load blowing Ronnie to pieces. His father had gone indoors for something or other and was unharmed, but devastated.

Jean had resisted the pressures of my mum and dad to be evacuated, but enough was enough, and that very same evening my dad took Jean to Paddington station and bought a one-way ticket to Dulverton with a quickly written letter to the council offices explaining her circumstances and requesting they find employment for her in service. Normally, Jean would have put up considerable resistance to this, but her recent experience had subdued her, and anyway her home no longer existed. She was found a position with a famous author, Roland Pertwee, who had a large house on the hillside above Exebridge and my mum and dad had come down to see how she had settled in. (The Pertwee family were into acting, writing, and the arts, one later playing Doctor Who).

*   *   *   *   *

I was never to live in Greenwich again. Many of the houses in Glenister Road were damaged to the extent whereby they could be rebuilt, but our house, No 43, and immediate neighbouring houses were beyond repair and replaced after the war by a new housing development. I had lived all of my pre-war years in that house and my memories are of amusing and pleasant times even though things were tough for my parents.

The terraced house we lived in was similar to thousands built throughout London, having a bay window, and a recessed front door, which would have opened directly onto the pavement except for about two feet of frontage which was enclosed by a small brick wall topped with ornamental iron railings, and a wrought iron gate. (Incidentally, they removed all of the wrought iron at the onset of war for the manufacture of munitions).

Inside, a passageway led from the front door through to the kitchen at the rear of the building, sidestepping the facing stairs which led up to three bedrooms.

Behind the bay window was the front room, and squeezed between that and the kitchen was a middle room (known as the sitting room) which like the kitchen had a window with a bleak view of a narrow passageway leading to the very small backyard and the outside toilet.

My father had lived all of his life there, and as a boy, with his parents, five brothers, and two sisters, you can bet that all rooms were needed, and more.

When my mother married my father she moved in with him and undertook the responsibility of running the household, his mother being no longer alive, and his elder sister and brothers having married and left home. Looking after his father must have been no mean feat for a young woman of twenty-two as he was a heavy drinker, frequently coming home drunk, and as an ex-Sergeant Major not one to have his home organised and run by a young slip of a girl. However, he came to appreciate her before he died of bowel cancer when she nursed him through the trauma and the messy difficulties associated with that disease.

She also cared for my father's younger brother Arthur and his sister Winifred, and in my earliest memories they formed part of our family.

The house was always well occupied because even after Winifred and Arthur moved out my mum took in lodgers to help pay the rent. I know this was always hard to find because on many occasion when the landlord came for his money my mum didn't have it. She would grab Jean and me, and we would all hide quietly in a spot where he couldn't see us. It was obvious he knew we were in because he shouted words of that nature through the letter-box and persistently rapped the knocker, and looked through the front window. It was often under that very window in the front room that we were hiding and we could see his shadow on the opposite wall when he was peering through.

Lack of money or not, the house always had a happy atmosphere. We were one of the few houses in the street with a piano and frequently on a Saturday night neighbours and friends would come in after the pubs had turned out and the house would be 'jumping'. There was always somebody who could knock out a tune on the piano and plenty ready to sing the old melodies, or popular songs of the day, with every one joining in the choruses. Jean and I would creep out of bed and sit on the stairs in the dark and enjoy the merriment, looking at the scene through the banisters until we were spotted and packed off back to bed. My dad was always the life and soul of the party and watching him perform a monologue, or sing a comic song, was amongst my greatest pleasures.

My mum would sometimes insist that the party be held somewhere else and then the men would lift up the piano and carry it into another house nearby. Nothing could stop a party on a Saturday night.

Our house was next door to Morton's grocers shop on one of the corners where Glenister Road and Armitage Road crossed, and with barely any traffic using these streets, just the occasional horse and cart used by tradesmen, and on rare occasions a car, this junction was a playground for all the children living nearby. There were also shops on two of the other three corners; Kites the sweetshop, and Maxwell's (bag-wash) Laundry. Kites had my ha'penny pocket money each day which bought an ounce of sweets, but often I only ended up with half-ounce having been tempted to gamble on a lucky dip. The lucky dip comprised of a box filled with dozens of envelopes each of which had an amount written under the flap, such as 1oz, 2oz, 4oz, and on up to 16oz, but the vast majority of them had half-ounce We all knew that the gamble wasn't worth it and would give it a miss, but every now and then someone would have a big win and come out of the shop with sixteen ounces of sweets which suckered us back. My sister Jean was one of these rare winners and blew it all on sixteen ounces of jaw-breaker toffee, which my mum was not too pleased about as she had false teeth top and bottom. Sometimes my ha'penny went on a quarter of a pound of broken biscuits from Morton's which he served up in a large cone of paper – good value for money.

Inflation was non-existent in those days and my pocket money always remained at a ha'penny-a-day with a penny on Saturday. Each day my mum would give me the ha'penny, but on Saturday I would receive the penny from my dad when he finished work at mid-day. This was known to me as my Saturday's penny, and he always managed to find one that was brand spanking new.

I would eagerly await him to turn the corner at the end of the street then run to meet him. He would hold his arms out and I would run into them to be swung round and round before being placed on his shoulders to be borne home as a 'flying angel'. Knowing almost everyone in Glenister Road he would exchange cheerful banter with the many people we passed.

He worked as a process worker at The Tunnel Glucose Refineries and felt lucky to have got the job when the factory opened in the early thirties having been on the dole for a long period during 'The Depression'. I never heard him complain about his work, which was routine and humdrum, but I know that it never fulfilled him like the artistic requirements of sign-writing and coach-painting which had been his craft before the slump.

He still kept his hand in, and made himself some extra money painting names and logos on shop fronts in Greenwich taking great pride in pointing them out to Jean and me when we passed one of his works of art.

One Sunday morning I was watching him paint the facia board of George's Café at the end of our road when George called him down from the ladder and said, "Come in Alf, I've boiled you an egg."

My dad said, "Thanks George, that's decent of you," and he went into the café, followed closely by me.

Seeing the egg we both fell about laughing, it was huge and instead of an egg-cup it was mounted on a thick china mug – it was a swan's egg.

My memories of those pre-war years are of happy and amusing times filled with interesting and fun-filled pastimes and events. I was allowed to play out in the street from as early as I can remember. Both Glenister and Armitage Roads had an abundance of children of all ages and there were so many games to play, handed down from one generation to another.

In my infancy it was Statues; Touch, and its variations such as Off-ground Touch; Kerb and Wall; Fairy Steps and Giant Steps; Queenie; Hide and Seek; Hop-scotch; then as I got older, the games became more robust, such as Hi Jimmy Knacker; Tin Can Copper-man; Kingy; Releaso; Cannon; and Tip-it. (See Appendix 1).

Then there was football and cricket, both played with a tennis ball. The cricket bat was cut and shaped by someone's dad out of a single piece of wood, and the wicket chalked onto the wall, thus any argument about whether the ball hit the wicket was easily determined by an examination of the ball for tell-tale chalk marks. There was always plenty of chalk around for this, and for marking out hopscotch, just a short trip to the shoreline of the River Thames where big lumps of it could be found.

Other pastimes came around at different times of the year known as crazes, such as marbles, whip-and-top, and cigarette cards.

Marbles was played in the gutter where the cobbled channel was ideal for an intriguing game. The 'glarnies' as the glass marbles were called would act uncontrollably in the joints between the cobbles, making it harder for you to hit your opponents marble. One or two kids liked to play 'lenders' where you all got your marbles back at the end of a session, but most of us played 'keepers' which gave the game an edge.

Almost every child had a whip and top and this craze hit the streets at least once a year. The tops were of various shapes but the favourite was one known as a window-breaker. It was shaped like a mushroom and when whipped to keep it spinning it would soar above the ground and could be kept spinning from one end of the street to the other. Everybody customised their top with a colourful design which gave a rainbow effect as it spun flew through the air.

The pastime that gave the widest range of pleasure and amusement involved cigarette cards; I had stacks kept in a biscuit tin. There were various games that we played which required the ability to flick a card both a good distance, and with correct aim. The games were usually played from a standing position in the gutter towards a wall at the back of the pavement with the object to get your card nearest the wall, the winner keeping both cards. An alternative game was to overlap another card, or knock down a card that had been pre-positioned leaning against the wall.

Cigarette cards came in a huge variety. The numerous tobacco manufacturers each had many brands and every packet of cigarettes had at least one picture card inside depicting a range of subjects; sportsmen, ships, animals, soldiers, film-stars; the different categories seemed endless. Collecting new cards and arranging them in sets was therefore another activity and undertaken on a rainy day, or when nothing better was happening.

With no-one smoking ready-made cigarettes in our house (my father rolled his own using loose tobacco) I had to go begging for new cards. It was a common and accepted practice for children, and I was no exception, to stand outside a tobacconist's shop and approach a customer as he emerged, usually unwrapping a packet of cigarettes, to politely ask, "Can I have the card please, mister," which invariably he would give to you.

There was a certain joy in anticipating what card you might get. Most often it would be a single card from a packet of ten Will's Woodbines, or Player's Weights, which were the cheapest cigarettes, and the ones most frequently bought in our neighbourhood, but occasionally someone would buy twenty Craven A, or Kensitas, or one of the many other more expensive brands which held two superior and rarer cigarette cards.

I realised the advantages of living in a street with little traffic and dozens of children to play with when I palled up with a boy at school whose father owned a classy sweetshop in the main road. When he first invited me round to play I thought that it was heaven. He lived in a flat above the shop and had an assortment of toys that I could only dream of, what more could a boy want. A lot as it happened, he was an only child and not allowed out in the street, and after a while playing with his toys in the flat I realised he wasn't in paradise - compared to me, he was in prison.

In the summer holidays I would be taken almost daily, weather permitting, to Greenwich Park. My sister Jean, being nearly six years older than me, together with some of her friends of a similar age, would be in charge of an entourage of smaller children of various ages, one or two being pushed in a pram. Jean and I each had a penny to spend, some sandwiches, lemonade powder, and an empty bottle. We would stop on the way to buy halfpenny-worth of sweets with the intention of making them last all morning, but they were usually gone by the time we reached the park gates.

On entering the park we would put some of the lemonade powder into the empty bottle and join others milling around a large drinking fountain to fill it up with water to make a lemon drink. This would be repeated throughout the day until the lemonade powder had run out. It would have lasted longer had we not constantly dipped our fingers into the lemonade powder and then into our mouths which left us with bright yellow tongues, and fingers.

The drinking fountain was huge and made of marble, or stone. It had a circular trough about four feet off the ground with numerous water outlets operated by brass buttons, also, cast iron drinking cups attached by a chain. On a hot day it was chaotic around the fountain as there could be about twenty children filling bottles, drinking water, or just splashing the water on themselves, with small children plonked in the trough to keep them cool.

We would roam the park, or play games organised by the older children until mid-day when we would have a picnic, then it was back to the park gates, where Mick the ice-cream man had his barrow, to spend the remaining ha'penny on an ice cream cone.

Greenwich Park is arguably the finest park in London with its flower gardens, variety of trees, and hilly open spaces, but more importantly, as far as we were concerned, it had a 'swing park' second to none. Apart from swings, there were numerous roundabouts, a rocking horse and a rocking boat, contraptions which seated six to eight children and swung to and fro, a maypole, sky-high slides, and apparatus for the gymnasts. It was a health and safety nightmare, and there to oversee and attend our cuts and bruises was one woman who we knew as Mrs Brown. There was also a sandpit, a paddling pool, and a boating lake which offered three types of craft for hire; canoes, rowing boats, and paddle boats.

A roundabout toured our streets in the summer months. It was horse-drawn, with seats arranged around a circular base having a canopy above and steps at the back which led onto this appliance. The whole ensemble was painted in gaudy colours, mainly of red, yellow, and blue, and as the horse pulled the contraption along, the circular base revolved and fairground type music blared out. The cost of a ride was one small jam-jar, (returnable at a grocers shop for one half-pence); a large jam-jar would get you two rides. A ride on the roundabout would take you spinning along the street for about one-hundred-and-fifty yards. A miserable gipsy looking man who took the jam-jars would lead the horse while his wife sat up in the driver's seat holding the reins. Every now and then he would crack a long whip right around the back to discourage free-loaders from riding on the steps at the rear. With this danger element, stealing a ride on the steps was almost as much fun as riding on the roundabout.

On very hot summer days the tarmac surface of the road blistered and a mobile tanker came around sprinkling water to cool the surface. This slow moving vehicle had a pipe fitted horizontally along the back with holes through which water was jetted and children would quickly don their swimming costume, or strip to their under-pants, and walk behind enjoying a cool shower, The water left the pipe forming an arc making it possible for someone small, like me, to run in from the side and walk behind this waterfall fully clothed without getting wet, so long as you kept at the same pace as the vehicle. It was too good to be missed, and that is what I was doing on one occasion when I passed my mum gossiping on the corner by Kite's sweetshop.

"You Rexy! What are you doing?" she shouted. I immediately stood stock still and got soaking wet.

Early memories in life are usually there due to something very special happening, sometimes pleasant, or emotional, and sometimes exciting, or shocking. In 1935 such an occurrence happened to me. It was during the run up to the general election when my father and a lot of other parents in our locality had high hopes of a labour government being elected. A march was organised in support of the Labour Party, not for adults but for children, and was to start in Armitage Road, just around the corner from our house and finish outside of the Greenwich Conservative Party campaign offices. The idea of a crowd of children marching was probably to arouse an emotive response and about forty children started off. My dad had made a drum each for Jean and me out of biscuit tins which were tied around our necks with string, other children had similar instruments; whistles, horns, anything which made a noise. It was all to be a bit of fun and in this fashion we all started off in high spirits chanting a short verse in support of the local Labour candidate....

"Vote, vote, vote for Mister Palmer,
Chuck Hopwood Hume out of the door,
With his high topper hat,
And his belly big and fat,
We won't vote Tory any more."

.....after which we banged our drums, blew horns and whistles, and gave a rousing chorus of "Vote for Labour."

The march took us around the network of streets comprising our neighbourhood, then finally up Blackwall Lane to it's junction with Old Woolwich Road where we converged on a very large house being used as the Conservative's headquarters. By the time we had reached our destination the number in the march had doubled and now included a lot of older teenagers and young men, and when we congregated on the deep pavement outside the front gates of the premises they started to make a lot more of the demonstration than was intended. They climbed the surrounding fence and broke down the hoardings and signs which were erected in the front garden, and threw stones at the house, the whole scene turned nasty.

Greenwich Police Station, also in Old Woolwich Road, was only a short distance away, and within no time at all a squad of policemen appeared on the scene with there truncheons drawn and looking very angry indeed.

Jean grabbed hold of my hand. "They're going to arrest us," she said, and we started running. It was most frightening and we never stopped running until we reached our front door.

That was the last general election before the war. George Hopwood Hume won the seat in Greenwich and a Conservative government was elected.

Ironically, the house which was used by the Conservatives for their election headquarters and which was vilified by a vast number of the residents of Greenwich was sold off and a cinema built on the site which became a venue for many happy moments for the people living thereabouts.

The opening of the 'Granada' cinema was done in style. The film being shown to celebrate its opening was Sabu the Elephant Boy and Sabu himself was there to perform the opening ceremony. He came out of the foyer riding splendid on top of an elephant clad in ceremonial Indian dress complete with a turban. The outfit was pristine white from head to toe, with red, blue, and gold decoration. His elephant was adorned with similarly coloured drapes, carrying an ornate carriage high on its back in which he was seated - it was breathtaking. Sabu dismounted and paraded in the semi-circle of space that the crowd had been marshalled to form. I had squeezed myself to the front and was almost in touching distance as he smiled and waved to us. I saw the film later that week with my mum and dad; a treasured memory.

There were two other cinemas in the area, the Trafalgar, also in Old Woolwich Road, and the Roxy in Blackheath, but the Granada was one of the new super-luxury-cinemas being built throughout London which were offering a bit more than just movies. When you went to the Granada in the evening you reckoned on having at least three hours of entertainment, and often more. There would always be an 'A' film and a 'B' film, together with a short comedy film or cartoon, and the newsreel.

Occasionally, on a large stage in front of the screen, they had professional entertainers, or held talent shows. My dad, the would-be thespian that he was, soon put his name forward and was duly invited to appear on one of the Monday shows. He had chosen to act out dramatic sketches from well known novels, and also tell a monologue.

With my mum, Jean and I gained seats near the front, and after the first film was shown the manager presented the talent show.

My dad had drawn the short straw and was first on, but unfortunately for him the microphone was not. The manager must have switched it off after introducing him and before leaving the stage. Completely unaware of this he launched himself into his first sketch, which was a scene from Trilby by George du Maurier. He adopted the mantle of the wicked hypnotist Svengali expressing his love for Trilby, and going down on one knee he mouthed a passage from the book, pleading with her, and offering words of endearment, then clutching his heart he keeled over. Gasping, and gurgling, he gave his best impression of a dying man. However, nobody, except possibly those in the first few rows, would have heard, or understood any of it.

He portrayed Fagin in his second sketch teaching Oliver how to steal a handkerchief. Walking back and forth across the stage with the imaginary Oliver taking a handkerchief from his pocket, and speaking with a Jewish accent that nobody could hear but which I knew included the words, "Good boy Oliver, here's sixpence," having heard him practice it many times indoors.

By this time the audience had become restless. Having not heard a word, nor understood what 'the idiot on the stage' was doing, they joined in a protest that was started by a group of my dad's mates who were shouting, "Switch the mike on! Switch the mike on!" at which the manager came back onto the stage, switched the microphone on and apologised.

Fortunately, the audience could then hear my dad give his monologue 'Spotty' (Appendix 2) which was well received judged by the applause he got. Needless to say he won no prizes and possibly took another year off of my mum's life -- red faced with embarrassment she had 'puffed and panted' throughout the entire performance.

One evening each week, apart from the normal cinematic programme, an organist would play a musical selection. The large white illuminated organ was something special, a wonderful spectacle to see as it rose out of the ground from a pit in front of the stage with the organist playing his signature tune. Dressed in a spotlessly white suit he would introduce himself to us, his audience, and then play a medley of popular songs which we would all sing along to. There was no need to know the words because they were printed on the screen. We, my family, loved a sing-song and always arranged to go to the pictures, which was a weekly occurrence, on the night that the organist was there.

I also went to the Saturday morning programme which was arranged for children only, with films to suit, like Hoppalong Cassidy, (a cowboy saga), or Buck Rogers, (spaceman). It was run as a club, 'The Greenwich Granadiers', and had its own song which was sung each week to the tune of The British Grenadiers. It went like this:-

> We're all for one and one for all,
> The Greenwich Granadeirs,
> We play the game of work and fun,
> The Greenwich Granadeirs,
> And when the clouds are overcast,
> We find the silver lining,
> You'll know us when we shout I SERVE,
> The Greenwich Granadiers.

The manager was known to us as Uncle John and each week he would give out a few prizes to children holding admission tickets having a lucky number. On occasions he arranged a competition, one in particular I can remember distinctly – the Bif-Bat Competition.

Bif-Bats were all the rage, a craze that swept through London at the time. It was the simple commonplace arrangement of a rubber ball fixed to a length of elastic secured to the centre of a small round bat. Bif-Bat was a proprietary name and produced two types, a utility model, and one for the keen enthusiast which was more expensive and far superior. This bat, made of wood and painted bright red with the Bif -Bat logo blazoned across the back, was over half-inch thick with an easy-grip handle and when you hit the ball it had a solid feel to it which in capable hands ensured optimum performance. The lesser bat was made of thin plywood, unpainted except for the logo, and the performance of this bat was reflected in its cheap price: poor. Jean had a red bat, I had a plain bat. We both entered the Bif-Bat competition which was held in Granada's car- park.

The object of the competition was to keep hitting the ball with the bat continuously for the longest period of time. In preparation of the contest, along with all of the other kids in the street, we had been practising for weeks, even indoors, with mum and dad getting fed up with the sound of the thud-thud-thud of Jean's bat, or the slap-slap-slap of mine. It was, "For Christ's sake, can't you put those bats down for five minutes, they're driving us mad." So when the day of the competition came we were each primed to our own level of competence.

All of the competitors, dozens of us, were made to stand in a line with our backs to a wall at the rear of the car-park, and at a given command the batting commenced. Adjudicators were posted every twenty feet or so, and when a ball was missed the defaulting competitor was removed from the line. I never felt that I gave my best as I missed the ball after about two hits, and trying to cheat by re-hitting the ball I missed again and got the elastic tangled around my wrist. I was ignominiously pulled out.

Jean was Bif-Batting like a champion and was still in the game when it whittled down to the last six. She was the only girl left in the competition and I was getting very excited as the prize was a brand new bicycle and she had promised me her old one if she was the winner.

At this point they stopped the contest and re-grouped the six so that they were all much closer together having become spaced out across the total span of the car-park. They were then re-started.

The contest was tense, and the huge crowd of onlookers, and failed Bif-Batters, were shouting and geeing their favourites on. Jean was going great guns, her ball going backwards and forwards in a straight line from her bat in a regular pattern, and her concentration unfazed by the noise and distractions. The practice was paying off, she was going to win -- I knew it.

Jean was about thirteen at this time and highly popular amongst the girls and boys in our neighbourhood. She was the only girl in the street who could keep up with the boys of her age on roller skates, and could also, with her drill-slip tucked into her knickers, shin up the lamppost on the corner and turn the gaslight on. Many of the boys could not do that.

One by one the Bif-batters failed until there were only three of them left, two boys and Jean standing just a few feet apart, with each ball on bat following a similar rhythmical motion. Then disaster struck, Jean angled her bat slightly causing the trajectory of her ball to change, she tried to correct it but the strict control of her wrist action was lost and the erratic behaviour of the ball caused her to miss it. No tears from Jean, she had done her best and that was that, and we both had to stick with our old bikes.

The following Saturday morning mid-way through the cinema programme, Billy Lambert, the winner of the Bif-Bat competition, was called onto the stage to receive his prize, a brand new Hercules Bicycle with three speed gears. The runner-up, a boy unknown to me, received a pair of skates. The second prize held no appeal for Jean anyway because she always bragged that her skates, brand name 'Union', were the best that you could buy, although I always argued, without any foundation, that my 'Speedfast Self Guiders' were superior.

Billy Lambert lived in Armitage Road and was well known to us. His father was our insurance man, distinct in the neighbourhood not for this reason but for the fact that he only had one leg, having lost his other in France during the First World War. He never seemed impaired by it as he got around with ease on a pair of crutches with which he could move with alarming speed, when going full tilt it was a job to keep up with him. On one occasion I was enthralled to see him run for a bus which had moved away from the bus stop as he approached it. Chasing it down the road in giant strides, with his unbuttoned raincoat flared out behind him like Superman's cloak, he caught up with it before it fully accelerated and launched himself like a pole-vaulter onto the platform, his crutches gripped under his arms as if attached there.

About this time cables were being laid in trenches down the streets to provide electricity to each house, lighting and plug points being appropriately fitted. We had no appliances to make use of the electricity, nevertheless, my mum soon got herself an electric iron and not long after a Goblin vacuum cleaner. Up until then our means of lighting had been with gas mantles which were fixed high on the wall in each room and gave out a very dismal light, electric light bulbs were a vast improvement.

It was in the autumn and the workmen (trench diggers, and cable layers) had erected a shelter in Armitage Road, close to it's junction with Glenister Road, in which they could eat their food and relax during lunch and tea breaks. There was a long table down the centre with a bench either side, and outside, close to the entrance, a brazier was kept burning which wafted heat into the shelter and on which they boiled a kettle for their tea.

After the workmen left each evening a night watchman came on duty to keep an eye on the site. He was an old man who liked the company of children, and when in the darkness of early evening we were drawn to the warmth of the brazier burning brightly he invited us to sit in the shelter. At his suggestion we each brought a large potato which he arranged on his brazier baking them until their skins were burnt and crispy. We ate them oozing with butter. I had never had potatoes baked in their jackets before, either because I had not been offered them, or perhaps I had refused to eat them, but in that old night watchman's tent with my sister and all the other children sitting at that long table, it rates amongst the best things I have ever tasted. Those evenings when the tent was in that location must have solved a problem for my mum who had a job getting food down me, for apart from the potatoes, she encouraged me to take other things to eat.

The old night watchman had a wealth of stories that he liked to tell us, all adventures with himself as the central character, and each evening we sat around enthralled, pleading for more.

In the spring of 1939 I became free to go to Greenwich Park and other places that were previously restricted to me without my minder – Jean. She had left school and started work at a shop called Sydney Green selling a range of items such as underwear, children's clothes, bed-linen, and towels. I recall my mother taking me there to buy a lumber-type jacket, maroon coloured, which I thought made me look like a cissy, but with a few favourable comments I soon got used to it.

That summer I was playing in Greenwich Park with some friends when we noticed workmen digging up grassland close to the Maze Hill entrance that we used. The development of this, observed on subsequent visits, resulted in huge trenches some six feet across and about ten feet deep criss-crossed over a large area; wire-bound chestnut paling was erected around to bar entry. Of course this was never going to stop us from getting in to enjoy a most bizarre experience playing within this high walled labyrinth. Our fun was to be short lived however because our shrieks of amusement were heard by park keepers who quickly arrived on the scene and told us in no uncertain manner to "Get the bloody well out of there." We did not give ourselves up meekly, running away from park keepers was an annual event anyway when they chased us during the conker season for throwing sticks high into the horse chestnut trees, but getting us out of the trenches was a different matter. After we ignored their calls to come out several of them came down the gradient leading to the lower level and with some difficulty, due to the maze of corridors, cornered us one by one. We each got a good clump around the head, which was par for the course in those days, and led by our ears to the gates of the park with a stern warning of what lay in store for us should we be found in there again.

As the weeks passed by the trenches were lined with concrete, complete with a slab across the top. Earth was then put back to the original level and grass laid on top to restore the area to much as it was before except for a number of air vents and an entrance to this underground chamber. Preparations were being made for war, which I had become increasingly aware of, and I had observed one of the first communal air-raid shelters being built.

Individual shelters for personal use were being built in back gardens throughout London, but our back yard was so small that it was not a consideration. Being only six feet wide across the back of the house it just about took a short line of washing. It really was of no more use than a passage to the outside toilet, except for my dad who had installed free standing cupboards at each end in which he kept paints, varnishes, brushes, and associated items. He had, at about that time, acquired a book on 'marbling and graining' and had been practising the art of reproducing the various marble patterns, and the varied wood grains, on the insides of the cupboard doors. On my final return home from Hastings I found that the front door, always nicely painted, now had a wood grain with a shiny varnished finish.

When I left a few days later to live with my Aunt Violet, and subsequently leave for Dulverton, that would have been the last thing I saw of our house in Glenister road.

*   *   *   *   *   *

Within a short time of my father approaching Mrs Grant, the billeting officer, George and I, were in her car one Saturday morning in early March leaving Mr and Mrs Rough's house and heading for Crewses Weir, the location of our new homes. Sylvia was with us because for some time she had been unhappy in her billet with Mrs Gibson and it was an opportune moment for a family to be found who could accommodate her and George together. There was no room in their new house for the three of us so a home was found for me close by.

At Crewses Weir I was the first to be dealt with and accompanying Mrs Grant I approached the gate which led directly from the main road to the house where I was to live. It was only when I reached the gate that I could see more than the roof of the house as it had been hidden by a large thick hedge and built on ground some twenty feet or more directly below. Dropping down to the bottom was a steep and treacherous set of stone steps and a path leading to the back door where waiting to greet us was a tall woman wearing glasses and a big smile. With her were three very inquisitive children, two boys and a girl.

Mrs Grant wasn't one to stand on ceremony and having introduced me to Mrs Stark, my new foster mother, she was back up the steps to sort out Sylvia and George.

Mrs Stark took me and my belongings through the back door which opened into the kitchen. It was the door mainly used by everyone, family and visitors, the front door was rarely used.

I followed Mrs Stark through to the living room which was warm and inviting, heated by logs burning in the grate of a large shiny black cast iron range in the oven of which something nice was cooking, it filled the room with a pleasant stomach- teasing aroma. There was a large well worn deal table in the centre of the room with six chairs around it, and upon the table stood an oil-lamp about eighteen inches high. Two large wooden armchairs breasted the hearth and I also noticed a piano against one wall.

Mrs Stark then introduced me to her three children. "This is Pamela," she said, glancing down at her daughter who was blushing and trying to lose herself in the apron her mother was wearing.

"And this is Michael," He was obviously the youngest, a couple of years behind Pamela and a well built lad.

"And Ashley is the oldest." Ashley was about two years younger than me, but just as tall, and much stronger built.

All three children looked the picture of health – they were children who were born and bred in the heart of the country, and looked like children born and bred in the heart of the country.

Mrs Stark then picked up some of my things while I took the rest and she led me upstairs to a small bedroom which was to be where I would sleep and keep my belongings. From the window of this room could be seen a pair of houses, just short of hundred yards away, and similar in many respects to those of Mrs Stark and her immediate neighbour: it was to one of these that Sylvia and George had been taken. Their foster parents were a Mr and Mrs Aplin who had a very small daughter named Rosemary.

The four houses, together with Weir Farm close by, nestled in a valley through which flowed the river Exe, close to where it was joined by the river Haddeo. With the exception of fields close to the rivers, they were completely enclosed by wooded areas. This small settlement had a degree of isolation being about a mile from any other dwellings, or farms.

I found out all this later after I had settled in and was able to take in my surroundings, but at that moment in time I was confused, and lonely, being without George for the first time since we had come to Dulverton.

Mrs Stark asked me if I knew the children who were being billeted with the Aplins. I told her that they were my cousins and related to her the circumstances that had resulted in us being re-housed. She knew about the death of Mrs Pike and sympathised with me when I told her how I was present when she died.

Mrs Stark must have guessed that I was curious to know how George and Sylvia were faring and suggested to Ashley that he take me around to the Aplins place to find out. I now knew where their house lay and was surprised when Ashley took me in the opposite direction down a path between his family's vegetable garden and that of his next door neighbours, whom he informed me were a Mr and Mrs Crossman; the path was some eighty yards long and ended with a small gate.

Through the gate we turned left, and left again, following the fence skirting Mr Crossman's garden, where I could see that we had turned completely about and were now heading through a field towards the back door of Mr and Mrs Aplin's house. This was the route generally used in and out of the houses except when direct access was required to and from the main road. On nearing their house I was surprised to see Sylvia and George coming towards us with a small girl who turned out to be Rosemary. They were on their way to see how I was getting on.

Sylvia and George were not disappointed with their new home, and were pleased to meet Ashley, who I am sure was equally pleased to have more children of a similar age to himself living close by. He had difficulty in hiding his initial shyness and a huge smile upon his face was accompanied by a deep blush, and in the months and years that followed I saw that blush many times due to all sorts of reasons. Nothing wrong with that, he wore his heart on his sleeve, and he was a friendly boy with a big heart.

I was then taken to meet Mr and Mrs Aplin, a pleasant young couple in their mid-twenties, after which we all made our way back to Mrs Stark where I introduced her to Sylvia and George. They had already met Pamela and Michael who, unable to stem their curiosity, had followed Ashley and me.

At lunch-time I met Mr Stark who had been working at Weir Farm where he was the Cow-Man. I was to learn that he took pride in his responsibility for the husbandry of a herd of cows which provided the milk and dairy products for Pixton House and other folk living on the Pixton estate. He would have been up since the crack of dawn to milk the cows, and then after turning them out to pasture, which could mean driving them to a field half-a-mile away, he would have cleaned out their stalls and laid out their feed; silage or hay. That evening he would bring the cows back in from the field and milk them again, this he did seven days a week, fair weather or foul. During the whole time that I was living with Mr and Mrs Stark I cannot recall him being absent from his duties for more than the occasional day, and they were few and far between. He was an average sized man, but strong; both morally and physically.

That afternoon Ashley took me to see the interesting aspects of Crewses Weir. The first, an item high on the agenda of importance, was the toilet. This was outside and at the remotest part of the garden, an alarming one hundred yards from the house. It was without the convenience of a water flushing system being just a bucket in a box with a toilet seat contrived above - our outside toilet in Glenister Road was a luxury in comparison. A serious call of nature in the late evening on a cold and windy night was not something to look forward to. I found out later that when the bucket needed emptying Mr Stark dug a hole in a small plot of land close by and buried the contents. By rotating this procedure around the plot, which took a very long time, the contents dug out of each new hole, were completely rotted and ready to be used as manure for the garden.

Through the back gate at the end of the garden there was a half-acre of land; a long strip with rough grass and trees skirted by a private road to Weir Farm. On this piece of land Mr Stark had a chicken run, and a line of hutches housing rabbits. The chickens roamed the area during the day doing what chickens do, as well as being chased by the one and only cock that ruled the roost. At one end of this plot were several sheds and at the other end a very large open sided barn filled with straw. This area turned out to be where most of our play and leisure activities were carried out.

The road to Weir Farm led over a small humped bridge under which flowed the River Exe, at this point only about eight feet wide. Running parallel to the river was a small canal alongside a timber mill, and a carpentry workshop, both receiving power from a turbine driven by a water wheel mounted in the canal.

Settling in with a new family is not easy as you have to fall into their routine, awaiting for them to tell you what to do; waiting for an invitation to join them in any activity they are undertaking, or intending; looking for guidance or instructions on simple tasks; but I knew this from past experience and let things fall into place.

After answering numerous questions about myself, my family, and my background, I was at a loss to know what to do with myself when Mr Stark suggested that I went with him and Ashley to get the cows in. It surprised me when we reached the field where the cows had been grazing to find them waiting at the gate ready to be driven home, and when the gate was opened how they all trouped through and walked without guidance in the right direction. They wandered along with very little coaxing, just enough to keep them on the move, then when they reached the farm and the cow-shed they each entered their own stall where they waited to be tethered up.

At that time milking was done by hand and I watched as Mr Stark settled onto a stool with a bucket between his knees and draw milk from the cow's swollen udders by gently squeezing each of the four teats in turn, each hand moving downwards with a gentle rhythm.

After a short while he said, "Would you like to try your hand?"

I thought it looked quite easy and was pleased to have a go.

He put his cap on my head, back to front as he had worn it, sat me on the stool and buried my head in the cow's groin.

"Right, I want to see that bucket filled," he said.

I took a teat in each hand, squeezed tight, and pulled. The result was pitiful, no more than a teaspoonful.

"Try again, only this time squeeze with a gentle downward movement," Mr Stark advised.

A few more miserable attempts, and a couple of more spoonfuls of milk, proved to me that I didn't have the knack, and I gave up.

Mr Stark gave a wry smile, took back his cap, sat back on his stool, and beckoned me to come close to see how it was done. I bent down to have a good look and with that he took a teat in his hand and squirted warm milk into my face. It was done in good humour and we all had a good laugh when we arrived back at the house later and it was related to the family. It also helped break the ice, for as it turned out all the children had had that prank played on them at some time or another.

By the time we got back it was getting dark and Mr Stark lit the oil lamp which sat grand in the middle of the dining table. Lighting the lamp was a slow process and followed a procedure which I saw him do countless times after. The large ornamental glass bowl and tube were removed and reassembled after lighting the wick, then left on a very low flame for several minutes. It would then be turned up just a little bit more, and then again, little by little until a full flame was reached with the lamp providing its full luminosity: this all took at least fifteen minutes. The reason for this was to allow the paraffin, which is drawn up the wick, to burn without smoking and so avoid blackening the glass components of the lamp and the ceiling above. Mr Stark never commenced lighting the lamp until the natural light through the window was failing, and that period, sitting in semi-darkness, seemed an interminable length of time especially when I was half way through a gripping story in my comic, The Champion - Rockfist Rogan of the RAF maybe, or Fireworks Flynn.

Once the lamp was burning on full flame the glass dome on the lamp would glow and give out a good light which spread to most parts of the room, it was certainly better than the light provided by our gas mantles at home before electricity was installed. Venturing to other parts of the house required the use of candles and there were several candlesticks available for this, I found that out on going to bed that night.

I went up at the same time as Ashley, Pamela, and Michael. Ashley led the way with one candlestick and Mrs Stark followed in the rear with another. The candles gave a flickering light causing two sets of our shadows to dance on the walls which was quite spooky. Adorning the walls of the staircase were glass cases holding stuffed animals, a fox in one and a pheasant in the other; also a set of antlers, which added to the amusing, albeit eerie, atmosphere

We all went into a large bedroom directly above and the same size as the living room. It had a double bed which Ashley and Michael shared, and a single which Pamela slept in. Pamela had carried her cat up the stairs, which was warm from sitting in front of the fire, and she thrust it between the sheets of her bed. This turned out to be her usual practice in the cold weather, and when she got in she would push the cat down to the bottom with her feet where it would be happy to spend the night keeping Pamela warm. The loud purring which emanated from the cat told you that it was very content to be there. I found out later that the cat was not without fleas (is any cat?) because a regular pastime of Pamela's was laying the cat flat on it's back and catching the fleas as they passed across the sparsely haired part of his belly. The cat, ginger in colour, was very large and had a pastime of its own; catching rabbits. It would often return home from one of its sorties covered from head to foot in mud where it had been down a rabbit hole, his trophy clamped in its jaws.

Mrs Stark then took me along to my bedroom and left me with one of the candles. The room was freezing cold and on getting into bed I kicked my legs about and wriggled my body until I was warm enough to settle down to sleep, only I couldn't sleep, without George alongside me I felt lonely. I knew that it was right that he should be with his sister, but being in a strange house alone a wave of self-pity washed over me and I lay there feeling sorry for myself, wishing that I was home with my family. I wondered how long it would be before I went home; if I would ever go home; and where was home. It was bombed and not there any more, and in this maudlin state of mind I cried myself to sleep.

Up the next morning, and at the kitchen sink for my wash, it was like being back home, the luxury of a bathroom and running hot water a thing of the past. I took my turn at the sink in the scullery prepared for a freezing cold wash from the single tap but was pleasantly surprised to find a jug of hot water thoughtfully provided by Mrs Stark. Yes, just like home.

Porridge for breakfast, I was surprised to see how popular it was. By now I was cured of my fussiness concerning the food placed in front of me, even porridge which at one time I could not stand, put off by servings of the lumpy variety, but I never expected to witness an argument over whose turn it was to scrape out the remains of the pot it was cooked in. But then again, I had never lived with children who had such voracious appetites and I could see why they were all strong and healthy.

Lunch was the same, it may have been rabbit, cut up with the pieces rolled in flour before being baked in the oven, a very tasty dish and one of Mrs Starks specialities, but whatever it was it would have been followed by a dessert, and if it had a custard topping, which invariably it did, each of the children would again make a claim on the pot from which it was served leaving their mother to determine whose turn it was to spoon out the remains. I envied them the custard pot but refrained from joining them in making a bid for it as I did not think it right for me to do so, but every now and again Mrs Stark would ignore their pleas and give it to me.

Now living beyond a reasonable walk from Dulverton - it was over two and a half miles by road, although you could cut it down to about two miles if you took a short cut across Pixton estate - I was excused Sunday church parade with the school. I was a happy heathen once again, well almost, Mr and Mrs Stark, with their children, did attend Brushford Church occasionally and I obviously went with them. Not on that first Sunday though, but I did have to put on my best clothes after dinner to join the family for a walk into Bury where I was to meet Mr Stark's parents, and Mrs Stark's mother, very warm and pleasant people. They resided in two of the half-dozen cottages which formed the crux of this small village, which included a small recreation hall (known for some reason as the Reading Room), a small chapel, and a blacksmiths shop: no public house. This part was Upper Bury and a hill led down from there to the river Haddeo at which point a ford allowed vehicles to cross to Lower Bury where there were some more scattered dwellings.

Mr Stark's parents lived alone, but Mrs Stark's mother (Mrs Bristow) had her son George and daughter Mary living with her. George had a progressive crippling condition which at that time was in its early stages and although he walked with some difficulty he had a personality that made him the 'life and soul of the party' amongst the young men of the village. He was also the tallest, and the most boisterous, and it was sad to see him as I did on a visit many years later unable to walk, and housebound. The condition that George had was one of those which are hereditary where it is handed down through the female side of the family but only affects the males; fortunately it never happened in every case as both Ashley and Michael were unaffected.

Nanny Bristow, as she was called by Ashley, Pamela, and Michael, (and later by me), was a gentle and reserved lady who wore a velvet band decorated with a small jewel of some sort around her neck to make the goitre she had less conspicuous. Her house was most interesting. It was built on a large rock at one end of the village with the front door being some ten feet off the ground and reached by a set of stone steps. The cosy parlour had a fireplace set in the centre of an ingle about five feet across where you could sit either side of an open log fire. In the summer with no fire in the grate you could look up the wide flue of the chimney and clearly see the sky above.

Granddad and Nanny Stark lived in a small mid-terraced cottage which even on a mid-summers day, with its narrow front door and tiny windows (curtains half drawn) challenged the sunlight from entering. The interior effect was not unpleasant being cool in the summer, and warm in the winter.

Nanny Stark, a small old lady with grey bushy hair had a jolly disposition and would tease me about my London accent. Grandad Stark stood much taller with a moustache adding character to his friendly face.

We saw a lot of Grandad Stark as he worked round and about Weir Farm; invariably spending his mid-day break with us sitting in one of the large wooden armchairs positioned either side of the range eating his lunch. Except for a cup of tea he never imposed upon Mrs Stark for food, always producing bread, cheese, and an apple, wrapped in a large red and white spotted handkerchief from a voluminous pocket in his jacket, the type worn by poachers. He would then use a large pen-knife to cut the cheese and the apple in turn, spearing the pieces with the tip of the blade and popping them into his mouth along with the bread. It fascinated me to watch.

The children from Bury, and the countryside around, attended Dulverton School and a bus made a circuitous trip to pick them up in the mornings and deliver them home in the evenings. One of the last stops was Crewses Weir to pick up Ashley, Pamela, and Michael; the passenger list now included Sylvia, George, and me. The drop-off and pick-up point in Dulverton was opposite the Rectory and just down the road from the Rock House Inn, the closest the bus could get to Dulverton School. After school all those catching the bus would congregate at this point and when the bus arrived, the driver, having allowed time for all it's passengers to be ready to board, left almost immediately, so if you dallied, or got detention, you suffered a long walk home. Also, the driver was a tarter when you were on the bus; he would think nothing of chucking you off if you mucked about, or kicked up a rumpus. I know, because I often suffered the long walk home after having missed the bus, or after being chucked off it.

I soon settled in with my new family joining the children in their pastimes and helping them with simple chores like feeding the chickens and rabbits, or collecting and sawing wood for the fire; in the dark evenings we played cards or indoor games. If we were not in bed by nine-o-clock we had to remain quiet while Mr Stark listened to the news on the radio (along with most of the nation apparently) broadcasted at that time each evening on the Home Service of the B.B.C. His wireless (as the radio was then called) was economically used and seldom turned on for music or light entertainment as it relied on an accumulator for its power. This unit, made of glass, was not unlike a car battery and required frequent recharging. A service was provided for this and each fortnight a man would tour the outlying farms and houses in a van with fully charged units which he would exchange for those with their charge depleted.

Mrs Stark was making a large rug she had ordered from a catalogue which required thousands of short lengths of coloured wool to be threaded on to a stiff mesh by using a special hooked tool. This was an absorbing task carried out on-and-off during the winter months and occupied each of us at some time or another. I never did see the finished article.

Pamela was learning to play the piano, under duress I think, because she never seemed to enjoy it. She was made to practice each evening for an hour, and unfortunately for her, and dare I say it, for the rest of us, the piano was in the living-room. It is impossible for almost anyone to learn a new piece of music and play it in a smooth and pleasant fashion without hitting a wrong note occasionally, and Pamela was no exception, which made her self-conscious when we were all in the room. Her mother was aware of this and except in the severest of weathers Ashley, Michael, and me were ordered out of the house.

Sylvia and George would join us in the area near the hay barn where we would play various games and the open sided barn in particular had a certain fascination, especially on rainy days when you could play games like touch, or just mess about without getting wet. We would climb onto the top of the straw directly under the high, slanted, corrugated iron roof, a height of about twelve feet, and jump or slide into straw at the bottom.

On one occasion we thought it would be a good idea to tunnel our way into the main body of the straw. What the consequences of that might have been I shudder to think, but fortunately for us Mr Stark and Mr Aplin happened to pass by on their way to Weir farm. They told us what 'bloody idiots' we were in no uncertain terms during a short but stern dressing down. The exact words have escaped me but I will never forget the astonished look on their faces when they first found us several feet into the straw, and the last phrase uttered by Mr Stark, "If we had passed by five minutes later than we did, we would probably be digging you all out dead."

Coming home from school one day whilst still living with Mr and Mrs Pike, George and I stumbled across a skylark's nest as we were walking through the bracken. We told Mr Pike about it and asked him if we could start collecting bird's eggs which although taboo now was a popular hobby at that time. He agreed as long as we promised to take no more than one egg from a nest and then only when there was a full clutch of eggs. With Ashley now our friend, and also an 'egg collector,' we continued this activity together which took us all over the place, near and far, to add to our collection. We would scour the hedgerows where we knew blackbirds, thrushes, finches, and tits, built their nests; mossy banks for wrens; river banks and ponds for moorhens, coots, and ducks; pastures and wooded areas for pheasant, partridge, and grouse; with the treetops for pigeons, rook, magpie, crow, and various birds of prey. The fun was really in the 'search and find' and the out-of-the-way places it took us to, for as our collection grew, apart from interest in the commonplace birds, we were looking for those hard to obtain, like buzzard hawk, or heron.

I was the best climber out of the three of us and would climb to the top of the tallest trees, even though I had suffered a nasty fall earlier when I was living with the Pikes. I had observed a pigeon's nest at the top of a medium sized fir tree and on investigation found a pair of infant pigeons on a flat bed of twigs barely big enough to hold the two of them. I was surprised to see how big the young pigeons were and would have taken them to be fully grown had they not been sitting there with beaks wide open waiting for food. I mentioned it to a boy in class, an evacuee like myself who knew very little about birds, and he showed an interest with an eagerness to see them. Later, I took him to the tree and he climbed up after me until he was able to observe the nest and the baby pigeons for himself. I was above him when we started to descend and foolishly threw down a challenge, saying, "I'll beat you down." Although he was slower than me, and more careful, he used the advantage he had by blocking my path down the tree as I tried to manoeuvre past him. In an attempt to climb around him I lost my hold, and my footing, and plunged through the flimsy branches towards the ground. Somehow or another, my body turned through ninety degrees and I was falling horizontally when I hit the bottom and thickest branch of the tree with my midriff which broke my fall, and almost my ribs. Whether this was better than hitting the ground I will never know, but it knocked all the wind out of me and it must have been a good two minutes before I got my breath back, during which time I rolled about in stinging nettles and badly stung my legs, arms, face, and neck, and the bruise that resulted below my ribs stayed with me for a couple of weeks. Still, I was first down the tree.

I had another fall from a tree whilst trying to add a tawny owl's egg to our collection - not an easy one to get. We had observed the owl in an old oak tree for some time and became aware that it was building a nest. The trunk of the tree rose about eight feet before it split into two main branches, one forking out with healthy foliage, the other rising almost vertical with limited growth and truncated after a further eight feet. This branch was seen to be hollow, and a hole in its base where the branches forked gave access to it. It was from this hole that we had seen the owl popping in and out.

With the help and encouragement from Ashley and George I managed to scramble into the fork of the tree and look into the hole, but could see nothing. I put my arm into it, but could feel nothing. I then climbed to the top of the hollow branch where it was truncated and peered down. It was like a chimney about six inches in diameter, and there at the bottom I could clearly see a nest holding a clutch of eggs, but there was no way that I could reach them from there. I came back down to where the branches forked and with some difficulty put my arm back into the hole right up to my shoulder, but the hole angled in such a way that I could not reach the nest. The owl must have been somewhere in the hollowed space all the time and fed up with the intrusion, because it attacked my arm which I quickly withdrew. The owl followed, lashing me on the face and neck with its wings, which knocked me out of the tree. Whether it attacked me, or was just fleeing to safety, it was a decisive victory for the owl. Fortunately, I had a reasonably safe landing, while Ashley and George had a good laugh.

Each week I received a parcel from my parents which contained a letter, a comic or two, chocolate or sweets, (their rations), and a shilling pocket money. I looked forward to receiving it very much, and on its arrival Ashley, Michael, and Pamela, always gathered round to see what I had got even though the contents seldom varied - I like to think that I shared my sweets with them.

They were eager to know what was written in the letter, especially after they had got to know my mum and dad, but showed no interest in the comics. These were, The Wizard, The Hotspur, and my favourite The Champion. All held adventure stories (without pictures) and after receiving them I was non-communicative for at least an hour as I joined Rockfist Rogan of the R.A.F, or Fireworks Flynn, on one of their thrilling escapades.

My dad wrote the letters and would always write at least three pages telling me of all the interesting things that were happening. I can picture the scenario where he would be sitting at the table writing the letter with my mum sitting across the room in the armchair saying, "Have you told him this?" or "Have you told him about that?" and my dad would say, "Why don't you write the letter," and my mum would reply, "You know I can't write letters, I never know what to say."

On receipt of my parcel Mrs Stark would make me sit down and write my weekly letter in reply, a poor specimen it was too, usually no more than two pages and I regret to say that I found it a chore, even though I knew that my mum and dad looked forward to receiving it, and cherished every word.

I had been with the Starks for about two months when the letter from my mum and dad informed me that they were popping down for a long-weekend. Mrs Stark told me to tell them that she could put them up if they so wished which pleased me no end. I lost no time in writing back with the good news, and subsequently when they arrived a few weeks later Mrs Stark generously provided them with board and lodging. This was not done for any commercial gain for I remember my dad saying that when he asked Mrs Stark how much he owed her she blushed and was obviously embarrassed at having to suggest an amount. He paid her what it would have cost them to stay at The Rock House Inn but I know one thing, the food served up in the 'Rock', however good, would have fallen far short of that which Mrs Stark provided. When it came to good old fashioned English meals Mrs Stark was in a league of her own, using vegetables direct from the garden, eggs from her own chickens, dairy produce and meat from neighbouring farms, and cooking skills learnt when she was young in service and honed by a desire to give her family the best.

My mum and dad fell in love with Crewses Weir the moment they set eyes on it, and came to love still more Mr and Mrs Stark and their family. On that first occasion they were only down for a few days but during that time they were able to see that I was in good hands and immediately hit it off with Mr and Mrs Stark and became life-long friends.

On the Saturday evening Mr Stark took my dad on the mile and a half walk to the Carnarvon Arms, close to Dulverton Station in Brushford, where they got to know each other over a pint or two. According to Mr Stark my dad struck up a rapport with the locals immediately, and knowing him he probably took centre stage telling some amusing anecdotes and singing a song or two; he would hardly have needed much encouragement, if any. I know that he was impressed by the postman who was in the pub at the time; riding a push-bike that day he had delivered post to various farms over a wide area, invariably being offered, and drinking, a pint of rough cider at each one, which by the end of his stint ran into double figures, and there he was in the bar, still standing, drinking pints of the same.

Whilst they were at the pub my mum and Mrs Stark had a cosy little chat, probably, amongst other things, concerning my welfare and needs. I knew that Mrs Stark considered that the trousers and shoes I possessed were not fit for the rugged everyday country life I was now leading (Sundays excepted) for after my parents had gone home Mrs Stark took me into Dulverton and got me fitted out with tough corduroy trousers, and strong leather boots which Mr Stark immediately reinforced by hammering steel tips and studs into the soles and heels to stop them from wearing out too fast. He also smothered the new leather tops with dubbin to stop water penetration.

Mrs Stark must have been very persuasive because my mum hated boots. She was made to wear them when she was a young girl living in Poplar, and I recalled her answer a few years earlier when I asked if I could have a pair of boots like some of the other children in our street. "No!" She said emphatically, "Boots are clumsy and too heavy for small children, besides with your thin legs you'd look like Mickey Mouse."

On the Sunday evening when it was time for my mum and dad to go home we all accompanied them to Dulverton Station. My mum held my hand all the way and I had the feeling that she did not want to let go. I knew that she missed me very much because I had overheard her telling Mrs Stark how the war was depriving her of my childhood and the joys of motherhood. Having seen how well I had settled in with Mrs Stark and her family she must have been thinking as we walked along that I was happier to be there than at home and not want to return with them even if I could, because she said to me, "Would you like to come home with us?"

I was stunned to hear her say this, and stumped to know what my answer should be, because I had often heard my mum and dad agree that with the bombs dropping day and night I would be a constant worry to them and was better off out of London. Added to this they still had no home to accommodate me.

Even at that age I realised that my mum was seeking reassurance from me that I would still prefer to be living at home with them, so although I was dying to say, "Yes. Take me home with you," I said, "I would mum, but I'll be alright for now, the war won't last forever."

I was quiet walking back from the station, unable to join the others in their happy mood discussing how pleasant the past few days had been with my parents staying there, as I was thinking to myself that the war did look like it was going to last forever. That night in my bed I cried myself to sleep.

On the overnight journey home my mum and dad would sleep on the train from Taunton to Paddington in a packed third class compartment, that's if they could get a seat, as the trains in wartime were always full of service men and women in transit, or going on or returning from leave. Then, Monday evening my dad would clock-on at his place of work for the night shift.

He had a very hard and dangerous job working as a smelter. This required him to wheel a barrow full of heavy manganese-ore up a ramp to a platform which overlooked a huge pot of this molten metal, the heat intensified by adding magnesium. He would feed the manganese-ore slowly into this inferno and at the same time add scrap aluminium to form ferrous-manganese which was used in the manufacture of munitions. Impurities in the materials caused the contents of the pot to spark, and spit angrily, all the time the process was being carried out, but none so much as when he scraped the slag off the top, and even worse when he had to tilt the pot and pour the finished product into a specialised railway truck.

No protective clothing was issued to him and he literally wore rags to thickly cover as much of his body as was possible, even so he frequently suffered burns to his body, legs, and feet. On one occasion during a later visit to see me he stripped off his shirt in the living room for my mum to dress burns which covered fifty per cent of his back. Seeing it made me wince, and realise just how perilous his job was, especially during air-raids when he was not able to leave the pot which once started had to be attended until poured, knowing that a bomb dropped nearby would cause him to be showered with molten metal. Bearing in mind that the River Thames was a constant target for enemy bombers, and his firm was on the riverside close to Blackwall Tunnel and opposite the London Docks, he must have lived in fear of his life at these times.

When I look back on the summers of my childhood, it seems that the sun was shining nearly all the time and the summer of 1941 was no exception. To help the farmers, daylight hours were extended by adopting double-summertime whereby the clocks were put forward by two hours instead of one; consequently with night-time coming two hours later the days seemed much longer.

At school Mr Searle decided that the sunny weather demanded an appropriate response, so he decided that every class would benefit from a day off studies and a visit to Tarr Steps instead, so on one early summer's day we all marched out of Dulverton on the long walk to see this ancient wonder. We were told that it was about five miles, and knew that five miles was a long way, but none of us visualised what five miles under a relentless sun, up and down hills, would really be like: it was purgatory. The first mile was not so bad, the road following the River Barle was pleasantly shaded and almost flat, but the next two miles were all uphill until we reached Exmoor, and by then we were well spread out. The senior girls and boys were a long way ahead, while the juniors, who included Sylvia, George, and me, took up the rear. We had each brought a packed lunch and I was carrying theirs, as well as my own, in a knapsack, which included a large glass bottle of drink (no plastic bottles in those days) and it was getting heavier by the yard, although we kept lightening the load by taking constant swigs from the bottle. It was no use expecting George to share the load, for although a tough lad, with his little legs he was really struggling, and Sylvia had her work cut out coaxing, and helping him with the progress he was making. We eventually arrived at Tarr Steps exhausted but as is the quality, and nature of children, within five minutes of paddling, and splashing about in the river, we were completely revitalised.

Tarr Steps is now a commercial attraction complete with car-parks capable of taking coaches and listed in all tour guides covering the area, but at that time, although a recognised ancient monument like Stonehenge, it was less popular due to its remote setting.

Enormous flat heavy stones are arranged to form a footbridge across the River Barle. Where they came from and how they were transported there can only be surmised, but one of the teachers informed us that folklore had it that the devil himself built it. Close by, a large indentation on Exmoor was known as the Devil's Punchbowl -- he needed a good drink after all that hard work.

The return journey was marginally better due to it being downhill on the latter part, but weary legs found us straggling into Dulverton too late to catch the school bus back to Crewses Weir. Although we were not strangers to the two and a half miles which now confronted us I do not think we ever found it so hard.

Shortly after this test of endurance I had a much better day out. A middle aged man, also from somewhere in London who we knew as Mr Williams, was in the habit of hanging around the Town Hall chatting to the students and teachers during mid-morning and lunch time breaks. He was well dressed with a pleasing manner, and seemed well to do. My impression, looking back, was that he had moved away from London to avoid the blitz and not knowing anyone in Dulverton found it easy to talk to us, having something in common. He asked George and me if we would like to go with him to the seaside, and furthermore when we said "Yes," he approached the teaching staff who, in light of the questions asked afterwards, surprisingly agreed. With the knowledge that our teachers had approved with this arrangement both Mrs Stark and Mrs Aplin gave their consent.

We met Mr Williams a couple of days later at Dulverton Station and caught an early train to Exeter, and then on to Exmouth, a beautiful seaside resort in South Devon on the mouth of the River Exe. We enjoyed ourselves exploring the area, playing on the large sandy beach and splashing about in the sea; with ice-creams and lunch at a beach side café the day passed all too quickly.

Afterwards, back at school, George and I were given the third degree by the very teachers who had given their assent; their questions concerned the behaviour of Mr Williams towards us. Perhaps they thought it a possibility that he was a paedophile, but it was too late to worry about that, they had taken a risk and fortunately for them, and us, he was just a very nice man.

A week or two later the schools broke up for the summer holidays and Mrs Stark took Ashley, Pamela, Michael, and me, on a picnic. I remember it clearly because it was such pleasant occasion and the spot chosen was ideal for the very warm day that it was – a weir at the head of the mill stream.

It was situated about half-a-mile up-river from the house and created a pool of still water about six feet deep at the weir-head diminishing to the river's natural depth; at that time of the year, an ankle-lapping six inches. I could swim enough to cross the pool and look over the edge of the weir, but even though it was a hot day the water was too cold to stay fully immersed for more than a few minutes.

Mrs Stark sat on the grassy river bank, where she had laid out a cloth on which was an array of sandwiches and cakes, keeping an eye on us whilst at the same time being amused by our antics as we paddled and splashed each other with the clear water.

We tried our hand at catching small fish, and skimming stones.

We raced twigs, dropping them in the river upstream then chasing along the river bank keeping an eye on them as they bobbed along, shouting with joy if in the lead, or complaining if they got snagged up.

In the field by the river we played touch, or a ball game, which Mrs Stark joined in, after which we were ready to do justice to the food. As we were enjoying this, the highlight of the day, Mr Stark appeared on the opposite side of the river, having strolled up the path alongside the mill stream from Weir Farm. He then walked through the shallows of the river in his dubbined boots to join us.

In my mind's eye I can see a picture of this scene on that sunny day, the beauty of which could only be portrayed by an artist with the skills of Renoir, or Monet.

The sunny weather continued and with it other summer activities, one of which was haymaking. I had never been haymaking before, nor seen haymaking done, but it proved to be my highlight of that summer. Tall grass is cut and left to dry to become hay, and haymaking is the process of collecting the hay and taking it to where it will be stored, in stacks, barns, or haylofts. There was no special machinery then which picked it up and baled it in one operation; it was all done by many hands loading it onto Mr Aplin's horse and cart, and Mr Stark's lorry.

It was hard, but jolly work for all the hands, helped by a flagon or two of rough cider which would always be close by in a shady spot. Long pitchforks were used to raise the hay from the ground to the wagon where a man on top would distribute it evenly and tread it down until the load was so high it became a mobile haystack. It would then return to the farm where further hands would transfer it to the barn, its passage back evident by hay festooning from the hedgerows.

All of us children were in attendance and given minor tasks, like raking the hay into piles to be pitched onto the wagon, or fetching the cider jar for one of the thirsty farmhands. It was a time to be enjoyed and nobody seemed to mind when we skylarked in the hay, sneaked the occasional swig from the cider jar, or dared each other to run under the horse's belly while he patiently stood waiting. It would have been fun to travel back to the farm on top of the hay but this was not allowed, being too dangerous, but we frequently walked back with the cart just for the return ride.

In late summer the blackberries were ripe and we helped Mrs Stark pick them locally from which, with apples picked from a nearby orchard, she made blackberry and apple pie. She also made a lovely whortleberry pie (in some areas known as winberries, and to the Americans, blueberries). Picking these required us to make a long walk onto the moors, which of course necessitated taking a picnic as the excursion took all day. We passed through Bury on the way to Haddon Moor, where we were joined by Mrs Stark's sister Mary. Both women knew by past experience where there would be an abundance of berries, and when we got to the site we each had a basin to fill.

Although the whortleberries grow in abundance they are only about a quarter of an inch in diameter and the bushes they grow upon hide amongst the heather. The first three dozen or so never reached our basins, being popped straight into our mouths. It took an age to fill a basin which must have held well over a thousand berries, and long before we picked that many we were bored to tears. Mrs Stark and her sister, like most women, could pick all day long without stopping, probably non-stop chatting helped, but with us children it was different, and Mrs Stark knew this, so after a while our basins were emptied into a basket lined with greaseproof paper, brought for the purpose of carrying the berries home, and we got down to the serious business of playing; the heather was ideal for hide-and-seek and tumbling about in.

After the holidays there was a sudden change in my schooling arrangements. The headmaster, Mr Searle, announced during assembly that all the teachers were returning home due to the majority of pupils having already done so during the break. The upshot of this was that I, together with the rest of those staying, was transferred to a school which had been evacuated from Leyton, equally decimated by its pupils having returned home.

If I knew the name of the school I have forgotten it, but it was generally known as Fisher's School, after the name of the colourful character who was its headmaster. The school was housed in a hall constructed of corrugated iron and located in a lane running down the side of the rectory; it had some connection with the church. There were just two classrooms, one in the hall itself, which was where I was located together with about thirty others of various ages up to thirteen, and a smaller class of older students in a room on a mezzanine floor above. Apart from Mr Fisher there was only one other teacher, Mrs Taylor, and they alternated between classes depending on the subject being taught.

He was not a churchgoer, come to that nor was Mrs Taylor, but he always took religious instruction, giving an unbiased view some might consider controversial. He sowed seeds of doubt in my mind concerning stories in the bible, his interpretations stripping them bare of their mystique. Concerning Samson, for example, who lost his powerful strength after Delilah cut off his long flowing hair, rather than the cause of this being that his hair held a magical power, he put forward the theory that the loss of his hair led to him getting a chill, influenza, or even pneumonia, which left him extremely weak.

During the First World War Mr Fisher was a fighter pilot and it was not difficult to persuade him to depart from the lesson to tell us of one of his many exploits. On one occasion he had been shot down, the consequence of which left him almost stone deaf, but he had designed and built a hearing aid which he was never to be seen without. Not a miniscule instrument that fitted in the ear, such devices were yet to be invented, it was a wooden box the size of a small suitcase, complete with handle, which held a complexity of valves, condensers, and other paraphernalia, including a large battery. From this a wire snaked up to a pair of ear-phones through which he enjoyed passable hearing.

He was not as handy with the cane as Mr Searle, and I learnt this in the early days at the school when being sent up to him by Mrs Taylor for some minor misdemeanour. How surprised I was at his way of dealing with me.

I climbed the stairs, knocked on the door, and entered his classroom where he was addressing about a dozen senior boys and girls.

"Ah! Young Wellard," he said. "What can I do for you?"

"Mrs Taylor sent me, Sir," I replied.

"Did she, and for what purpose?"

"For making this," I said, handing him a dart that I had made from a pen. (I had snapped the end off the nib which left two sharp points and cut a cross in the wooden shaft into which I had fitted a flight made from a sheet of paper from my exercise book).

"And was Mrs Taylor impressed with your handiwork?" Mr Fisher asked, holding the dart up so that the class could see it.

"No Sir, she said it was wilful damage to school property."

"I see," Mr Fisher said. "But in making this dart I must presume that you wouldn't have a pen to write with. Is that correct?"

"No Sir," I replied. "I had already been given a new pen."

"Who gave you a new pen?"

"Mrs Taylor, Sir."

"But why would Mrs Taylor give you a new pen when you already had a pen?"

"It was too short to write with."

"How did it get that short?"

"I chewed it short, Sir."

"Are you telling me that you've eaten over half a pen?"

"Yes Sir," I said.

By now, the class was finding my dilemma amusing and Mr Fisher in toying with me was playing to his audience.

"Just the right size for a dart," he said, and held it up again for all in the class to see, at which there was a burst of laughter from them. He then came around to the front of his desk saying, "I'm sorry Wellard, but I can't let this go unpunished." Then after a short pause he added, "Bend over."

I bent over and steeled myself for the cane or a whack across the backside with the blackboard cleaner, a little surprised as corporal punishment was not his style. To my further surprise, he picked up a piece of chalk and drew something on the seat of my trousers. It was a target.

The class was now in an uproar with laughter which grew in intensity when he walked back a few paces with the dart in his hand and took aim at it.

"Prepare yourself Wellard," he said. "I throw a good dart and from this distance I can't miss."

I tensed myself and waited for the dart to strike, but it never came. He was satisfied that the humiliation he had imposed upon me was punishment enough, with the added humiliation of returning to my own class with the target still on the seat of my trousers knowing that they had all heard the laughter.

Another incident occurred whilst with Fisher's school. I had gained the wrath of Mrs Taylor for another transgression, talking maybe, just before the whole school was going out for the afternoon on a nature ramble, the result of which found me staying behind writing an essay titled - Pay Attention or do Detention.

All by myself in the building the time passed slowly. The door wasn't locked, and with the essay completed I wandered up and down the lane by the vicarage, but with nobody about it was boring and by four-o-clock I was fed up to the back teeth awaiting my class to return. Looking through the doorway I saw Mrs Taylor enter the lane and to make her think that I had been hard at it I returned to my desk only to hear the door shut and the key turned in the lock. I ran to the door and called out loud, but she never heard me. I was locked in.

I thought that she would be back in a short while but I thought wrong. I tried shouting but the hall was in an isolated spot and no-one could hear me. There were no windows that could be opened, they were all located high up on the walls with wire mesh fitted to the outside to stop them being broken by stones.

The time had passed slowly before, but the next hour really dragged and I started to get fed up because I had missed my bus and faced a long walk home. Mrs Stark would not be expecting me for an hour or so as I had often been late before due to missing the bus, so with no one to raise the alarm I anticipated being in there for a long time.

It started to get gloomy, so I switched on the lights in the hope that somebody might notice when passing the end of the lane, and also to keep my spirits up, as being in that building all alone in the dark was quite spooky.

Two hours later, and worried to the point of tears with the expectancy of spending the night there, I heard a key turn in the lock and the door opened with Mr Fisher making an appearance.

"Come on Wellard," he said, "I'd better get you home before they get the bloodhounds out looking for you."

As we walked down the lane to Fore Street where his open top M.G. sports car was parked he told me that whilst having his evening meal with his wife, and Mrs Taylor, with whom they shared the house, they were discussing the days events when she suddenly remembered that she had locked the doors of the hall without checking whether I was still in there. Probably hoping that I had left before, which in hindsight I wish that I had done.

I had never been in a sports car, or driven fast in any car, but to be driven at breakneck speed, sometimes touching eighty miles per hour; down country lanes in a car driven by an ex-fighter pilot was an experience that was worth being locked up for and one that I will never forget.

Sylvia and George were only at Fisher's school for a very short time when, with their mother, they left Dulverton to join their father who was working at an American Air Force base on a long term contract. With George gone, Ashley and I, already good friends, now relied upon each other all the more for our companionship, and pastimes.

About this time I had a belated birthday present from my mum and dad, a bicycle with the stirring name 'Coventry Eagle', but with no gears the only time it flew was when it was going down hill. However, unlike other bikes being produced in wartime, which were utility models and all black, it did have chromium plated handlebars, pedal-arms, and wheels, and being brand new it certainly looked the part.

Ashley had the use of his father's bike, a celebrated 'Sunbeam'. Not a racing bike such as the 'Claude Butler' which was the dream of teenage cycling enthusiasts at the time, but a sturdy bike ideal for the countryside made to the highest standards and a dream to ride. It had Sturmy-Archer gears which together with the chain ran in a bath of oil, and with its shiny black stove enamel frame emblazoned with a flash of gold it was considered the Rolls-Royce of bikes.

Mind you, it was not meant to be subjected to the kind of treatment that Ashley and I put it through. Just across the road from our house was a small forest built on the side of a steep hill at the top of which was the site of an ancient castle with a rough track leading up to it. We would wheel our bikes to the top and then freewheel back down again at breakneck speed, twisting and turning to avoid the holes and exposed tree roots, finishing with a thrilling climax where the track passed above, and alongside, an old disused quarry. The knowledge that one small error would send us flying over the top made it all the more exiting.

The castle itself was interesting in an historical way (even with my childhood imagination I saw it as little more than a mound of earth) and on one or two occasions we visited the site with digging implements hoping to find unearthed treasures and become very rich, but if there were any we never found them.

Each Saturday Ashley, or I, sometimes both of us, had to cycle into Dulverton to collect newspapers and shop for various small items. There was a choice of two routes, one across Pixton Estate, the other by the main road, but whichever one you took it was necessary to climb uphill for the first half of the journey and downhill for the second part, obviously the same coming back. Going into town I invariably went by road, but for the return journey I always took the gravelled drive which ran for a mile through a wooded area of the Pixton Estate. It was the final part of the return trip and downhill all the way until arriving at speed, and a skid finish, at Weir Farm to deliver the first paper to Mrs Goss, the farm manager's wife.

On taking this route for the first time I was unaware that halfway down the drive there was a hairpin bend, by which time, even though I was only free-wheeling I was going very fast, and a tentative attempt to break on the gravel surface told me that it was a dangerous thing to do, so instead of taking the bend I drove straight on and up over the bank which fringed the road. Fortunately, the bank was not too steep at this point and I took a large semi-circle dodging the trees and undergrowth until I rejoined the road about a hundred yards further down. I told Ashley about this manoeuvre, and how hair-raising it was, and of course it appealed to him and this became our normal way of negotiating this hazard.

We would use our bikes constantly and on one occasion when almost home, after returning from a cycling trip, an amusing incident gave everybody indoors a good laugh when Ashley told them about it; the laugh being at my expense. On climbing the hill which led to the front door of Cruises Weir I was standing on the pedals for maximum effort with my head over the handlebars and approaching Mr Aplin who was trimming his hedge. At the very moment I reached him he raised his right leg high in the air such that his shiny corduroy-trousered backside was almost touching my face and emitted a well-timed loud rasping fart.

One Saturday evening in early autumn an annual 'Social and Dance' was held in the Reading Room at Bury, and people living in the surrounding farms and houses converged on this small building and filled its hall, and adjoining yard, with many more spilling into the village road outside. Those in attendance ranged from the very young, to the very old, all hell-bent on enjoying themselves. A variety of food was prepared and brought by the womenfolk, whilst a barrel of beer, and one of cider, were set up in the yard to provide the stimulus for the men to lower their inhibitions.

Arriving early with Mr and Mrs Stark and their children, I watched farmers, farm-workers, wives, and girlfriends, from miles around coming together for this annual event to enjoy the occasion, as well as to exchange greetings and news, many not having seen each other since the previous year.

As things warmed up during the course of the evening the small hall rang out with singing, and the floorboards rattled from dancing feet. To see those farmers, some of them real heavyweights, scrubbed up, out of their Wellington boots, and in their Sunday best, cavorting around the room performing the Lancers, the Military Two-step, and other old country dances was a sight to be seen. Mr and Mrs Stark were no strangers to these dances and displayed a dexterity which surprised me.

103

It was about this time that my sister Jean decided that she had had enough of being a servant in the Pertwee household and did a moonlight flit. She saved up enough money for her train fare back to London and on the pretence of having an early night went to her bedroom and packed a case which she lowered from her bedroom window. Then changing into her outdoor clothes, slipped out of the back-door, and walked through the dark country lanes to Dulverton Station where she caught a train to Taunton, then a further train to Paddington.

Imagine how surprised my mum and dad were the following morning when they emerged from the communal air-raid shelter, where they spent each night, to find Jean waiting there to meet them. Fortunately for Jean, a pre-conceived plan to join the Woman's Land Army met with their approval and it was not long before she was heading for a farm in some other rural area to milk cows, tend pigs, and till the land. She had just turned sixteen at the time.

Boils showed their ugly yellow heads on my body again, surely not still due to the country air, and good food, as claimed previously for their emergence. My fear of going back into The Retreat again made me conceal them from Mrs Stark until she became aware of the discomfort I was in.

"Will I have to go into The Retreat?" I asked her.

"Of course not," she replied. "We'll soon clear them up."

Dealing with the first boil she took a tin of Kaolin from the cupboard and put it into a saucepan of water on the range until the water boiled, then made preparations for applying a poultice. I watched the water simmering and the Kaolin getting hotter knowing what to expect, as a few years earlier I developed an abscess under my chin and my mother treated that in a similar manner.

Mrs Stark tested the heat of the Kaolin with her elbow a few times before she had satisfied herself that it was sufficiently hot and then spread it on to a piece of lint. I was dreading it, knowing that the heat on the swollen and tender area of the boil would be painful, but even so, I never visualised just how painful it was going to be. With all the family looking on I was determined to be bold, but when it was applied I screamed out in pain, and broke down in tears; it was excruciating.

Mrs Stark told me not to be such a baby, but when she took the dressing off the next day she was most remorseful and apologetic as the skin around the boil was blistered. She hugged me into her apron with an out–of–character show of affection which meant more to me than her words of apology. The poultices were continued, but never so hot again, and the boils cleared up without the barbaric practice of squeezing. Fortunately, after this bout they never returned.

Christmas came and went with life continuing much the same in the following year with no sign of the war nearing its end and my returning home. I was aware of the progress of the war by overhearing the news each evening as Mr Stark listened to the wireless in deep concentration, never missing a word.

Although I was now one of the family and likely to remain with Mr and Mrs Stark, my surrogate parents, for some time to come, I still addressed them as 'Mr and Mrs Stark' which was very formal considering my relationship to them. When my mother and father had first met them it was Dorothy and Walt / Jenny and Alf from the word 'Go', and bearing in mind that 'auntie' and 'uncle' is a familiar form of address used by children in respect of friends of the family I could easily have been steered in that direction, which I would have liked, but it never happened. I was to call them Mr and Mrs Stark until the day I left.

Mr and Mrs Stark, like my mum and dad, were not demonstrative in showing their affection, or expressing terms of endearment, love being inherent in their actions, but I knew by what they said, and the way they treated me, that they liked me, and were happy to have me around.

A letter from my mum and dad in the New Year informed me that they had moved to a new house in Charlton and when they came down to see me in the spring they described it as a small modern three bedroom semi-detached house. At least now, when the time was right, I had a home to return to.

They had managed to acquire the property by becoming squatters, which became a practice for people who had become homeless due to the bombing, and my father was amongst the first to take advantage of this. He found a house which had been left empty, where the occupants had moved away from London to avoid the blitz, and then with others in a similar situation made representation to the local authority that they should be allowed to occupy such dwellings until the owners returned. The Council agreed, but when the war ended the returning families were unable to re-occupy their homes until those squatting had been re-housed, and in the case of my mum and dad this was not until 1953 when they were found a new council flat.

Finding different things to do indoors during the wintertime was not easy but like all children we were innovative and imaginative using simple items at hand. One such activity during the cold early months of 1942 greatly diminished Mrs Stark's assortment of cottons by making 'tanks' from cotton reels, which had become the latest craze. We would take the wooden reel on which the cotton was wound and cut notches in the edges all around the circumference on each side. An elastic band would then be threaded through the hole in the cotton reel and anchored on one side, then on the other side it would be passed through a washer of wax (a thin slice of a candle) before being looped around the end of a match. When the match was rotated it wound the elastic band which drove the 'tank' along. We would then race the tanks against each other with minor obstacles for them to climb.

Making things was as time-consuming and as pleasurable as the use we got out of the articles we made. One such endeavour by Ashley and me was to make a catapult. We scoured the forest and hedgerows for suitable 'Y' shaped branches, cut them off to size, then took ourselves off to Dulverton where we purchased a length of quarter-inch square rubber and a ball of string from Germans the hardware shop. We notched the wood for the rubber to pass over, then after binding it, found and fitted a suitable piece of leather for the sling. By the time we had knocked off a few tins balanced on a tree stump a new craze had come along.

I think that was the pop-gun. Back along the hedgerow with the penknife to find an elderberry tree, and in particular lengths from one of its branches about a foot long and an inch thick which we could fashion into a barrel each for our guns. Wood from the elderberry is very hard but has a soft core of pith, and when this is removed a smooth round hole remains down the centre. To remove the pith Ashley heated up a long thin poker in the cooking range until it was glowing cherry red and pushed it through the lengths of wood while I held them fast on the garden wall with my foot.

Ramrods were then required to fit the barrels of the guns for which a small branch from an ash tree suited the purpose. Precision was required so these took a lot of careful whittling, not without mishap and repeated effort, but eventually we had our finished articles. To ensure that enough pressure was produced to fire a pellet when the ramrod was pushed down the barrel it was necessary to chew the end of the ramrod until it was frayed, leaving it soaked with spit to provide lubrication.

Armed with our new weapons Ashley, Michael, and I, dodged about between the trees and bushes firing pellets at each other, facial hits being the prime target. The pellets were made of paper, masticated and soggy with saliva so that they made a tight fit when plugged into the business end of the barrel.

Another craze that we latched onto required a further trip to Germans the ironmongers. This time for a quantity of carbide, a grey compound in the form of small rocks which was used to produce a gas which served the flame in carbide lamps hung on carts by some farmers when on the move in the dark.

We had a different use for carbide, not so practical but more fun. We took a Tate and Lyle Golden Syrup tin, which has a tight fitting lid, made a hole in the bottom and placed inside two or three small rocks of carbide. We then added a good quantity of spit and pushed the lid back on tight. (Water added to carbide creates a gas). The gas expanded inside the tin which created a pressure that forced a jet of gas through the hole, and when a lighted match was applied to the jet it caused an explosion within the tin which resulted in the lid flying through the air.

Of course, after using the Tate and Lyle tin for some time we graduated to larger tins which culminated in us eventually using an old two gallon oil drum. We drove a nail through the bottom to make a hole, then poured a small quantity of water onto carbide rocks inside (spit was no good this time as it needed more than we could produce between us) then pressed down the lid. It took some time for the gas to build up sufficient pressure for it to be emitted with force through the hole during which time we mounted it at an angle of about forty-five degrees between the vee of a sawing horse which stood permanently in the area. Ashley held a box of matches at the ready but when the gas started hissing he got cold feet and was unwilling to ignite it, chary of the outcome. We tried to persuade Michael to light it, but although somewhat younger he was not that naïve and refused. I reluctantly took the box of matches with more than a little concern not knowing exactly what the result would be, and put a flame to the jet of gas which was now hissing wildly. Immediately there was a tremendous explosion within the drum and the lid was driven high into the air which soared over the tops of the trees, and the hay shed, towards the river, never to be seen again, even though we scoured the area looking for it. The force of the explosion caused a backlash which propelled the drum backwards and nearly took my hand off, well not quite, but a kick from a horse would have been less painful.

In the early part of that summer the bombing of London had eased and my parents thought it safe enough for me to go home for a short visit, so with a few clothes in my case, and a packed lunch, I left on an early train from Dulverton to be met by my mum in the afternoon at Paddington Station. This interminable journey with a train-change at Taunton is erased from my memory, being so mind-numbing.

We could have taken a shorter trip from Paddington to Charlton, but my mum wanted to show me the damage done by the bombing to the East End of London, and in particular Poplar where she was born and where I went frequently with her before the war to see her mother, (my grandmother), so we went by bus which took us through that area.

There was a lot of bomb damage to be seen from the moment that we started the journey, but nothing could have prepared me for the devastation that met my eyes. When we passed through Limehouse, Stepney, and Poplar, there was hardly a house standing, and you could see right across to Whitechapel, and Bow, where the houses had been razed to the ground.

At Poplar we boarded the 108 bus which took us through Blackwall Tunnel to Greenwich where we got off at a stop close to Glenister Road as I wanted to see what was left of the street which featured so much in the memories of my childhood.

My mum and I stood hand in hand on the pavement looking at the rubble on the site where our old house once stood without saying a word. What was there to say?

My mum broke the silence. "Come on," she said. "Let's go home to our new house, you'll like it."

Although our new house was quite small, with its mod-cons I did like it, and was pleased to see that some of our old furniture had been salvaged, including the 'battle scarred' piano which was brand new at the beginning of the war. None of my toys had survived.

It was nice to be home with my mum and dad, and they did their best to keep me entertained, but I had no friends. and unlikely to make any in the short term there, so when it was time to return I did not feel as bad as I thought I would.

There was an added reason; whilst I was home there were several air-raids, probably only minor in the scale of things, but enough to give me a taste of the dangers that people in London were living under and letting me know the fear of being bombed. In the middle of the night, when the sirens screamed out warnings of enemy aircraft approaching I was dragged out of my bed by my mum and dad and taken to the shelter in the garden. This was a heavily built brick building without windows and the size of a medium sized shed. There was no door, just a wall of sandbags about two feet in front of a doorway, and inside two mattresses on the floor, together with blankets. However, it was difficult to sleep due to the sound of bombs exploding, some quite close, but mostly around the area of London docks, a mile or two away. There was also extremely loud explosive noises of the anti-aircraft guns nearby, one mounted just across the road on waste-land.

The shelter, with its concrete floor, and bare brick walls, was most uninviting, and my mum and dad only went in there when the raids were most severe. Some people made their shelters home-from-home and retired to them in the early evening and stayed there all night. My mum's brother Bill, who lived in Dagenham, adopted this practice. He had an Anderson shelter which was comprised of curved sheets of corrugated iron which after construction lay half buried in the ground with at least a foot of earth on top. They were prone to water seepage, and dampness, but he overcame this with panelling, carpeted floorboards, and four bunk-beds. Added to this he ran electricity for lighting, heating, and a wireless, giving the whole interior a degree of luxury where he and his family felt comfortable and safe.

A few days before I returned to Dulverton my sister Jean came home on leave. She had left the Woman's Land Army and joined the A.T.S and was now in the army as a P.T. Instructor. During the course of her stay my mum showed her a dress that she was making for Pamela. It was almost finished, tacked before final stitching.

She held it up saying, "I hope it's the right size."

"How big is she?" Jean asked.

"About as big as Rex," mum replied. "She's a big girl for her age."

"Well, that's it, Rex can try it on," Jean concluded.

"I'm not trying it on," I said, surprised that this should be suggested.

"Don't be silly," Jean said. "It'll help mum finish it."

"It won't take a minute," mum added.

I protested but they continued to press the issue, with Jean pointing out how selfish I was, until I reluctantly agreed. "But be quick," I said.

They put the dress on me and my mum made adjustments, pinning the material together as necessary until she was satisfied with the end result. I was then made to stand in the dress whilst they examined the front, then the back, and everything would have been fine if my sister had not remarked, "Doesn't he make a lovely girl, let's call him Rosie?"

This amused my mum, and they both had a good laugh calling me Rosie repeatedly; embarrassed I tore the dress off.

My embarrassment never ended there because later when my mum posted the finished dress to Mrs Stark she informed her that it should fit as a girl named Rosie, who was about the same size as Pamela, had modelled it. A few pertinent questions of me and Mrs Stark soon found out who Rosie was, and so did everybody else.

My most embarrassing moment up until then had occurred several years earlier. A girl that I knew invited me to her birthday party where I happened to be the only boy. That was bad enough, but during the evening I needed to use the toilet, which like our own was in the back yard, and having waited until the last minute I found it occupied so decided to pee in a drain-hole close by. Whilst I was doing so, a small girl came out of the toilet, passed me, and went indoors immediately telling the other girls of my dirty deed, upon which they all came out and pushed me into the toilet shouting, "Use the lavatory you filthy boy."

If there had been a back door from the yard I would have gone home, but there was not, so after dithering for some time I went back to the party and suffered the scorn, and teasing, which I knew was coming.

A few weeks after I returned to Dulverton, Ashley and I were meandering through the forest along a private drive which ran from Crewses Weir toward Bury. The road ran alongside a very steep bank which fell towards the edge of a field which apart from grazing was used as a breeding area for pheasants. For reasons to do with their breeding a cartload of straw had been tipped from the road whereby it had tumbled down the bank to a ditch at the base. We were not aware at this time of the reason for the straw being there but immediately perceived that some fun was to be had by jumping into it and sliding down to the bottom.

This source of amusement continued over the next few days with the straw gradually moving down the bank until it was in one deep pile at the bottom. It then became a single jump from the road into this big heap of straw.

It rained once or twice between our escapades in the straw and although it was damp it did not concern us much, but one thing we noticed was that it was getting quite warm. It got much warmer still; it got red hot and burst into flames, but fortunately at a time when we were not there. In fact, nobody was there, but the flames were noticed before it became a serious incident by somebody passing who raised the alarm and rounded a team of men, including Mr Stark, who brought it under control.

A post-mortem was held, with Mr Crossman the gamekeeper (and tipper of the straw) being the main inquisitor, where he more or less accused Ashley and me of having started the fire as we had been seen playing in the straw by various people. He must have had me down as a pyromaniac because he brought up the previous fire George and I started at Pixton House. Fortunately, when we proclaimed our innocence most vehemently, and pointed out how hot the straw was getting the last time we were messing about in it, they concluded that it had self-combusted.

My dad asked Mrs Stark if it would be in her interest to provide holiday accommodation for people he knew who were looking to get away from London for a week or so. Mrs Stark readily agreed that it would, with three children and me to support the money obviously came in handy; subsequently numerous people came to stay, including my Aunt Win and Uncle Bert. However, the first to arrive was a lady who worked in the canteen of the Tram Depot in Charlton with my mum called Mrs Sweeny, and she arrived with her son Graham, a real pain in the neck and a boy with very few favourable graces. He was overweight, flabby, and spoilt, and we were expected to keep him amused by including him in our games and pastimes, but he would not run for a ball, and he could not walk for more than a few hundred yards.

He was also very greedy, and the first night there he was vying with Michael, Pamela, and Ashley, to spoon-clean the custard pot, a privilege that in my mind was clearly theirs and the same with the porridge saucepan at breakfast the next morning. No meal would go by without him making a claim for 'more of this' or 'the biggest of that'.

Mrs Stark, always respectful, humoured him throughout his stay giving in to his demands, seeming even to find his avarice amusing; more than I could say for the rest of us.

On the last day of their holiday, following dinner, Mrs Stark brought in a large jug of custard followed by a tray of apple dumplings. They varied slightly in size depending upon how big the apple was, except for one which was half as big again as the others. It was huge; a big golden ball of beautifully baked pastry, shining where it had been brushed with milk before it went into the oven. As soon as the tray was placed upon the table the boy Tweeny screamed out, "I want that one! I want that one!" Pointing to it as Mrs Stark knew he would.

She put it on the extra-large dish which she had brought in especially for it, and then distributed the remaining dumplings before going around the table pouring custard over all of them. One small dumpling remained on the tray.

Young Tweeny swiftly attacked the large dumpling with his spoon only to find that the pastry broke away to reveal a tight ball of newspaper. He pushed it away in disgust, angry at being hoodwinked, whilst the rest of us howled with laughter, even his mother thought it funny.

Mrs Stark had a broad satisfied smile on her face as she replaced his newspaper dumpling with the small apple dumpling remaining. Hopefully a lesson was learnt, but I doubt it.

Fisher's school closed down and after the summer holidays, I, together with a handful of evacuees still remaining, were absorbed into Dulverton School, a proper school with an assembly hall, classrooms and a playground.

Mr Weaver, a short elderly man, was the headmaster, he may not have been that old but with his tweed suit and staid manner he seemed it. Like Mr Fisher he also took a class, but unlike Mr Fisher he lacked wit and humour, making his classes pretty dull. He was also handy with the cane, which I soon found out, and during my time there my hand and his cane became very familiar with each other. Unlike the canes generally used which were thin and swished as they arced through the air leaving a painful stinging sensation, the cane that he used was short and thick with a knob at one end which resulted in a bruising effect.

Apart from Ashley, Michael, and Pamela, who attended Dulverton School I already knew boys there, so fitting in was not too much of a problem, but unfortunately, there is always someone who you fall foul of and within the first few days I was involved in a punch-up with a lad called Cross. He was about the same age and stamp as me, and after a lengthy exchange of punches it ended with no clear winner and was broken up by one of the teachers. Ashley was in the crowd watching and was most impressed with my performance as he knew that the boy had a reputation for being useful with his fists.

Later, an occasion was to present itself whereby I was to come into contention with him once again, an incident which favoured him, much to my chagrin, and envy, but which also gained my begrudging admiration of him. A flag which flew at the top of a thirty-foot mast just inside the school gate was stuck, and Mr Weaver standing at its base with other teachers, and a crowd of children, was jiggling the ropes to free it. Having no luck he asked if any boy could climb up and sort it out. There were only two volunteers, Cross and me. The headmaster chose Cross, knowing his capabilities, who effortlessly shinned up the pole and freed the flag to great applause.

Twice a week, on Tuesdays, and Fridays, a screen was erected on the stage of the Dulverton Town Hall with rows of fold-up seats arranged to form a cinema, and one Friday evening as a rare treat Ashley and I went to see a horror film called The White Zombies, starring Bela Lagusi. Because we were returning after dark, and our bikes were not fitted with lamps, we walked the two-and-a half miles into town.

The film, which was already over ten years old, was one of the first talkies and set in Haiti where the owner of a sugar mill (Bela Lagusi) had the supernatural power to re-animate dead bodies into zombies which he used to work his mill. The lifeless human forms would be brought to the mill at dead of night from a large old ramshackled spooky house which stood remote from the mill on high ground. They were marched in single file down a steep slope outlined against a part-cloudy moonlit sky staring straight ahead with vacant looks.

The storyline continued with Bela Lagusi, not satisfied with the corpses of people who had died from natural causes, mercilessly murdering innocent victims to provide more zombies to satisfy the output needed from his mill.

The film concluded with a few brave heroes, and heroines, eliminating Bela Lagusi and his zombies, but not until after a nail-biting finish, because the zombies, being already dead, could not be killed with a bullet, or suchlike. When shot they would lumber forward even though riddled with holes.

Bela Lagusi was one of the most frightening characters ever to appear on the silver screen, and he together with the zombies in a grainy black and white film made it terrifyingly scary.

We left at the end of the show with trepidation as we started the long walk home in the dark through the lonely countryside, but after only a few strides we were joined by Mrs Farmer whose house we had to pass. She lived in a lonely spot at the bottom of The Cleave (a steep hill covered with bracken) which led to the drive approaching Pixton House and in her company any frightening effects that the film had had on us we were able to keep under control, discussing it, and even laughing at it. But on leaving Mrs Farmer, with still about a mile and a half to go, it was a different matter; we had left our boldness with her.

We climbed The Cleave and skirted Pixton House, taking the road around the back of the stables which led us directly onto the park. It was when walking across the open pasture that we realised how similar the scenario was to that in the film. There was a thin layer of clouds with a weak moon flitting in and out, large trees silhouetted against the sky, bats flying about, the whole panorama in shades of black and white, and there before us was a hill sharply outlined against the thin moon. "Look Ashley," I said. "That's just like the hill the zombies walked down to the mill."

The response from Ashley was a quickening of pace which I was not slow to follow, possibly quickening the pace still further, and by the time we reached the forest, which we had to pass through, our walk had become a run. The path through the forest was quite narrow and with the moonlight barely entering it was difficult to keep to it, yet the fear that we had built up within ourselves spurred us on still faster.

The gate out of the forest brought us to the top of a very steep field which led directly to Weir Farm at the bottom. Bursting through the gate we careered headlong down the hill unable to keep on our feet due to the forward pitch and momentum of our bodies, stumbling, sliding, falling, until we scrambled through the lower gate, almost home, just a sprint across the bridge and a dash to the finish. I cannot recall that Ashley was naturally a faster runner than me, or whether on this occasion he was more frightened and so produced more adrenalin, but he was half way up the garden path before I reached it. Out of habit he shouted back, "Shut the gate." The gate never got shut that night.

Mr and Mrs Stark were surprised to see us burst into the house all flushed and out of breath, and I suppose we should have kept the reason for our obvious distress to ourselves, because when we blurted out the gist of the film, and our reaction to it on the way home, they both found it very funny, which was a bit embarrassing, and later on reflection we both felt a little bit silly. There were to be no more horror films for us.

During the summer when I retired for the night, usually about nine-o'clock, my small bedroom was a pleasure to be in as I was able to read my comics or a book for an hour or so due to extended daylight hours. Now with winter, and the clocks going back, my bedroom was looking less inviting once again, so I was pleasantly surprised when Mrs Stark said that she would like me to share the large bedroom with Ashley, and Michael, allowing Pamela to have a room of her own. Having experienced how cold that room was in the winter, like an icebox, I could not swap quickly enough. I had no pangs of guilt with regard to Pamela's welfare as I knew she had heating arrangements which were not available to me - a hot-water bottle and her ginger cat.

Otherwise that year passed with all the calendar arrangements I had enjoyed the previous year repeated and now behind me, such as, picnics, whortleberrying, haymaking, the Bury Social, and I was now approaching my third year with Mr and Mrs Stark, and their family.

I knew that my mum and dad, who had been visiting me three or four times each year, thought the world of them and had never held any qualms about me being there, in fact, I heard my dad say to my Uncle George on one occasion that if he scoured the country looking for a better location, together with a more suitable family for me to be living with, he would be pushed to find it. Even so, now that the bombing had eased in London I was aware that they were looking forward to me being home with them.

Early into 1943 and after Ashley's eleventh birthday we both joined the Boy Scouts. We would cycle into Dulverton at least one evening each week for meetings and activities under the direction of the Scoutmaster who was Mr Harding, the owner of the town's sweetshop and tobacconist,

In cold and wet weather, meetings would be held in the scout hall where we would learn the various disciplines to gain proficiency badges, or charge around playing British Bulldog, or some other physical game. When it was fine we would be out and about in the countryside nearby on various activities.

Ashley soon got fitted out with his uniform to which he sewed on the badges that he had earned, but it was not thought worth me having one, being likely that my scouting days were numbered.

One proficiency badge that Ashley would not have earned was for eliminating a wasp's nest without getting stung, not that they gave out a badge for such a thing but at a mad moment he decided to take up this challenge.

The wasps had built a nest in a bank opposite the house and were nuisance enough for Ashley to do something about it. I went along to help but like Pamela and Michael, I was more of an onlooker. His bravery bordered on stupidity as he got a stick and poked numerous times into the opening where the wasps were going in and out. The wasps obviously took umbrage to this and came out on the attack from which we all fled, none of us getting stung at this stage.

Ashley was not going to be beaten and went back armed with some sacking and a box of matches, this time with my help to hold the stick whilst he lit the sacking which emitted a lot of smoke. He then pushed the sacking with the stick into the entrance of the wasp's nest but could not have blocked the opening properly because the wasps came out in their droves, flying around us in a fury with their barbs at the ready. They got me in five places, but Ashley was stung fifteen times. Pamela and Michael sped at the first sign of trouble and got away scot-free.

Our next venture was not so traumatic – we built a raft. From the saw-mills we obtained two empty forty gallon oil drums and a few planks of wood, then with a length of rope we lashed the planks to the oil drums before taking it down to the river. We chose a spot where the river was deepest, then with some difficulty forced it through the trees and shrubs growing along its bank where we tied it fast.

Thinking about it afterwards, we realised that we should have part-filled the drums with water to lower the centre of gravity, because the top of the raft was a couple of feet above the surface and very unstable, which meant that getting on the raft was a tricky affair, and no mean feat..

Ashley was eager for me to try first, obviously anticipating the likely outcome, so I gripped one of the branches hanging over the raft and gingerly put one foot on the planking, with the other foot still on the bank. The raft immediately moved away leaving me straddled between the two. Ashley managed to pull the raft back in and I was able to put my other foot onto it, but no sooner had I done so, and transferred my full weight onto the deck, the ropes binding the planks and drums together loosened, and the whole caboodle came apart. I frantically tried to keep it all together with my feet but to no avail, the drums and the planks drifted down the river leaving me dangling from the branches with my legs in the water. There was no way back and I had to let go, the result a good soaking.

In late June of that year my parents decided to take me home for good. It was almost three years since I first arrived in Dulverton spending most of that time living with Mr and Mrs Stark. I had mixed feelings about returning to London, not concerning the bombing which had more or less ended, but once again confronting the unknown; the strangeness of my new surroundings; a new school; new friends to make. Here, in the house at Crewses Weir, Ashley, Michael, and Pamela, were like brothers and sister to me, and I knew that I would miss them greatly, but on the other hand I looked forward so much to be living with my mum and dad again, and I knew that they had been longing for that too.

My parents came to get me, and stayed a couple of days during which time I was able to say my many goodbyes and take a last look at the paradise I had been living in. Mr and Mrs Stark, with Ashley, Pamela, and Michael, walked us to the station, with Ashley and me taking it in turns to ride my Coventry Eagle – it was also London bound. Promises were made by my mum and dad at the station that we would be back soon to visit and that all being well would keep coming back throughout the years ahead. We then made our tearful and heartfelt farewells.

After settling in at 20, The Heights, Charlton, arrangements were made for me to attend Fosdene Road School where I was put into a class in the final year under a Mr Melanaphie, the nastiest and most brutal teacher I ever had the misfortune to be taught by. He would use the cane for the slightest digression, and use it with the utmost force. To maximise this he would stand upon the dais supporting his desk whilst his victim would be positioned on the classroom floor some six inches lower. On one occasion when I was unlucky enough to be on the receiving end I had a blue welt across my hand which remained there for days. I had to hide it from my mum for fear that she would make a complaint to the school, not wanting to be seen as a wimp who could not take his punishment. Whether she would have gone as far as Ginger Johnson's mother I very much doubt it.

Ginger Johnson, one of the smaller boys in the class, was subconsciously tapping a ruler on the desk whilst working out his sums which caused Melanaphie to shout out, "Who's making that tapping noise?" This resulted in the whole class looking around including Johnson who was still subconsciously tapping. "It's you Johnson, bring that ruler out here".

Johnson went down to the front or the class and Melanaphie took the ruler from him. "Hold your hand out," He demanded, which Johnson did. "Not that way," Melanaphie said, grabbing his wrist and turning it so that the knuckles of his hand were uppermost. He then raised his arm and brought the edge of the ruler sharply down on the back of Johnson's hand where it struck the bones with a loud crack. Ginger gave a cry of pain and ran from the classroom.

A short time later, after the class had settled down and Melanaphie was back behind his desk the door burst open and Mrs Johnson, with her face as red as her ginger hair, flew into the classroom and whacked Melanaphie around the head and shoulders relentlessly with a cricket bat she had brought with her for that purpose, at the same time calling him all the names under the sun. Caught by surprise, all he could do was raise his arms to protect himself, which also took a battering. The class was in an uproar cheering Mrs Johnson on.

It was nearing the end of term with most of the class leaving to start work and Ginger Johnson never came back. Incidentally, I was later to become very friendly with him as like me he joined the Royal Navy and we were often on leave at the same time.

One occasion comes to mind when we were returning home along the Old Woolwich Road after a night out. Walking, because we had missed the last bus, we passed a house that was throbbing from the music and singing coming from within.

We could see that a party was in full swing which looked most inviting, and both of us having a bit of cheek, and not yet ready for the evening to end, we knocked at the door on the pretence that that we knew a lad that lived there, hoping that we would be invited in - nothing ventured, nothing gained.

We were both in our navel uniforms and people were friendlier disposed to service men at that time, so a few minutes later found us in the front room of the house with a glass of beer in our hands joining in the merriment. I sang a few comic songs, some learnt in the navy, some borrowed from my dad, and before long we were not only welcome but on first name terms with everybody there. It was most enjoyable and going well until some joker had a trick to play on someone and unwittingly I became the victim.

Standing on a chair, he took a glass of beer which he held against the ceiling with a broom handle. "Hold on to this while I get down, will you Rex?" he asked.

I naively took the broom handle from him whilst he alighted from the chair which he then placed against the wall some distance away from me. He then, quickly followed by the others, took pleasure in my predicament - standing in the middle of the room with a broomstick in my hand pushing a glass full of beer against the ceiling. After an interminable five or six minutes with everybody laughing, and dancing around me, I thought, 'enough's enough,' and pulled the broom handle sharply away, at the same time attempting to catch the glass without spilling too much of the beer, especially over me. It was a catastrophe, the glass immediately tilted sideways with the beer going all over the place and the glass smashing into pieces on the floor.

Not only were we shown the door but all those not living there were thrown out too. Party over.

I left Fosdene Road School the following year at the summer break, one month after the first V.1. Flying Bomb landed in East London at Grove Road near Mile End Station on the 13th June 1944. It caused quite a stir with questions and rumours running rife – it was known to be a plane as many people had clearly seen it, but was it driven by a suicide pilot; guided by remote control; or had the pilot baled out by parachute? These were the questions and theories being asked and bandied about. After a few more had arrived and exploded it was found out that they were pilot-less and projected towards London from 'ski-launch' sites along the French and Dutch coasts. Apparently, only twenty-five per cent of the 10,000 launched toward London reached their target, nevertheless over 6,000 people were killed by them with some 18,000 injured.

The V.1. Bombers were nicknamed Doodlebugs, which was the term of reference usually used, but early reports in the papers called them Buzz-bombs due to the buzzing sound they made. Buzzing suggests the sound a bee makes, but my dad blew a good long raspberry with his tongue when emulating the noise coming from them, this was a much better impression.

Our house at The Heights was one of the few finished houses on a new site when building works were stopped at the start of the war. A large remainder of the site was barren except for one house which was left partly built and stood isolated in the middle of this large vacant plot of land. During the school holidays that summer, I would climb onto the timbers which formed the roof of the house (without tiles it was open to the sky) and watch the doodle-bugs, with their fiery tail, fly overhead. From this viewpoint, high above the River Thames I was able to see up-river and observe the flashes, and flames, caused by the explosions when they landed in The City, or The East-End; sometimes closer.

When a doodlebug started to descend, the engine cut out and it fell to the ground in silence. On one occasion, I was alone indoors when this happened, and rushed into the garden. Looking up I saw it diving out of the sky directly towards me, and fearing for my life, I rushed into the shelter and threw myself onto a mattress. Pulling a pillow around my head I expected to be blown to pieces. The explosion came very loud shaking the ground, the shelter, and the houses around, but not delivering the death-dealing blow that I expected.

I went into the street where I met Mr Green, a neighbour, who had been braver than me and watched its final descent.

"We were lucky there," he said, "That one looked like it had our name on it, but at the last minute it veered to the right."

Not quite so lucky for my mum who arrived home a short while later from a shopping trip to Woolwich looking shaken up, her stockings and dress both torn with her arms and knees bleeding. Alighting from a bus, close to the spot it landed, she was caught by the blast which blew her back into the bus. Still it could have been worse.

I had a similar experience a few days later when on my way to see a friend who lived a few streets away. The air-raid warning sounded, so I started running back towards home and had not got far when a doodle-bug spluttered and made its deathly dive. Seeing it loom large above me I knew it would land close by, but not exactly where. Fortunately, a man running towards me, who had obviously assessed its point of landing better than I had, swiftly turned me around to run in the same direction as him. Barely a few seconds later the doodle-bug hit the ground and exploded. It made a tremendously loud bang, followed immediately by a wind force that lifted me and the man off the ground sending us flying through the air for a distance of twenty feet or more. At the same time the vacuum caused by this brought the glass from all the windows crashing around us. Luckily, although shaken up, both the man and I walked away without a scratch.

Like everybody else, I was just getting used to the doodle-bugs dropping spasmodically on random locations when on the 8th of September the first V.2. Rocket landed. Unlike the doodle-bug this was too serious to be given a nickname. There was no tell-tale sound warning of its approach, just a gigantic explosion when it landed, leaving an enormous crater and people invariably killed or wounded.

On leaving Fosdene Road School at fourteen my mum was not too keen for me to start work straight away, not so much due to my lack of educational attainment, but more to do with my size. "Whatever job you get," she said, "They'll have to stand you on a box." So she set about finding me further education.

There were a number of children around at the time that had not had the chance to take the thirteen-plus examination which existed for entrance to colleges giving training in technical and commercial subjects, such as building/engineering, or typing/cookery, and to compensate for this Day Continuation Schools were set up. It was to one of these, located at St. John's Wood, near Lewisham, that I started after the summer break.

I had only been at the D.C.S. (Day Continuation School) about five weeks when plans for evacuation were made due to the constant interruptions caused by the V.1s and the V.2s, and the dangers they presented. The upshot of this was that a couple of weeks later I was standing in a hall of the Working Men's Club in Glanamman, South Wales, waiting to be fostered once again.

My new home was with a Mr and Mrs Hopkins, an elderly and childless couple who were kind to me from the very beginning and were to treat me like a son they never had. Living with them in their large stone built semi-detached house was Mr Hopkins' sister, younger but still elderly. The house, called Bryn Rhos, was not far from the centre of Glanamman which proved to be a small town that ribboned along a road that ran parallel with the River Amman. It was a mining community which was readily perceived by the mountainous slag heaps which towered above and behind the houses.

I found out later that Mr Hopkins had been a miner, but due to silicosis (a disease caused by coal dust in the lungs) he had been found work above ground. His main task was to ensure that the miner's lamps were fully charged and in good working order for each shift. He gave one to each miner as they entered the mine and noted their return when they came up so indicating when a miner had not resurfaced. His secondary job concerned the well-being of pit ponies. Unlike deep-bore mines reached by lifts, where the ponies stay underground all their working lives, this was a mine where the entrance was set into the hillside and sloped down to the numerous coal faces, and like the miners they went in and out at the beginning and end of each shift. He enjoyed his work which was reflected in his pleasant and amiable manner.

Mrs Hopkins was quick to proudly let me know that her brother was James Griffiths, a prominent member of parliament for Llanelli who was to become a major player in Clement Attlee's Labour Government after the war. Within a short time of being in her care she asked me if my parents voted labour, which I thought unusual, but I was able to relate my childhood experience where I paraded the streets banging a biscuit tin and shouting "Vote for Labour," which she found pleasantly amusing and agreeable.

The morning after our arrival we reassembled in the hall of the Working Man's Club where arrangements had been made to accommodate us in rooms adapted for use as classrooms. It was a strange environment for schooling where we mixed daily with the men of a mining community who used the bar and snooker hall when they were off shift. The bar-room was off bounds, together with the snooker tables within it, but there were two tables in a separate room, one of which was allotted to us - even modified by raising the floor around it so that we could lean over the table and cue properly. Admittedly, the cloth on the table had seen better days, being worn, patched, and badly repaired; nevertheless it was always in great demand.

Normal lessons quickly resumed, and furthermore, within a week or two, singing lessons were introduced – it must have been the Welsh influence. These were given by a Mr Woodhouse who although none of us had heard of had a degree of fame as a serious singer on the radio. It was a bit of a shambles at first, the girls were eager and willing but the boys were reluctant and needed a lot of coaxing, but eventually, he licked us into some sort of shape because it culminated in us contributing to a concert given by the miners and others in the local community. At that time I was one of the few boys whose voice had not broken and I was given a solo part in the song 'Old Father Thames' singing a section where the melody rose to notes on a higher scale.

In the first week after joining the Day Continuation School I palled up with an easy-going lad named Ronnie Adams, and although he had been the first to be fostered and I was the last, and bearing in mind that the billets were scattered over a large area, we were lucky to find ourselves living almost opposite each other. Unlucky however, that both families had strong religious leanings which resulted in us spending a major part of each Sunday in church..

The school assembled every Sunday morning outside the Working Men's Club and marched to the local church on the opposite side of the river to attend morning service there. The man Ron lived with, Mr Fuller, was a Lay Preacher who read a passage from the bible at that service. He also read from the bible at the evening service and suggested to Ron, not expecting 'no' for an answer, that he came along to that as well.

The Hopkins also went to pray each Sunday, but they attended chapel. Miss Hopkins also taught Sunday school there in the afternoon and made it clear to me that it would please her if I attended that, so a deal was struck between Ron and I whereby he came with me to Sunday school and I went with him to church in the evening; not my idea of making the most of a free day but our hands were tied. In the five months spent in Wales I must have sang every hymn, listened to every parable, and heard countless passages from the bible.

The first time that I entered the chapel, not having been in one before, I was rather surprised, for unlike the sombre interior of a church it was bright and very colourful with a balcony around three sides. Very much like a small music hall, but not quite so jolly.

My bedroom was at the front of the house overlooking the main thoroughfare through Glanamman and contained a most generous sized single bed with a deep feather mattress which was like sleeping on a cloud; so soft and enveloping. I have heard it said many times that feather mattresses are unhealthy – unhealthy or not, once in it I slept like a baby. However, there was one exception when I had a very bad dream,

Very few dreams stay in my mind longer than a few hours after I wake up, but during a bout of flu, when running a high temperature, I had a nightmare from which I woke up screaming and wet with perspiration to find Mrs Hopkins bathing my face with a cold wet flannel, and Mr and Miss Hopkins standing behind her looking concerned. To this day I can remember every detail.

In my dream I was strolling around a fairground when I was aware of people scattering in all directions running away from a huge man wielding an axe. For some unknown reason he targeted me, and frightened, I tried to run away, but could not move, I was running on the spot and he quickly bore down on me.

The scene then changed and we were both on an extremely long swinging boat pivoted high in the sky travelling through a very wide arc. The axe-man was close behind me as I scrambled in fear, and with great difficulty, along this unusual craft, climbing as it rose, and falling as it dipped. After what seemed a terrifyingly long time, with him close behind and breathing down my neck, I reached the end of the boat and did the only thing that was left for me; I climbed over the edge and hung there by my finger-tips. The madman loomed over me and brought his axe down with the intention of cutting off my fingers. I let go just before the axe fell and tumbled down, down, down. That is when I woke up screaming.

It is not my habit to analyze dreams but this one may have had its foundations in something that happened to me at the fair on Blackheath the previous August Bank Holiday. I was standing with some friends when a boy known to me from the time I lived in Glenister Road approached and asked if anyone would go on a

126

swing boat with him, his treat. All of the others declined, but I liked the thrill of the swing boats and accepted.

"Don't go on with him," one of my friends whispered. "That's Smudger Smith, he's a bloody lunatic." But I replied, "What harm can come from it, he's sitting in the boat with me."

By experience I knew that he was a thief. When I was coming out of a sweet-and-tobacconist shop in Old Woolwich Road one day he was outside with another rogue, Tommy Tantony, both several years older than me, and both as it turned out, destined for Borstal.

They confronted me and enquired, "Did the old man leave the shop?"

It was the custom of the old man who owned the shop to sit in a curtained off room at the rear when he was not serving, making his appearance as soon as a buzzer sounded, which was triggered by a customer treading on a mat just inside the door.

"Yes," I replied. To which they both entered the shop, stepping over the wide mat, to emerge only seconds later with their arms loaded with boxes of cigarettes and ran off up the road. Having told them that the old man was not in the shop I felt implicit in the crime and quickly made myself scarce as well.

But that was a long time ago, and although a thief it did not make 'Smudger' a lunatic so I went on the swing boat with him.

A swing boat holds two people, usually in a row of six, hanging from the horizontal cross member of an 'A' frame constructed of wood. It is about fifteen feet high and the boats are propelled to and fro by pulling on ropes.

On climbing into the swing boat and getting seated we each grabbed hold of a rope and started pulling. We had hardly got the boat swinging when Smudger let go of his rope, and holding on to the steel rods that the boat was suspended by, stood up on the seat. He shouted, and beckoned for me to do likewise, which I did.

Within a very short time the swing boat had reached a point where it was horizontal and could go no higher. Standing on the seat I was now above the top of the structure and in a horizontal position myself looking down at the ground when my side went up, and hanging by my hands from the steel rods when his side went up. Frightened, I carefully sat down again, but that was worse. After slipping into the well of the boat onto my back, and then nearly going over the end, I stood up again. I just held on tight and made no contribution to the momentum of the boat, but there was no need, Smudger was quite capable of doing it all on his own. In fact, he was more than capable because the steel rods were hitting the top horizontal bar harder and harder each time we reached the upper limit. If it had been possible I am sure we would have turned full circle.

The whole wooden framework was rocking, and shaking, with people in the other swing boats screaming and shouting at us. A large crowd had gathered and the man running the appliance was yelling at us to stop, but Smudger had no intention of stopping. He was fearlessly leaning forward as his end of the boat fell, and stretching back as it rose.

At the base of the structure, directly beneath each boat, a length of wood is hinged and when lifted scrapes along the bottom of the boat to act as a brake. The man hoisted this on to his shoulder to perform this operation but the tremendous force of the downward motion of the boat made him buckle at the knees. Seeing his plight, several men working on adjacent fair ground appliances rushed over to assist him, and between them held the wooden brake until our swing boat was brought to a standstill.

The fairground-men manhandled us from the boat and I was glad when I managed to break free from their grasp and lose myself in the crowd. From this vantage point I was able to see Smudger remonstrate and argue with the men before swaggering off. I was not surprised to learn later that he was committed to Borstal for his involvement in a serious robbery.

Miss Hopkins had a room on the ground floor at the front of their house for her own private use in which there was a piano. I happened to mention that during the past year I had been taking piano lessons upon which she expressed an eagerness for me to continue and urged me to write home immediately and ask for my music sheets to be sent. When these arrived arrangements were made with a piano teacher who lived just a few doors along the road and I continued from where I had left off.

I omitted to tell her that my mum was on the point of cancelling my lessons.

"I'm wasting my money," she had said. "You don't practice all the week until an hour before your next lesson, what good's that I'd like to know – and what must your music teacher think?"

Well I knew what my music teacher thought because she had warned me that if I came to her each week without practicing she would no longer continue giving me piano lessons.

Things proved to be a lot different with this new arrangement. The music teacher was not stricter, if anything a bit easier on me, but my practice session each evening was serious stuff. It was overseen by Miss Hopkins who would sit in a chair nearby reading a book whilst at the same time giving an ear to my performance, and progress; a bit disconcerting but it kept me up to scratch and I made a marked improvement.

I would start by practicing my scales, and then play the latest piece I had been given, followed by a number of pieces that I had learnt and needed to improve upon. By this time I would be looking at the clock anticipating some tacit agreement from Miss Hopkins that I had done enough, knowing that Ronnie Adams would be waiting for me, but it never came unless, or until, I had completed at least one hour. If under the hour I would hear her say, "You haven't played Handel's Largo yet, Rex." Or, "It would be nice to hear the Poet and Peasant Overture, Rex."

She knew every piece of my repertoire and made sure that they all had an airing at some time or another, but on top of that I would often receive an added request from Mr or Mrs Hopkins, who had been listening in whilst reclining in their armchairs in an adjacent room. With them showing such an interest I would feel obliged to return to play 'Nola' or 'Glow-worm' or some other such melody that they liked, and not included in that particular session. I may have wished at times that I had never mentioned that I was taking piano lessons, but when I look back I can only applaud Miss Hopkins for her patience in listening to me practice, bearing in mind all the wrong and discordant notes played while learning each new piece.

For recreational purposes, apart from the snooker table, the Working Men's Club also provided us with a room in which we could play table-tennis, cards, or just meet up. The town also boasted a cinema; a far cry from the plush Odeons, Granadas, or Gaumonts, which had sprung up in all of the major cities just before the war, but a big step up from the arrangements in Dulverton Town Hall. Named after its owner, the James Picture House was a long semi-circular building of corrugated iron construction built for the very purpose of showing films, and did that each day except Sundays, changing the programme twice a week. The films shown were a year or more behind those on view in London, but they were all new to me.

A few of us joined the Army Cadets and once a week attended the local drill hall which with its rifle range was one up on the Boy Scouts. The uniforms were a bit naff, off the peg from the Quartermasters Store and re-issued time and time again. They were well worn, probably not as clean as they could be, and in my case, being a bit on the small side, fitted only where it touched – I could almost turn around in it.

The novelty of marching routines, and rifle drill, soon wore off, but the gymnastic equipment, and the shooting range, kept us interested, as did the manoeuvres which took place out and about in the countryside.

The tedium of Sunday was relieved by taking a bus ride in the evening after church to a spot near Gwaun-Cae-Gurwen, a town a few miles away famous for its choir, but it was not that which drew us there, the attraction was a dimly lit stretch of country road known locally as 'Monkey's Parade' which was a rendezvous for teenage boys and girls who gathered there from miles around.

Like all the other lads there, Ron, and I, would stroll up and down hoping to 'pick up' a couple of girls with the hope that it would lead to a snog, which wasn't too much to ask for considering the amount of snogging that was going on. That was what everyone was there for. I must confess however, that neither Ron, nor I, had anything more than a modicum of success, we were at the wrong end of the teenage scale (even too young for girls of our own age) and our chat-up lines were rubbish, we were also disadvantaged by not being Welsh. Still, it was fun trying.

By mid-March 1945 the doodle-bugs and rockets had stopped and along with all of the other students of the D.C.S. I returned home, but not before Mr Hopkins took me down 'his' mine. In a pair of borrowed overalls I travelled, like the miners did, in one of the trucks used to bring coal to the surface which ran on railway-lines and was pulled by a pit-pony. The shaft of the mine we were in terminated about half-a-mile from the entrance and we got out of the truck within fifty feet of the coal face at a point where the pit-props and railway track ended. From there the shaft narrowed down to a space where the miners were on their knees digging coal from a narrow seam, really dirty, dangerous, and back-breaking work. We stood well back while a miner drilled a hole in the coal-face into which he placed a stick of dynamite. After exploding this from a safe distance and when the resultant coal dust had settled, they handed me a pick and I spent a short time digging out some of the loosened coal, a lump of which I kept as a souvenir taking it home with me in a Shredded Wheat box.

When I arrived home a surprise awaited me. Jean was now out of the army having been discharged due to being pregnant. She had married a sailor, who also lived in The Heights, but unfortunately it was a poor match, incompatible from the start they were already separated.

I had been home with my family for about five weeks when early one Monday morning, at daybreak, we were all woken up by a cacophony of noises coming from the river. The boats moored on the Thames were all sounding their steam horns in a variety of unorchestrated sounds of deep and high notes, some in short blasts, and others long, or continuous. Many giving hoots emulating the V (for victory) in Morse code – hoot, hoot, hoot; h-o-o-t, h-o-o-t, h-o-o-t; hoot, hoot, hoot.

"That's it!" My dad said. "The war's over."

We all went out into the street. The sun was shining with almost everyone milling about, smiling and talking; congratulating each other on surviving the war, and praising our soldiers, sailors and airmen for achieving victory. The date was the 7th of May 1945 and cessation of fighting was confirmed in an announcement that evening, although the next day, the 8th of May, officially became Victory in Europe (V.E.) Day. Needless to say, I never went to school that day which judging by the number of people out and about was deemed to be a public holiday, and deservedly so.

Jean suggested to me that if I wanted to make the most of V.E.Day I should go to the West End and join in the celebrations up there, so together with my friend Darryl, that's where I went.

We caught a train from Charlton, to Charring Cross Station, and walked along to Trafalgar Square, which was so densely crowded with happy people that the buses and taxis had to slow down to a crawl. A great many were waving small Union Jack flags; or red, white, and blue streamers; with everybody having a good time singing and dancing or just soaking up the atmosphere.

From Trafalgar Square we squeezed our way down The Mall to join the thousands in front of Buckingham Palace, and with great difficulty, determination, and dexterity, gained a vantage point high on the plinth of the Queen Victoria statue. The crowd were chanting for the royal family to make an appearance, their voices reaching a decibel level which I have only heard equalled at Wembley cup finals.

When the royal family came out onto the balcony of Buckingham Palace, accompanied by the Prime Minister, Mr Winston Churchill, their appearance gave rise to loud cheering and flag-waving – years of tension being released.

It was late in the afternoon when we left Regents Park and pushed our way through the hordes of people (the numbers seemed to be growing all the time) to Piccadilly Circus where singing and dancing were in full swing. The statue of Eros had been taken down and removed for safe-keeping during the war and to safeguard the supporting structure it was clad in hoardings kept in place by scaffolding and sandbags. This was now covered with young people. A sailor was balanced precariously at the very top loudly singing and waving his arms as if leading an orchestra.

Strains of band music were coming from the direction of Shaftsbury Avenue so we eased our way towards it. The American Forces had a club across the road from the Windmill

Theatre called Rainbow Corner and the music was coming from there. The sash-cord windows on the first floor were all open as wide as they could be with a gramophone mounted in one of them blaring out popular music to the enjoyment of the crowd below; the other windows had soldiers leaning out of them calling to girls in the crowd.

In the street, although jam-packed, dancing was in full swing and at one time a long conga line was snaking its way about. The many American, and English, servicemen there were having the time of their lives on this lovely hot summer's day kissing and being kissed by all the smiling young ladies in their pretty summer frocks.

To add to the excitement, every now and then, the American soldiers would throw a large fire-cracker from a window of the Rainbow Club into the street and although it seemed impossible an area of about twenty feet around the fire-cracker would be cleared immediately. At least that was the case most of the time but on one occasion a middle aged couple passing slowly through had a very nasty shock. The man was wearing a loosely fitting woollen jumper and one of the fire-crackers went straight down the V-neck and exploded, blowing a large hole in it.

Surprisingly, although shaken he was unharmed, the explosion taking the path of least resistance, but his wife was most annoyed pointing to his chest and remonstrating. It seems cruel but I couldn't help laughing, that was the sort of day it was.

On the way home, through the windows of the train we could see preparations being made for huge bonfires on the many bomb-sites. Timber, together with old or damaged furniture from the bombed-out buildings, was being piled as high as possible, which in some cases was over twenty feet.

It was well into the evening when we arrived back home and I joined my mum and dad at the local pub where they were celebrating. The pub was so full it would have been difficult to find them had my dad not been wearing a huge paper-mache head. The pubs must have been hoarding beer for the occasion because previously it had been in very short supply; this certainly was not the case now as my dad was merry enough on leaving to shin up a very high lamp-post still wearing the 'big head'.

Celebrations went on well into the night with people singing and dancing around the bonfires, their flames lighting up the skies all over London. My dad had invited a crowd home from the pub which included English and American servicemen who were strangers to him before that evening, but there were no strangers that night, everybody was every one else's friend. One of them, a Sergeant in the American Army, played 'a mean' piano and we partied until the morning.

The war was not over for many people who still had sons and relatives fighting the Japanese in the Far East, but it was for us. We were a family once more, ready to face whatever the future had in store.

Addendum

Being separated from their parents over a long period had a traumatic and lasting effect on many of the children evacuated during the war. Some were billeted with foster parents who used them as servants or cheap labour, and it came to light after the war that quite a few had been physically abused. Many had fathers serving in the armed forces which meant that they seldom had visits from their parents, and in some cases their parents could not afford to visit, or simply chose not to.

I was fortunate for the most part, to be well looked after, and had parents who made an effort to see me as frequently as they could. They wrote to me every week with news of relatives and friends, keeping me in touch and never letting me forget that I was loved, and sorely missed. This, together with my own resilience, meant, that unlike many who blamed the war and evacuation for blighting their life, and the cause for holding them back from achieving better things, I always looked upon it as an adventure.

The friendship that had developed between Mr and Mrs Stark and my parents continued after the war and by the time I joined the Royal Navy a few years later I had been back to Crewses Weir with them several times. They continued their visits off and on until they were quite old and corresponded frequently, always keeping them informed of my whereabouts and wellbeing.

Never having lost touch myself, when I learnt to drive, and owned a car, I took my family to stay with Mrs Stark (unfortunately Mr Stark had died earlier) and my children were able to live for a couple of weeks in a manner that I had lived, visit my old haunts, and share some of my more pleasant memories. Mrs Stark had moved to the house previously occupied by the Aplins which now had electricity, hot and cold water, and a flush toilet, so it was not quite the manner in which I had lived.

We continued to visit now and again but unfortunately Mrs Stark was not getting any younger and she was required to move from Crewses Weir to a small pensioner's bungalow a short walk from the town centre. Taking our holidays in Cornwall at that time we would pop in to see her on our way home and was still making the occasional visits, and corresponding with her right up until the time she died, which fortunately was at a ripe old age.

When I left the Hopkins household I intended to keep in touch and did write one or two letters, but as is often the case with good intentions I failed to keep it up; I was a teenager and that is my pathetic excuse. Many years later journeying back from a holiday in Tenby we made a detour to take a look at Glenamman but I misread the map and took a road which led me to Brynamman. As it was getting late I left it for another time, somehow that time has not yet arrived, and perhaps now it never will.

Part Two

DON'T FORGET YOUR PAYBOOK

After a hard day's work labouring on a building site at New Cross Gate, a suburb of South-East London, I was travelling home through Deptford on a No 38 tram reading a discarded Evening Standard when the headlines of a recruitment advertisement for the Royal Navy caught my eye.

Oiling at Sea
Seeking a Life of Adventure?

JOIN UP NOW!

It had been running in the papers for a few weeks and included a picture of two ships in choppy seas sailing close to, and parallel with each other. A hose was stretched between them with sailors active in oiling a ship at sea.

This was late November 1947, five months before my eighteenth birthday when I would be called up for National Service with the likelihood that I would spend two years in the Army; possibly the R.A.F. Very few conscripts were selected for the Royal Navy.

It had been my desire to be a sailor for many years and only weeks before I had been through the process of entering the Merchant Navy only to fail the medical. The reason was not given to me and on a subsequent visit to my doctor he gave me a clean bill of health.

I had already ascertained that a recruitment office for the Royal Navy was located at Lewisham and on the spur of the moment I jumped off the tram at West Greenwich where I could readily board another which would take me there.

The recruitment drive was for stokers, and the chief petty officer holding the interview gave an encouraging picture of life in this branch of the service, which was good enough for me to agree on taking the next step – a simple aptitude test.

This caused me no problems, nor the medical examination which followed, and I left knowing that I had passed the only obstacle between me and a 'life on the ocean waves'.

It came as a bombshell to my mum and dad when I told them on arriving home.

"Are you in any sort of trouble?" My dad asked.

"No, of course not," I said, and explained to them my reason.

I suppose that I was a bit of a disappointment to them in a way but they never said so. They were easy going and always accepted each decision I made with very few adverse comments.

If they were disappointed they had every reason to be so, for on leaving school at fifteen I was found a very good job as an engineering apprentice with a large manufacturing company. The training included two days each week studying for meaningful qualifications at the South-East London College of Engineering and I had left after only six months to work as a labourer on a building site.

Everyone told me that I should think of the future, but I was more interested in earning the big money that was on offer in my new line of work. I was following the adage, 'live for the moment'.

After six years of war this attitude was commonplace and typified by a friend of mine working as a telegram boy. "A secure and steady job with a pension on the end of it," his father had advised him, a long time Post Office worker himself.

He hated it, and one bitter cold day, climbing uphill on his heavy standard issue bike, with the wind and rain in his face, he thought to himself, 'I'm only fourteen, what am I bothering about a pension for, I've got fifty years of living to do before that.'

He delivered his last telegram that same day.

My first steps onto a building site were tentative; seeking a labouring job I naively thought that little experience would be required, just hard work. I later found out how wrong I was.

The foreman of the site looked me over, without seeming too impressed (at just under nine stone I hardly looked the labouring type) and asked me where I had worked before. Prepared for this

I gave him the name of a large building site I had passed only minutes before.

He said, "Can you use a Kango hammer?"

Having no idea what a Kango hammer was, I sensed that without this item of knowledge there would be no job, so I said, "Yes." Thinking, 'My dad will know.'

"O.K," he said. "Start at seven in the morning. The rate's one and ninepence an hour with an extra penny for using the Kango hammer."

Later at home, my mum and dad were really surprised at my news.

"You a builder's labourer," my mum said. "You won't last a day." Very encouraging.

On top of that my father had never heard of a Kango hammer and found great amusement in my dilemma.

Early on site the next morning I reported to the ganger (foreman of the site) who took me into a large empty chamber on the ground floor of the building being constructed where he introduced me to a workman of Irish extraction.

"This is Paddy, you'll be working with him," he said.

The room was about ten feet high with the walls, ceiling, and floor, all of concrete construction. Boarded scaffolding spanned the entire area to enable work to be done on the ceiling. I was soon to find out what this work was.

Paddy took me up a short ladder to mount the platform where he picked up a Kango hammer, which turned out to be a hand-held pneumatic drill. He then set it into motion and proceeded to randomly chip small holes in the concrete.

"This has got to be done over the entire surface of the ceiling, and then the walls," said Paddy, "and in case you're wondering why, it's for keying in the plaster. "

It was not until some time later when I saw the plasterers in action that I understood fully what he meant.

Paddy got me chipping the ceiling from one end, while he chipped from the other, meeting in the middle. The concern I had regarding my lack of knowledge of the Kango was unfounded as it was simple to use, the problem was finding the strength and stamina to keep going. It seemed to get heavier, and heavier, with

141

the vibrations pounding my arms, and shoulders. By the time tea-break arrived my whole upper body was aching and by the end of the day I was ready to drop, but I was back on site the next morning determined not to let it beat me.

On the third day, having matched Paddy in the amount of work done, he asked me, "How much are you getting paid?"

"One and nine pence an hour, plus a penny for the Kango," I said.

He immediately got down from the platform and left the room, returning after about ten minutes.

"The Ganger wants to see you," he said.

I found the Ganger in his office and without ado he said, "From today I'm putting your rate up to two shillings and threepence an hour, plus a penny while you're on the Kango."

I thanked him, and he said, "Paddy's the one you've got to thank." This I did on my return to work.

Tea and lunch breaks were taken in a hut at the rear of the site and I got to know the other labourers, and artisans, working there; bricklayers, plasterers, and carpenters. The majority of them had only recently been discharged from the army and between them they had a wealth of stories about their experiences in the war which I soaked up. Although working hard I was enjoying the experience.

There were many times that my inexperience displayed itself and it was not long before it became evident that I had not worked on a building site before, but I was willing to learn and always tried to match the effort put in by the other labourers.

The first time this happened was when the combined efforts of the labour force were required to fill a lorry with debris resulting from the demolition of the old building. Joining the others I took a shovel and drove it into the pile of rubble, then attempted to toss its contents over the side and onto the bed of the lorry. This resulted in a shower of dust, together with pieces of brick, and concrete, falling on the men around the truck who reacted with an angry roar of four letter words in disapproval.

Mick (another Irishman) quickly pulled me to the far side of the pile and gave me a lesson in shovelling. He showed me how to get the maximum load onto the shovel by keeping the blade on the ground and pushing the handle with my knee, then when throwing the load onto the lorry how to sharply drop the business end of the shovel at the end of the toss to keep the contents flying through the air together. A few practice throws and I was back with the gang filling the lorry up.

They liked to tease me and put me to the test. One such occasion occurred when there was a delivery of bricks. The men formed themselves into a chain, standing about five feet apart, which extended from the lorry to where the bricks were stacked. The bricks were then thrown from one to the other, the driver of the brick lorry making the first throw with the last man neatly stacking them. I was given a pair of leather gloves and positioned midway in the line.

I managed to catch the three bricks being thrown and toss them on to the next man easily enough. No problem. The driver then increased the number of bricks being thrown to four, which I managed, but with some difficulty.

Bricks are thrown horizontally and the technique is to catch the outer bricks whilst at the same time press inwardly to hold the inner bricks. This requires strong arms and wrists, which mine, although developing, were definitely not. Nevertheless, with all eyes on me and waiting for me to fail, I was holding my own, until the driver, upon a wink from one of the labourers, upped the number to five. The five bricks thrown to me ended up on the ground at my feet, luckily without crushing my toes. (I was only wearing shoes). Several more throws were made in swift succession and the pile of bricks at my feet grew bigger, with all the men in fits of laughter at my predicament. Having had their bit of fun they reduced the number of bricks being thrown back to four.

It was shortly after this that I nearly killed the ganger.

We had dug a hole ten feet deep to accommodate a three foot square copper plate to provide an earth for a lightening conductor which was to be buried in concrete at the bottom.

The concrete mixer stood on a pathway some thirty feet from the hole and planks were laid end to end on the rough surface in between for the barrows of concrete to be wheeled along. I was responsible for one of the barrows.

143

Wheeling a barrow filled with sloppy wet concrete on a sound flat surface is in itself a difficult task as a slight tilt to one side, followed instinctively with a reactive movement to the other, causes a wobble which invariably results in spillage. Doing it whilst balancing along a line of planks is considerably harder.

Following Paddy's advice I gripped the handles of the barrow firmly by my side and looking straight ahead walked quickly until successfully reaching the end of the last plank, whereupon I upturned the barrow and shot the contents into the hole. Unfortunately, I had overrun the end of the plank and the barrow followed, almost taking me with it.

I tentatively looked over the edge and to my relief the ganger, who had deemed it necessary to do that part of the job himself, was still in one piece, looking up covered in cement and aggregate mix.

On the advice from one of the labourers I vacated the site and returned about half-hour later when he had cleaned himself up. Lucky not to get the sack I remained on the site until all major works were completed.

The experience had been good for me, it had been hard work but I had enjoyed it and was sorry to leave. Although still skinny, weighing less than nine stone when I went for my naval medical, it had toughened me up – but not tough enough according to my next employer

This was Mr Brierly of 'Brierly and Grey' - copper-smiths to the brewery trade. Their premises were modified railway arches and I was there just three days. The longest three days of my life.

Within a short time of arriving at seven o'clock on the first morning I was handed a leather apron and given the job of cleaning a huge piece of copper pipe in the form of a bend. It was two feet in diameter and soot black where it had been in a furnace, for the task I was given a wire brush and a few sheets of emery cloth.

"Bring it to a shine," Mr Brierly said, before he disappeared into his grubby office in the corner of the workshop.

Whilst scratching away with the wire brush I chatted briefly to a lad who was an apprentice there, but after just a short time he left with a fitter and Mr Brierly to carry out some work in a local brewery. This left me with two very old men who were working slowly but consistently on the other side of the workshop.

After several hours of non-stop work I had barely made any improvement. Scratching away with the wire brush, followed by circular rubbing movements with the emery cloth, not only showed little for my efforts, but was also extremely tedious.

During this time I had taken stock of my surroundings and assessed it to be the dirtiest and most depressing place I had ever been in. There was barely any colour other than grey and black. With a small furnace burning in a forge it reminded me of a blacksmiths shop but without the pleasing presence of a horse. A cubicle in the corner of the room housed a toilet; a tap with a bucket underneath, just outside the door provided washing facilities.

I tried to engage the two old men in conversation but they did little more than grin and nod. I did however manage to get an answer when I asked them what time we stopped for a tea-break.

"There is no tea-break," one of them said. "We have an hour for lunch at one-o-clock."

"Well I'm going for a tea break," I said. "A.E.U. rules state that you're entitled to a tea break if you work a period longer than four hours." (I had been a junior member of the Amalgamated Engineering Union whilst apprenticed at Molins Machine Company).

With that I washed my hands in the bucket and went to a nearby café that I had noted on my way there.

On return I continued to clean the copper bend until lunch time and again throughout the afternoon.

Speaking to my parents that evening about my day, I mentioned that no tea-break was given. My dad was most surprised and wondered what Mr Brierly was doing with the tea and sugar ration that he was allowed for his employees.

The next day, and the day after, was exactly the same, scratching with the wire brush and burnishing with the emery cloth; it was soul destroying and the job was nowhere near completion.

We finished each day at five-o-clock, and on the third day, Wednesday, I was washing my hands ten minutes before time when Mr Brierly came out of his office, saw me, and bellowed, "I pay you until five, wash your hands in your own time. Get back to work."

"Surely I am entitled to clean up before I go home," I said.

"You can, but not until after five; and while I'm about it, you can stop taking tea breaks over the café in the morning." This had obviously been a bone of contention and I had given him the opportunity to raise it.

This made me angry. "Well I won't be taking any more tea breaks because I'm leaving, you can make up my cards."

"I knew you wasn't tough enough for this job," he taunted.

"Not stupid enough you mean," I answered back.

All the men were standing stock still listening intently, and realising the inference in respect to their position I quickly moved on. "You don't deserve to have good people working for you, a man so mean that he doesn't provide a tea break for them; and come to that, what do you do with the tea and sugar rations that you get for your men?"

"You cheeky young sod," he said "You're just a stirrer. Go on, clear out."

I put on my jacket and left, returning in the morning for my money and cards. He gave them to me with barely a word said.

Shortly after that I received my call-up papers and on the 19th February 1948 joined a group of new entrants at the Royal Naval Recruitment Centre in Charring Cross Road.

From there we were transported by train to Corsham, near Bath, and then by coach to a nearby naval base. A large sign on the entrance gate told us that we were entering H.M.S. Royal Arthur.

It had been snowing hard all day and we alighted from the coach into snow six inches deep. Told to keep clothing to a minimum, as they were to be packed up and sent home once we had been kitted out with our uniforms, I was in light clothing – sports jacket and trousers. Cold and shivering as we walked along a road between mess-huts, heads poking out of open windows chorused, "You'll be Sorry!"

A few weeks earlier they had been receiving the same greeting, and a few weeks later we would be greeting further new entrants in a similar manner.

We were shown to a hut, which was to be our mess for the duration of our basic training, by a man in a jacketed type uniform with a peak cap who introduced himself to us as Petty Officer Nutbrown. He informed us that he would be our adviser and instructor whilst we were at H.M.S. Royal Arthur.

The hut was large enough to accommodate a total of twenty-four single beds (twelve each side) and after we had claimed a bed and deposited any belongings we had brought, we were taken to the canteen for a hot meal.

The next morning, after breakfast, we were marched to the purser's store to be kitted out with our uniforms and other items of clothing, from underwear to overcoat; also, a kitbag, a small case, and a name stamp. The store men were past masters at sizing up each person at a glance, which was not really too difficult as they only came in three sizes; large, medium, and small; except for hats and boots. The only exception was for anyone extra large, their suits being made to measure.

The uniforms were, without exception, a terrible fit, and a civilian tailor on the base made a good living out of re-tailoring at least one of everybody's suits. My conception of a sailor was that he wore a tunic so tight that it could only be removed with difficulty, he wore a round hat (often on the back of his head), and he had a blue collar. The tunics we had issued hung straight down from the shoulders, the hats were oval (to stop being worn on the back of the head), and the collars were so dark that they looked black.

Petty Officer Nutbrown informed us that after this first issue of clothing all replacement items would have to be bought, for this we would receive a kit upkeep allowance. He then told us that nobody he knew bought their uniforms from the pusser's store (he used the term pusser for purser as did everyone else in the service) and advised us to open an account with a naval tailor when we had finished our training. (I later allotted eight shillings each month to Coopers of Portsmouth which kept me kitted out for the rest of my time in the navy).

147

Assembled in our uniforms we were marched to the studio of the camp photographer where we each had a snapshot taken of our head and shoulders. The following day, along with all the others, I was issued with my 'naval pay and identity book' which had this photograph of me on the inside of its stiff blue cover.

After handing them out, P.O. Nutbrown addressed us with regard to their safekeeping.

"As you can see by the wording on the front cover, it is your pay and identity book. This is the most important document you will have whilst in the service and if you lose it you will be put on a charge. When ashore you must carry it with you at all times, and when on the base, or onboard ship, you must ensure that it is in a secure place. It is also your passport when travelling in foreign parts, so just remember, that whenever you leave the ship, don't forget your pay book."

All new naval ratings carried out a course of training at H.M.S. Royal Arthur, whatever branch they had enlisted for, and the three months spent there was to drill naval routine and discipline into you. From early morning when reveille was sounded until pipe-down in the evening the day was spent on the various aspects of marching, rifle drill, and physical exercise. It was a hard routine designed to knock you into shape.

I was unprepared for the rigorous routine of square-bashing; I thought that was the province of the army. Humping a rifle at the double around the parade ground or shouldering a full pack on a five mile march was not what I expected; still I endured it and became fitter for it. It was made easier by Petty Officer Nutbrown's cheerful and sympathetic manner; some of the instructors had a mean streak and took delight in making their charges suffer.

The senior command there had a penchant for boxing, and during the first week our group were lined up alongside one wall of the gymnasium in descending order from tallest to smallest with another group similarly lined up on the opposite side. Wearing boxing gloves, and starting with the tallest, a rating from each side was required to run into the centre and throw punches at each other non-stop for one minute. At the blast of a whistle they stopped and the next pair ran into middle to do the same, and so on until the last man had had his go. They called it 'milling'. It was hardly boxing; it lacked any art form at all.

It was a totally unfair method of pairing people up and to my relief I could see, by counting down the line, that my combatant was even skinnier than me, and when it came to our turn, I am ashamed to admit, that I took advantage of this and gave him a pounding.

Later that same day I was sitting in the mess-hut when a messenger from the physical training instructor (P.T.I.) entered and asked for me. A request had been made by the officer responsible for sporting activities to meet him at the rear of the gymnasium.

When I got there, he was standing on a patch of grass accompanied by the P.T.I. and a lad about the same size as me.

"Thanks for coming. What weight are you?" he asked.

"Nine stone," I replied.

"Good. Have you done any boxing before?"

"Not in the ring," I answered. "Just a bit of sparring at a youth club."

"I'd like to see how you get on with this young chap, are you happy with that?"

I thought to myself, 'Perhaps the P.T.I. saw something in my performance this afternoon.'

"I don't mind," I replied.

I put on the boxing gloves proffered to me, as did the other lad, and at a signal from the P.T.I. the pair of us started sparring and exchanging blows.

I was holding my own and quite pleased with my performance when they stopped the round after about two seconds.

We broke, and stood about six feet apart. I was left to stand alone whilst the officer and the P.T.I. went to my opponent's side and acted as seconds, offering him advice. Very sound advice as it turned out because when we restarted he performed one or two manoeuvres which left me open to a sucker punch to the jaw. My legs became jelly and I collapsed to the ground, surprised to find myself there as the punch did not seem to carry that much force. I rose to my feet quite quickly but the officer and the P.T.I. had seen enough.

They dismissed me, thanking me for my cooperation, and went off with their protégé. I realised then that I had never been in the reckoning; they had a likely contender on their hands and wanted to see what he was made of. I was just a patsy.

He turned out to be quite useful, winning the lightweight division of the camp tournament, and later, as a welterweight, representing the Royal Navy. Shortly after our little episode he told me that he had trained with an amateur boxing club in Glasgow.

My boxing career was not quite finished. Having impressed with my milling performance I was entered into that category in the camp tournament and furiously punched again for one minute, only this time against a more worthy opponent who out-punched me.

Four weeks into our training we were given a weekend off, and I, like all the others, decided to spend it at home. Before being allowed to go 'ashore' (even a land base is considered to be a ship – known as a stone frigate) the officer-of-the-day is required to carry out a dress inspection, so on leaving the base at five o-clock on the Friday evening I fell in outside of his office with the rest of my group. When he reached me, he tapped my shoulder and told me to stand to one side; the rest were allowed to go and filed out through the gate.

He turned to me and said, "The reason that I am sending you back is because your collar does not conform to regulations. It has been bleached, and badly at that."

We had all done it. Having been issued with two collars it seemed a good idea to bleach one of them to a paler shade of blue to make it look like you had 'time in', but it was poorly done and turned out patchy. I would not have worn it had I not loaned my other collar to a messmate who after constant badgering had returned it that same day badly creased, and dirty.

Disconsolate, I went back to the mess-hut where I was sitting on my bed thirty minutes later when Petty Officer Nutbrown happened to look in.

"Why are you still here?" he enquired.

"I've been stopped from going on leave," I said. And told him about the collar and the reason I had worn it.

"Where is your other collar?" Petty Officer Nutbrown asked.

I retrieved it from my locker and showed it to him.

"Bring your toothbrush and toothpaste, and come with me."

He led the way to the washroom and with a spot of toothpaste on the toothbrush he scrubbed the white stripes on the collar. I then followed him to the ironing room where he pressed the whole of the collar using a damp cloth.

"Have your mother wash it for you when you get home, it will pass muster for now," he said.

He had given me back the chance of going on leave when a few moments before all hope had seemed lost.

Now wearing my dark blue collar he took me back to the duty officer and addressing him said, "I have Stoker Wellard here Sir, he has changed his collar and requests permission to proceed on weekend leave."

The officer looked up from the desk he was sitting at and with barely a glance towards me gave his approval.

Arriving home that evening I enjoyed being greeted like a long lost warrior; cosseted, and praised for looking smart in my uniform.

Saturday flew by; the afternoon spent watching Charlton Athletic beat Aston Villa in a thrilling game of football, and later going to a dance at Greeenwich Town Hall where I met up with the usual crowd, many of them surprised to see me in uniform not knowing that I had joined up. But my crowning joy was going to the pub on the Sunday at lunch time and enjoying a pint or two of mild ale with my dad. Although not eighteen, the legitimate age to buy alcohol, in uniform, I appeared old enough.

In the pub my dad introduced me to a couple of his drinking pals and I remember one of them saying during conversation, "Going in the forces doesn't do a lad any harm, it makes him take personal responsibility for his own life; he goes away a boy, and returns a man."

During the month of May I reached the next stage of my training. I was now adept at parade ground routine and able to drill with a rifle. I could do my own dhobiing (clothes washing) and ironing. I was calling the floor – the deck, the ceiling – the deckhead, the walls – bulkheads, and the toilets – heads. I had concluded the first stage of becoming a sailor and I had not yet had sight of the sea.

That was soon to be rectified with my transfer to H.M.S. Raleigh at Torpoint (near Plymouth) for the next phase of my training, which was of a technical nature. A lot of the time was spent in the classroom learning about the function of ships machinery in its boiler-room, engine-room, gear-room, etc., but also included a month on a battle-cruiser moored in the estuary of the River Tamar for hands-on experience.

This experience was not only concerned with the engineering aspects, but also to get you used to living at sea and share a confined space around the clock with your messmates. The confined space that you live in aboard a ship is your mess, it is the place in which you have your meals, spend your leisure time, and 'sling your hammock' for a good night's sleep. (Once you get used to it).

A mess on board a ship is without luxuries. It is a steel box, evident by the rivets in the bulkheads, and bare of everything except essential equipment; long wooden tables with benches either side, both affixed to the deck; steel lockers for clothes; steel lockers for food, utensils, and cleaning materials. Hooks, and rails, adorned the higher level for hanging hammocks, and an area of the mess was railed off for stowing them in.

It was while on the cruiser that I had my first taste of naval punishment; not without reason, but for nothing more than a prank.

Sitting on the forecastle one summer's evening alongside another lad, Ron Warburton, with whom I had formed a close friendship, we were chatting about our ill luck at being stuck on board due to lack of money to fund a run ashore.

On this theme I threw out a facetious claim.

152

"Do you know what?" I said. "I'd jump off that high diving board at Plymouth Hoe for five shillings." (The diving board referred to was ten metres high).

Ron countered with, "Well, for that, I would swim from here to over there," pointing across the River Tamar to the opposite shore, a distance of about one mile.

Not to be outdone, I bragged, "I would jump off here for half-a-crown."

"Would you?" Ron said. "I'll see what I can do about that."

He then got up and went below returning after about ten minutes with a group of our mess-mates, a big grin spread across his face.

"You're on. The lads don't think you'll do it, so they've raised half-a-crown to challenge you."

Having made this brag without considering what it fully entailed I peered over the guardrail to the water below and estimated it to be a drop of over thirty feet. Furthermore, I had not considered how I was going to get back on board; I could hardly swim around to the gangway and tell the quartermaster that I had fallen in. However, looking for a way up I perceived that the ship was secured to a large buoy by two massive chains running together and connected to a capstan on the foredeck after passing through the hawser pipe (a hole through the bow). The links of the chain formed a natural ladder and with the hawser pipe being over three feet in diameter I had my answer.

Although fearful of going through with it I agreed, losing face would have been worse, so I went below to the mess-deck and donned a pair of trunks.

Returning to the upper-deck I lost no time in climbing through the guardrail and leaping into the sea below. I swam around for a while, mostly on my back to receive a few accolades being given, then climbed onto the buoy and up the links of the chains. The chains never went steeper than forty-five degrees and with each link being very large, and paired as they were; the ascent was made without difficulty.

When I emerged from the hawser pipe, Ron was in his trunks about to outdo my act of bravado and dive. He had been given

153

this challenge for a further half-a-crown and carried it out with some panache.

The next day he would not stop crowing about it until in the end I decided that the only way to shut him up was to better it, or at least equal it, so that evening I decided to dive off, but a little higher up the forecastle. I was not alone, another friend, Vincent Sennet, decided to join me.

Vince left the mess first, and when I reached the forecastle he was standing in the fading light on the outside of the guardrail looking down at the twinkling water a long way below, contemplating the feat in front of him. Having never dived from such a height before I knew that if I lingered, there was a possibility that I might lose my nerve and not dive at all, so I walked swiftly across the deck, ducked under the rails, and threw myself into space before I had time to change my mind. The dive was far from Olympic standards but, I had entered the water head first and was still in one piece without injury.

Pleased with myself, I swam around watching Vince still clutching the guardrail, plucking up the courage to join me. A large crowd had gathered urging him on.

At last he dived, and had hardly risen to the surface when the ship's tannoy blared out 'MAN OVERBOARD – MOTORBOAT'S CREW AWAY'. At the same time lights were beamed onto the water and the sound of voices and people were heard running along the gangway on the port side.

I quickly scrambled onto the buoy and climbed up the chain into the hawser pipe, with Vince close behind me. It was not a moment too soon, for just after, the officer of the watch arrived on the forecastle and a motor-launch rounded the stern of the ship with its searchlight on.

Apparently, the alarm was raised by two petty officers who were taking the air on one of the upper-decks when they heard a splash and saw a crowd of ratings peering over the side of the ship. That was probably the moment after I made my dive.

Crouching in the hawser pipe we could hear the officer of the watch asking questions of the crowd gathered there, and giving instructions to the coxswain of the launch.

Whispering to Vince, I said, "You stay in here and I'll make a run for it. He'll see me and without knowing there's two of us will look no further."

With that, I leapt from the pipe and ran across the forecastle toward the hatch leading to the deck below, jumping the breakwater on my way.

The officer caught a glimpse of me and shouted, "Stop! Come here!"

I had no intention of stopping and continued at a fast pace until I reached the bathroom where I took off my trunks and hid them.

After showering I waited awhile before returning to my mess. Bad news: Vince had come out of the hawser pipe and was now being held in the master-at-arms' office.

A short time later, when I was warm and dressed, Vince came back into the mess still in his damp swimming trunks looking cold and downhearted. He had refused to disclose who was with him but had been advised that if he continued with his silence it would be a lot worse for him. There was no way that I would let him carry the can alone so I went with him back to the police office and gave myself up.

As defaulters we had to appear before the first- lieutenant for him to determine our punishment. He was of the opinion that our misdeed was serious enough to go to a higher authority and put us on 'Captain's Report'.

This was a routine which I went through many times during my naval service. It is a small court held with the captain presiding. Sitting alongside him behind a desk, or table, is the first lieutenant, and arresting officer.

You wait in the gangway until your name is called then double into the office, or cabin, where it is being held, and up to the desk where the master-at- arms (or chief boatswain) brings you to a halt.

He then barks out, "Off cap!" (Off caps, in this case).

At this command you swiftly bring your right arm up to grip the left hand side of your cap and bring it down to your right hand side.

The master-at-arms then reads out the charge, followed by the arresting officer who gives details of the incident and any excuse, or explanation that you may have given.

The captain then asks his own questions to all concerned, which may include witnesses, to fully ascertain the nature of events.

Finally, he passes sentence, after which the master-at-arms escorts you to his office where he outlines the terms of your punishment.

Vince and I went through this procedure which resulted in us being given fourteen days No 11 punishment as detailed in the Kings Regulations and Admiralty Instructions, which were in force at that time. Listed in a numerical scale, the lower the number the more severe it was. (I do know that Number 16 was two hours extra work and Number 1 was execution).

The next day we started our elevenses (as No 11 punishment was known) and found out just what it entailed. At seven in the morning we fell in with other defaulters and were directed by the duty petty officer to scrub the quarterdeck for the next hour before we were free to go for breakfast. We then proceeded to undertake our normal duties until lunchtime.

Immediately after lunch we had to report to the P.O. in charge of the galley where we spent the remaining period of our break cleaning the soiled pots and pans.

Normal duties again until five-o clock, when with the other defaulters we were given an hours rifle drill on the upper deck which included running on the spot, and a further hour cleaning the heads before being dismissed for dinner.

At eight, we were back in the galley cleaning the pans until nine-o-clock when we were required to muster in full uniform and pass inspection by the duty officer when he carried out his evening rounds. By the time we returned to the mess it was gone half-past-nine. What was left of the rest of the day was our own.

The tasks varied, but other than that the rest of the fortnight was the same.

Midway through the course we were given leave, a long weekend from Friday midday until Monday morning. I invited

Vince to come home with me as he was not inclined to take the long and expensive train journey to Newcastle, where he lived, for such a short period. Ron, who came from Sheffield, envied Vince his trip to London so I invited him too.

To save funds we decided to hitchhike. Having got a bus to Plympton it was not long before we were in a car, and after several more lifts, and many hours later, we were in London being dropped off in Trafalgar Square.

We took the train from Charring Cross to Charlton station, which is in Church Lane, and walked up its steep hill to The Heights, arriving late that evening.

The next day, being Saturday, with Charlton Athletic at home, we went to the football match, but it was the evening that Ron and Vince were excited about. They were intent on going to the Hammersmith Palais where Ted Heath and his Orchestra were playing, they were big on the radio at the time with Dickie Valentine and Lita Rosa the resident singers.

Nothing that I could say would put them off.

"It's on the other side of London," I said. "That's miles away. Kenny Baker and his Dozen are playing at the Greenwich Baths."

This offer did not have the same appeal and at seven that evening we were queuing outside the Hammersmith Palais with hundreds of others after the long journey by train and tube.

It was a good evening, and dressed in our uniforms we had no problems in getting partners, but I warned Ron and Vince that it was not worth taking any of them home afterwards unless they were prepared for a long walk as the buses and the tube shut down about midnight.

Nevertheless, when we left the Palais it was well past eleven and Vince had a pretty girl on his arm having already made arrangements to see her home. We pleaded with him to say his goodbyes there and then but nothing we said would make him change his mind.

"I won't be long," he said, "Just give me a quarter of an hour."

We gave him longer than that, and just managed to reach the Embankment in time to catch the last tram returning to New Cross Gate depot.

We walked from there, through Deptford and across Blackheath, arriving home just after half past one, tired out ready for bed.

My mum shook me awake in the morning.

"Rex. Where's Vince?"

"Isn't he home yet?" I asked sleepily.

"No."

"What's the time?"

"It's just gone nine."

"I'll get up."

I had hardly washed and gone downstairs when Vince came in through the back door with quite a tale to tell.

Having taken the girl home to her front door she was very responsive to his amorous advances so it seemed worthwhile spending a bit more time developing their relationship.

"How did it go?" I asked eagerly.

"It didn't," Vince said. "Just as things were warming up her father opened the door and ordered her in."

On leaving her he lost his way back to the Palais arriving there well after we had gone.

Having no idea of where to go, or what to do, by the time he had found someone able to direct him the transport system had closed down for the night. Without the funds to hire a taxi he walked toward Central London and found himself in Trafalgar Square.

With a pointer now and again from late night stragglers he managed find his way across the Thames and onto The Old Kent Road which he had been told to follow all the way to the end. He eventually reached Greeenwich, and not knowing my home address called in at a police station in Old Woolwich Road to seek help. By then it was four-o-clock in the morning.

The policeman on duty listened to his tale of woe and not being inclined to pursue the matter at that unearthly hour gave him a cell where he could get his head down for a few hours. The policeman then rang H.M.S. Raleigh at seven-thirty who were able to give him my address. Fortunately, it was only a short distance from there.

We left soon after Sunday lunch that day and got a train from Charlton, changing onto the underground for Malden, the fares being paid for by my mum. From there, we could readily start thumbing a lift on the A3, which at that time was the main road out of London heading to the South West of England.

Luckily, a flat back lorry pulled up quite soon; not the most comfortable of rides but beggars can't be choosers. Vince rode up front with the driver whilst Ron and I roughed it out on the back, covering ourselves with an old tarpaulin when it rained. We were not sorry to get off at Chard in Somerset.

Things went from bad to worse with lifts few and far between, and only for a few miles at a time. By nightfall we were still a long way from Plymouth.

We sat on the side of a long straight road waiting for the next lift to come along, but unfortunately we all fell asleep. We were aroused from our slumber some time later by a police officer who had arrived in a Wolseley car which was parked close by with the driver still at the wheel.

"Are you trying to get yourselves killed?" he asked, not expecting an answer. "See that skid mark." He shone his torch on two black lines in the road which culminated close to our feet. "You nearly had your legs cut off, luckily the driver saw you at the last minute."

He took our pay-books into the car from which he wrote down each of our names and asked us the ship we were on before sending us on our way.

"What about a lift then?" I asked.

"You're lucky I'm not giving you a lift to the Police Station and a night in the cells," he replied. "Now get on your way."

We had not walked very far when we came across a hay barn on the side of the road. What a break! We climbed up onto the top of the hay, just under the roof, and slept until morning.

When we got back on the road again we were already adrift (late) but there was nothing that we could do about it. Luckily things changed in our favour and we were back on board before mid-day.

This resulted in another charge, for which we received the loss of two days pay and leave.

It did not end there however, a report from the police arrived a few days later concerning our brush with the law and we were further charged with bringing the uniform into disrespect. For this we were given two days No 16s. (Two hours extra work each day).

In September, having completed my training I was sent to H.M.S.Victory, the Royal Naval Barracks in Portsmouth, for a posting onboard a ship.

Before I could unpack my kitbag I was advised to look on the notice board where postings were listed and to my surprise I was due to join H.M.S. Suvla that same day. On reporting to the admin office, transport was arranged and I was taken to where she was moored alongside the wall in Portsmouth dockyard.

The ship's engines had already been warmed up and I had hardly got on board before the gangway was pulled away and it became sea-bound.

With kitbag and hammock I was taken below by the seaman manning the gangway and introduced to the killick (leading hand) of the stoker's mess which was located at the stern of the ship. Within a few minutes of talking to me he produced a pen, and a sheet of paper, on which he wrote the ship's address, and suggested that I write home to let my parents know that I was on my way to the Mediterranean and hopefully would be back before Christmas. The letter was taken off, with other official notes and correspondence by the pilot when he left the boat at Spithead.

Given a locker, I stowed my kit away and was shown around the messdeck. It spanned the width of the ship and was split into two messes, the seamen's mess on the starboard side, and the stoker's mess on the port side, with each mess having three tables long enough to accommodate ten men each. Separating them was an area railed off for storing hammocks, and a small clear space where a dartboard was mounted.

Meeting some of the stokers who were not on duty, I was chatting to them when the Chief Stoker P.O. came into the mess and introduced himself to me. After a few friendly words of greeting he informed me that I would be watch-keeping in the boiler-room, starting with the forenoon the following morning.

On leaving Portsmouth Harbour I joined a group on the upper deck and enjoyed the moment as we rounded the Isle of Wight and headed into the English Channel. That evening after dinner when I sat in the mess with members of the crew talking about the cruise ahead I felt on top of the world; this was what I joined the navy for.

I learned that H.M.S.Suvla was a Landing Ship Tank (LST), and that we were on our way to Tripoli to carry out exercises with the army. There were various types of landing craft but LSTs were the largest, able to carry and deliver tanks, and armoured vehicles, directly onto the beach.

The next morning I joined Petty Officer Cox on the plates in the boiler room at eight-o-clock sharp for the forenoon watch. (Decking in boiler and engine rooms is constructed of steel chequer plates; consequently being in either of these is termed - being on the plates). He was a very likeable man with a great sense of humour and we got along well together from the very start. Under his directions I soon picked up the duties expected of me, which although important, followed routine procedures like flashing up the oil fired burners, keeping a watchful eye on the various gauges, and making sure that the whole area was kept clean. Copper pipework and brass fittings had to be gleaming, made so by Brasso and elbow grease. During the night watches another important task was expected of me – making the cocoa.

Coming into the mess at midday after my first watch I observed a ritual which was being performed on every naval ship at that time of the day. Up Spirits - the issuing of rum.

Between eleven and twelve o-clock the coxswain, accompanied by a seaman, and the officer of the day, unlocked the spirit room and from a rum barrel drew off enough rum for the entire ship's company, excepting officers who were not entitled. They had a bar in the wardroom.

The pot containing the rum, known as the 'rum fanny' was then carried ceremoniously to a distribution point where it was poured into an oaken rum tub with shiny brass hoops bearing the inscription 'The King – God Bless Him'.

Neat rum would then be measured out for chiefs and petty officers before water was added to form 'grog' for the lower echelons.

A rum bosun from each mess, who was usually the senior kellick, would then be served with exactly the right amount for those eligible. Ratings under the age of twenty and men under punishment were not entitled.

On entering the mess with the rum he would find almost everybody waiting eagerly for his tot.

Seating himself at the top of the table the rum bosun would then arrange several glasses which the insides, like the rum fanny, were never washed, and proceed to dish out the grog.

He would take a small copper pot which held the exact entitlement, thee-eighths of a pint, and holding it with his index finger deep inside, dip it into the fanny and fill it to the brim before pouring the contents into one of the glasses. It would be grabbed, and downed in one, by the rating most eager to get it, but not before he had offered the rum bosun sippers, a polite formality.

After all tots were issued a quantity remained in the fanny due to everyone having been given short measure. The rum bosun would then drain this into a glass and pass it around for each to have sippers.

It would be difficult to describe the quantity you should take with 'a sipper' only with experience did you find out, although, it was in a recognised scale of measurements concerning a tot of rum.

Three sippers = one gulper.
Three gulpers = one tot.
Half a tot was another alternative.

Rum was fondly referred to as 'Nelson's Blood', but in the mess it was called 'Gibber Juice' to depict the way it loosened tongues.

Sailors would come into the mess at midday showing little emotion, but soon after the rum had gone down their throats, discussions, or arguments took place. It could be about anything; girls, football, religion, politics, and usually accompanied by pointing, arm waving, and other histrionics. A lively atmosphere was always present at tot time. .

If you chose to waive the right to your rum ration a daily payment of three-pence was made in lieu, but this was seldom taken up because a tot of rum was worth more in barter value. It was a form of currency. For a couple of tots you could find someone to do your watch; for three, scrub your hammock. For simple favours a gulper or two may suffice.

As I stood watching this for the first time I looked on with envy and was surprised to receive a few sippers, not unusual as it turned out, for such generosity with respect to men underage and those under punishment was commonplace.

A few years after this, and on another ship, I was to write an ode for a weekly radio show. It went like this:-

'Rum's up,' the cry, then the stampede,
First to the rum pot is speedy John Reid.
Next in line, is old Mickey Dunn,
Sippers to the bosun, then down in one.
Jimmy Johnson takes the next glass,
He's another, who drinks it down fast.
Unlike Yorky, who takes his time,
And spoils the taste, by adding some lime.
Then Chalky White, who is looking quite glum,
He lost at cards, and owes half his rum.
Two tots are owed by lazy Tom Green,
For a favour done, but his hammock is clean.
Standing in line, they queue one by one,
Until the last man, has knocked back his rum.
No one has moved, they are all waiting there,
To see what is left, they all want their share.
It's sippers all round, gulpers it's not,
'Don't hang about, pass round the pot.'
After the rum comes the afterglow,
You feel a tingle from head to toe.
It's dinner time too, and everything's fine
With rum in your belly, who needs wine?
Now everyone's talking, it's loosened the tongue,
On every subject under the sun.

Football, girls, and politics too.
Philosophy, religion, nothing's taboo.
It's getting quite manic, almost berserk,
But then it's over, we're all back to work.

The weekend found us in the Bay of Biscay which is notoriously rough, and although not the worst time of the year (this being the winter months, as we found out on the return journey) it was still very choppy. Being a landing craft, by necessity it has a flat bottom, so having no stabilising keel the waves tossed it about like a cork; rising and falling with every wave whilst rolling continuously from side to side.

It was like this on the Sunday morning at breakfast-time when a tray of eggs and bacon were brought down from the galley and placed on one of the tables in the mess. A few of the stokers were showing signs of seasickness and Pincher Martin, a long-serving killick and a bit of a joker, cut off two strips of fat from his bacon, poked a piece into each of his nostrils, and left them dangling there as he proceeded to eat his breakfast. This had the effect he was hoping for because a number of them pushed their plates away and left the mess.

"Sod you Pincher!" was a typical remark that was made.

Pincher, and a few other seasoned sailors, helped themselves to extra portions of bacon and eggs and they were all surprised when I joined them, helping myself to double rations. Being my first trip they assumed that I would be amongst those heaving over the guard-rail, but fortunately seasickness never troubled me. I actually enjoyed being in rough seas and standing on the upper deck with the wind in my face, and the waves rising and falling, I found it exhilarating, like riding on a roller-coaster.

We anchored at Gibraltar and stayed there for nearly a week, enough time to give all the crew a few runs ashore. Holidays abroad were very seldom afforded by working class people then so I felt lucky to be enjoying the chance that had come my way.

Eager to get ashore I was the first one on the liberty boat and the first one off when it tied up alongside the harbour wall and stood there waiting for my shipmates to join me, surprised that they were hanging back. I understood why when from the back of the boat the ship's engineering officer, in civilian clothing and the only officer going ashore at that particular time, was given gangway to alight from the boat before them. From the look that he gave me I knew that he was not pleased and that I would hear further about it. I had crossed the line with regard to the protocol concerning officer's precedence over ratings.

It was a pleasure to be on the 'Rock' enjoying its sunny Mediterranean climate and after climbing to the top, and feeding the Rock-Apes, I went down to the small but busy town and had a meal of steak, egg, and chips. I remember, as I sat there cutting into the steak, thinking how wrong it was that I had as much meat on my plate, probably more, than my parents were allowed in one week due to rationing which was still in force at that time.

It would have been nice to enter Spain, but servicemen were not allowed to cross the border in uniform, however, with the many kerbside bars all having attractive Spanish hostesses dressed in their national costumes luring you in it was easy to think that you were there.

With the alcohol cheap, and being unused to heavy drinking, I returned to the ship late that evening drunk and being supported by my shipmates, themselves well oiled but able to hold their liquor much better than me.

The next morning, as expected, I was summoned to the engineer's office. Knowing this was coming Pincher Martin had rascally pointed out that the engineer looked a bit like the canteen manager, both being middle-aged and portly, and suggested that I use this as an excuse by saying that I mistakenly thought it was him in the liberty boat and not the Engineer.

(Each ship carries a shop run by the NAAFI. It has nothing to do with the pursers ship's stores which stocks all basic needs for a ship and its crew to perform efficiently, but sells every-day items such as sweets and chocolates; toothpaste and soap; cigarettes and tobacco; and any other item that there is a call for. The man in charge of this enterprise is called the canteen manager and resides in the seamen's mess).

In his office the engineer asked me my name; this was the first time that he had spoken to me and I had been on the ship for over a week.

He then asked, "Aren't you aware that you should allow an officer to embark from a boat, or a ship, before you?"

I replied, "Yes Sir, but I never recognised you."

"But you knew that I was an officer. I was the only one in civilian clothes." (At that time ratings could not leave a ship in civvies without special dispensation).

"It was the civvies that threw me Sir; I thought you were the canteen manager."

Obviously not liking the comparison, he looked shocked, and blasted, "Do I look like the canteen manager?"

I thought it best not to answer this, and he dismissed me after a few more cautionary words.

Back in the mess the lads were surprised that I had adopted Pinchers suggestion as an excuse which amused them immensely and my standing amongst them rose considerably. Within a short time the details of this episode circulated around the ship and a few days later the canteen manager came up to me and jokingly said, "Hey! Are you trying to insult me? I don't look anything like that pompous sod."

The next port of call was Malta, and knowing our destination all the old hands were talking about 'The Gut' and the lascivious goings on that we could expect to find there. That may have been so in wartime, or it may have just been old sailors embellishing the truth to titillate young sprogs like me, but apart from middle-age hostesses in the bars cosying up for drinks I never found any of it, nevertheless it was the place where we spent most of our time when ashore there.

During my time spent in the Royal Navy I never found its equal when it came to bars, clubs, cafes, and mini-dance halls grouped together in one street. It was long, and unbelievably narrow, just ten feet across from one bar door to another.

Due to this, and because it attracted just about every sailor on shore leave from the ships anchored in Malta, all the premises and alleyways in the Gut were always packed, with barely room to move - a really wild place. Apparently, it very often got out of hand such that it was not uncommon for a large ship to be denied entry into Malta until another large ship already there had left to make room for more riotous and unruly behaviour. The sailors went there to drink and they did that to the extreme.

I was no exception and got very drunk each time ashore, although not quite as drunk as a lad I was with on one occasion. His name was Frank, and he was almost out cold as we made our way back to the ship. Barely able to stand, that alone walk, it meant that I had to manhandle him all the way up 'The Gut' to reach the top of a very long and steep set of stone steps which led to the harbour which lie at the bottom.

On reaching the steps, a wobble at the top warned me that we could easily come a cropper, either by tumbling down to the bottom or falling over the side into the water below. Drunken reasoning led me to believe that the best way to get him to the bottom was to pull him down by his feet. It was probably not, as his head hit every step.

To reach the ship, which was moored on the other side of the harbour, I dragged him over to a jetty where some other drunken sailors were negotiating the hire of a dghajsa. (A dghajsa pronounced 'die sa' is a water taxi built like a very large canoe with a post at each end, and colourfully painted. The oarsman stands up in the middle).

With my contribution a settlement was reached and they helped me get Frank into the vessel. He was still out cold then, but as we approached the far side he rallied round and for some unknown reason decided that he wanted to get off and stood up. In doing so he rocked the boat upon which the oarsman told him, in no uncertain terms, to sit down. He was slow to heed this advice upon which one of the other sailors grabbed his tunic and tried to pull him back onto his seat, but Frank yanked himself free, lost his balance, and toppled overboard. Fortunately, we were not too far from the opposite side and between us we managed to hold him by his collar and keep his head above water until we reached the landing stage. With great difficulty we managed to drag him onto it.

In the morning he remembered nothing of this and surprisingly, apart from a slight headache suffered little effect from the night before.

Our final destination was Tripoli, and once again we were sailing across the still blue waters of the Mediterranean.

It was common practice in the Royal Navy to stop the ship when sailing in tropical waters to allow the crew to bathe in the sea. The ship's motor boat would be lowered in case anybody got into difficulties and a rifleman or two would be conveniently posted to deal with any sharks that may be looking for a tasty meal. So it became routine for the captain to weigh anchor at four o'clock each afternoon when 'Hands to Bathe' would be announced over the Tannoy system. Ready and waiting, most of the ship's crew who were not on duty were lined along the rails prepared to make the jump over the side into the sea. With swimming trunks being optional the majority, including myself, were in 'the altogether' and the leap over the side gave me a feeling of vulnerability imagining a man-eating shark lurking, or some other fish with very sharp teeth, taking a fancy to my delicate parts.

A climbing net was hung over the side and for half-an-hour each afternoon men were leaping and diving from the ship.

On a later occasion when I was on board a ship in the Indian Ocean, the captain ordered two depth charges to be dropped, then returning immediately to the area gave instructions for hands to bathe and gather fish for our evening meal, of which there were now many floating on the surface. Together with all the other swimmers I was quickly overboard gathering them up and depositing them in the motorboat when I espied a particularly large fish, nearly three feet long and amply proportioned. Having collected it, I was swimming on my back, with it stretched out on my stomach as I made my way towards the boat, when all of a sudden; it gave me a solid whack with its tail and darted to freedom, its rough skin scratching my face. In shock, I swam back to the motorboat in a time that Mark Spitz would have been proud of.

We spent a couple of weeks in and around Tripoli where we undertook exercises with the army. On several occasions, a platoon of fully armed troops with their tanks and armoured vehicles would be loaded onto the ship, taken out to sea, and delivered to a remote spot further down the coast. The Captain, taking up a position perpendicular to the shore would then run the ship onto the beach where the squaddies rushed down the ramp screaming and shouting whilst at the same time firing rounds of bullets (probably blanks, but it all seemed very real) at another platoon (the enemy) already in position behind the sand dunes. The tanks, vehicles, and heavy artillery followed.

Our ship would then move to a position a few hundred yards offshore where we were entertained watching the various manoeuvres that followed.

My experience of Tripoli itself was not much to write home about. Apart from the seafront, and a large bar at one end, everywhere seemed to be out of bounds. My attempt to observe some of the local colour resulted in being driven back to the seafront by the Military Police and told to keep within that area.

The bar used by servicemen was housed on the first floor of a building which could have been a barn in earlier days, access to it being by stairs constructed on the outside. Drinking was the only facility available, the inside being bare except for crudely built tables and chairs, with Stella lager on draught being the only brew on offer. It was served in glasses, although I am loath to call them that, being bottles neatly cut in half.

Most of the crew had never drunk Stella before, at that time it was not a drink served up in English pubs. Old hands had warned us of how strong it was but this heeding was ignored and the quantities consumed very soon resulted in extreme drunken behaviour, with men being sick, fighting, and more than one falling off the staircase.

On one occasion the primitive urinals located in an outhouse in a corner of the yard below were blocked resulting in its sunken floor being flooded with urine. To avoid paddling in this the men were standing in the doorway and relieving themselves without entering. Doing the same, I had the misfortune to fall, or possibly I was pushed, into this foul smelling pool. Not that I was aware of it; I could remember very little of that evening after about five or six pints of Stella, but the incident was recalled to me by several witnesses the following morning after I had dragged my sorry stinking self back onto the mess. This was after I had spent the night in the paint locker which doubled up as 'the brig'.

'Off Caps' before the captain as a defaulter I was docked a day's pay and given three days extra duties with loss of leave. At the same time he gave me a stern lecture on my conduct with respect to my drunken behaviour. He was aware that I had returned to the ship worse for drink on every occasion that I had been ashore and advised me to change my ways and the company I kept.

He further said, "Whilst on this ship I am your guardian and do my best to ensure that you develop into a responsible adult, but I think that your parents should know the path you are taking and I will write to them and let them know."

With the town out-of-bounds there was not a lot to do in Tripoli so we spent most of our spare time swimming and sun-bathing. There were many sunken ships in the bay (there since the war) and we would swim from one to the other. One of these was a liner with its stern rising high out of the water, and having been hit by a torpedo had a large hole in its side several feet beneath the surface. By swimming down and through the hole, then working our way up to the part of the ship out of the water, we were able to dive off the wreck from various levels; all good fun.

We left Tripoli and made our way home, stopping again at Malta and Gibraltar.

Going through the Bay of Biscay in December was much worse than before. The ship still rode the sea like a cork, rolling and pitching, but now, with the waves mountainous, the ship heeled to an extreme angle as it rose to the crest of each one, and again as it slid down from the dizzy heights back into the heaving troughs. This continued without easing up for three days until we neared the English Channel.

During this trip I was transferred from the cosy little number I had in the boiler-room to replace the stoker in the port engine-room who was suffering such severs seasickness that he was unable to perform the duties required of him. Joining an engine-room artificer, (E.R.A.), and a leading stoker on the plates, I could see why.

H.M.S.Suvla was one of just a few ships in the Royal Navy to have steam reciprocating engines - the vast majority being driven by steam turbines. They had to be constantly oiled whilst running and my job was to do just that. I was the grease monkey.

Both port and starboard engines rooms had four steam cylinders to provide the drive which turned the propellers.

Each cylinder drove a six-inch diameter piston rod up and down which transferred its power through a crank rod to a crankshaft, very similar to a car engine but on a much larger scale. Unlike a car engine however, the moving parts were all exposed with the personnel in attendance only touching distance from its pounding machinery.

Applying oil to the moving parts was a dangerous task at any time, but in really rough weather it was frightening. There were oil cups fitted to the bearings which had to be topped up constantly and to reach them I had to stand on the bottom bar of the surrounding guard-rail and lean right into the middle of the engine. In doing this I had to hold on to an overhead rail with one hand whilst pouring oil from a can with the other. The oil cups, being between the pistons and the crank rods, were moving the whole time and all surrounding surfaces were covered with oil which made everything slippery.

It was obviously trickier when the sea was at its worst because as the ship rolled steeply to starboard the propeller on the port side came out of the water, and with no resistance the engine roared and raced at several times its normal speed. The best time to fill the oil cups was with the ship on an even keel which in these conditions happened only briefly as the ship righted itself before lurching in the opposite direction. I would do it as the ship rolled from starboard and was about to lean to port, this way if I lost my grip I would fall onto the plates and not into the engine. Even so, there were times when I was hanging in mid-air over the whirling machinery with the huge piston rods pounding close to my head looking down on the crankshaft thrashing in its bath of oil knowing that one slip and I would be crushed to death.

Arriving in Portsmouth by mid-December, I was home on leave for Christmas and the New Year.

Having a drink with my dad in his local, he brought up the subject matter of the Captain's letter. He was pleased that the Captain had my welfare at heart but knowing that it was not my intention to take a vow of abstinence advised me to drink in moderation.

The next few months were spent in Portsmouth where the ship underwent a refit. Apart from the usual things that were carried out, like boiler cleaning, routine maintenance, and painting, a rocket with its launching system was installed on the prow.

With the ship in good order we left Portsmouth and made our way along the English Channel and up the West Coast on our way to Scotland. After passing through the Irish Sea arrangements were made to launch the rocket and the ship was positioned about three miles off the coast with its bow pointing out to sea.

Two civilian boffins were on board to oversee the operation which was very hush-hush; the only information given to us was that we were taking part in an important experiment.

The rocket was about ten feet long, having mono-wings and looking very much like a small doodle-bug. The mechanism was set into motion and it was pointed upwards at an angle of about forty-five degrees. This was followed by a count-down at the end of which fire emitted from a tube at the rear and it whooshed into the air.

The whole ship's company was watching this spectacle and a huge cheer went up as the rocket left its pad. It took a forward and upward course before mysteriously arcing and taking a circular path back towards the ship. The cheering was muted when for a moment it looked like it would turn full circle and hit us on its return. This never happened and the rocket, flying upside down, flew over our heads toward the Scottish coast. The cheers rose again louder than ever.

The crew may have been cheering, as they usually did when somebody dropped a clanger, but the alarm shown, and exclamations made by the scientists, and officers, such as, "Christ Almighty, something's gone drastically wrong!" indicated that they were panic stricken.

As it disappeared over the mainland some wag shouted, "It's on its way to Glasgow to demolish the bloody Gorbals, we've done the Scots a favour."

It was not until several weeks later that we learned that it had landed in some bleak spot somewhere in the highlands without causing any harm.

Our final destination after passing through Clyde-mouth was Gareloch where we were to swing around a buoy in the Scottish mist for the next six weeks. The nearest sign of civilisation was Rosneath, a small village delightful for tourists but offering very little for sailors seeking their natural pleasures; wine, women, and song. For these it was necessary to travel into the nearest town which was Helensburgh, but not on a Saturday night - Glasgow was the place to be. It was returning from one of my jaunts there that I used up two of my lives.

For the many ships located jn the natural harbour that Gareloch offered, the local bus company provided two double-deckers at the railway station in Helensburgh to meet the last train back. I boarded the first bus which was already packed to the limit and consequently had to stand in the aisle downstairs close to the open boarding platform.

Halfway through the journey back to Rosneath, sleepy with drink, I was slumped in a relaxed manner when the bus, after slowing down whilst ascending a hill, sharply accelerated causing me to lose my balance, stumble onto the boarding platform, and fall off. Fortunately, I landed onto a grass verge and rolled into a ditch without knowingly hurting myself.

Dragging myself back onto the road, my main concern was the daunting prospect of facing a five mile walk back to the jetty and missing the last liberty boat, which was arranged to meet the bus and deliver all the sailors back to their ships.

The following bus came along and on passing me, like the first bus, it slowed down as it changed gear and before it accelerated I was able to leap aboard. Immediately after I did so, it braked hard and along with all the other standing passengers I was thrown toward the front of the bus. When everyone had sorted themselves out it became apparent that the bus had come to a halt because the one ahead had stopped and all its occupants were running down the hill. After a very short while those on the bus I was now on became curious and joined them; I tagged along too.

Milling around with the crowd, not realising that they were looking for me, I heard Doddo (Dodson), the friend I had been ashore with, call my name, so I stepped forward.

Surprised to see me in one piece he anxiously asked, "Are you alright?"

"I'm fine," I said. And related to all who had gathered round how I had scrambled from the ditch and threw myself on to the following bus.

"He's lucky to be alive," I heard someone remark as we all got back on the buses.

On arriving at the jetty we found the liberty boat already there waiting for us. It was a large heavily built motor launch capable of carrying all the sailors returning to the many ships anchored in the harbour.

When we drew alongside H.M.S.Suvla I was standing on the broad wooden gunnels of the launch ready to step from the boat onto the ship, it not being practical or expedient to use a gang-plank.

The deck of the ship was a foot higher out of the water than the launch and had the usual wire guardrail fitted which we were required to clamber through, so all those boarding were waiting for the launch to be secured. That is, all except me, for when the two boats touched I attempted to step across, a very stupid thing to do as the launch was only part way through its manoeuvre in closing with the ship. On touching, it moved away again and this left me gripping one of the wire strands of the ship's guardrail whilst my feet were still on the gunnels of the launch, albeit temporarily, for as the gap widened my feet lost their holding and I was left hanging there.

The launch, completing its manoeuvre, closed in on the ship again and I could see that if I stayed hanging there I would be cut in half, so I dropped into the sea.

It was the best thing to do under the circumstances, but I was not out of danger as I was still between the two vessels. The side of the launch did taper inwards very slightly, although I doubt whether it would have been enough to save me from a sticky end.

Above me, on the launch, I heard voices calling out, and looking up I could see many pairs of hands pushing on the side of the ship to stop the launch from crushing me. This was followed by a body leaning over with a strong pair of hands, which I immediately grabbed, to be yanked back on board. The hands belonged to Reynolds, a huge, strongly built, quick thinking stoker, and messmate, who casually remarked. "You'll get yourself killed, you will."

I was not sorry to leave Gareloch with its constant mist and drizzle, which we did in the middle of May. Before leaving we took on board a platoon of soldiers from one of the Scottish regiments together with their war machines. We also had two sections of a pontoon bridge strapped to the ship, one each side. We were to take them to France to join American forces, and others, for a re-enactment of the D-Day landings on 6th of June.

I was surprised at how many soldiers could be accommodated in the cabins which lined the sides of the forward part of the ship. I had not seen inside of the cabins before as they were generally kept locked, but there was nothing special about them, just large metal boxes housing bunks.

At first all went well. The servicemen taking passage were all in good humour until we reached the Irish Sea when it all changed.

The Irish Sea is notably rough, but on this occasion it was violent. The ship was tossing, and rolling, with huge waves washing over the sides of the ship whilst inboard it was difficult to walk down the passageways without losing your balance. It became impossible when the majority of the soldiers became seasick and the lower decks became slippery, awash with vomit.

To add to their problems, and ours, the pontoons strapped to the sides of the ship became loose. This resulted in them parting from the ship as they floated free on each wave, then crashing back with enormous force as the ship rose. The noise was horrendous and struck fear into the heart of everyone on board. Although the impact of hundreds of tons of steel crashing against the sides of the ship every few minutes was alarming there was nothing that could be done about it except reduce speed and make for the nearest port where remedial action could be taken. This was Milford Haven where we arrived many worrying hours later.

The soldiers, pleased to leave the ship, were transported by road to the Army Barracks in Aldershot from where they would rejoin us later; their vehicles stayed onboard. We docked in a naval yard sited close to a small settlement just north of the large commercial docking area where we remained for a couple of weeks while dockyard engineers inspected and repaired any damage caused by the pontoons. I never found out what their proposed use was, but they were removed and not put back on.

This turned out to be a lucky break for us for the location, although only a small place had two pubs and a working men's club where we had an open invitation to use the bar and its snooker tables. Also, on the Sunday, midway through our stay, a group of young ladies from a local factory invited those of us off duty to a picnic on a nearby beach. Who could ask for more?

The soldiers joined us again at Portsmouth and we took them to Cherbourg, a port close to the Normandy beaches where the allied forces landed in 1944.

On the day commemorating the invasion we joined a lot more ships and landing-crafts filled with servicemen from the many countries involved and stormed the beaches once again, only this time on a smaller scale and without loss of life.

There was a carnival atmosphere in Cherbourg that evening. All the bars were filled with soldiers and sailors from the different nations singing, dancing, and sharing bottles of cheap wine. Everybody was having a really good time.

One generous Frenchman, like us, very tipsy and in good spirit, got carried away with himself and invited a large group of us home for drinks, and a meal. At least that is how we understood it, his grasp of the English language being no better than our French, which amounted to no more than being able to order beer, wine, or cognac.

There were about eight of us, and having invited so many we were surprised when he led us to a small terraced house and planted us in the tiniest of kitchens. We had brought a few bottles of beer and wine with us and he provided cups and glasses.

Apart from a dresser holding a modicum of crockery there was only four chairs around a scrubbed wooden table in the room. A scullery led off this with little more than a sink and a gas stove.

When someone indicated that he wanted to use the toilet he pointed to the low butler sink and run the tap.

It soon became apparent that we had come to the wrong conclusion and realised that food was not on the menu, but by means of Pidgin English, and sign language, he indicated that with money from us he would go out and get more drink, and sustenance. We gave him all the Francs we had and waited for his return.

We waited, and waited, but when the door burst open it was not him returning with food and drink but a shocked, angry, red faced woman, presumably his wife.

Finding eight noisy drunken sailors crowded in her kitchen, many over six feet tall, ominous in dark uniforms, imbibing alcoholic drinks and piddling in her sink, she was entitled to be angry. We were slow to leave trying to explain our reasons for being there, together with pathetic apologies in a language that she could not understand, and still hopeful that her husband would return soon with food and drink, when she grabbed hold of a stick, the type used for disentangling the washing in the copper, and started to whack Reynolds, the biggest amongst us, about the shoulders. This was a definite indication that she meant business, so we got out of the house like a shot.

I dread to think what happened to her husband on his return.

H.M.S. Suvla stayed in Portsmouth for the next three months, so apart from enjoying the pastimes there, and those on the seafront at Southsea, I was able to go home for the weekends. All this required cash, which I never had much of, but I did have access to a means of getting it. Being on a sea-going ship I was entitled to purchase duty-free cigarettes from the on-board shop which when smuggled ashore sold easily and at a good profit.

This was obviously illegal and to discourage you from doing this police were on guard at every dock-yard gate and anyone caught was in for the high jump. You were allowed to take out forty cigarettes when going ashore for the evening, so being a non-smoker that alone would buy me a couple of pints, or a trip to the pictures, but more often than not I had in excess of that. It was nerve racking when you were pulled up and frisked, usually done with them running their hands down the side of your body. This happened to me several times, but fortunately, on each occasion I had them lined down my back, that is, with the exception of the two packets of twenty blatantly on show in my tunic.

Concerning this, a shaggy dog story was told to me about a sailor going ashore with a holdall filled with packets of cigarettes. Out of sight of the dockyard gates he took the cigarettes out of the holdall and put them in a suitable hiding place. He then went in search of one of the many cats which were always to be found hanging around the place, and on finding one he put it into the bag and continued on his way. On passing through the dockyard gates he was pulled over, as he knew he would be, by the official on duty who pointed to the holdall.

"Open the bag," he demanded.

"I can't do that," The sailor said.

"Why not?" The official queried.

"I've got the ship's cat in the bag. I'm taking it to the vet."

"A likely story, open the bag."

The sailor opened the bag enough to allow the cat to burst out in a snarling rage and bolt back into the dockyard.

"Now look what's happened, I'll have a job finding him now," The sailor moaned, and ran after it.

Back in the dockyard he retrieved his hidden cigarettes and after a reasonable time went back through the gate.

"You got him back then?" The official asked, as he let him through.

"Yes, but no thanks to you," was the cheeky reply.

During the summer of that year, Joan and I, having enjoyed each others company on a few occasions, promised to write to each other. This arrangement was to last a very long time, for shortly after, I was posted to the Far East where I was to spend the next two years. She wrote almost every week and her letters were most welcome; always witty, and amusing, with the occasional photograph.

The posting was in September, when together with a close friend, a tall, and heavy framed stoker known as Horse, I was detailed to join the crew of H.M.S.Concord, a destroyer based in Hong Kong.

We took passage on H.M.S. Ocean, an aircraft carrier which left from Plymouth. I had hoped to be taking it easy on one of the liners transporting troops to Kowloon, or Singapore, which were in service at the time and where I could have sat back like a passenger on a cruise ship, but no such luck, I was to work my passage watch-keeping in a vast boiler room.

The journey took us once again through the Bay of Biscay which was heaving as usual but being on a large ship its effect was incomparable with my previous experience, even so, there was still a lot of seasickness. Like me, Horse never suffered in the roughest of seas, but during my time in the navy I was surprised at how many seasoned sailors were affected when the sea was at its worst.

We passed through the Mediterranean, and the Suez Canal, before stopping at Aden to take on water.

Travelling through the Indian Ocean the following day an announcement over the Tannoy system drew everyone onto the upper decks to observe the largest school of porpoises imaginable, estimated to be well over one hundred.

Porpoises had been accompanying the ship since leaving Aden, swimming alongside, or zig-zagging across the bows, but this was a once in a lifetime sighting never to be forgotten.

Our next stop was Trincomalee in Ceylon (now Sri Lanka), where there was a small naval base. This was nothing more than a native village, like a scene depicted in the Geographical Magazine; white sandy beaches, palm trees, and mud huts. We were only there for a couple of days but long enough for me to fall down a palm tree trying to relieve it of a bunch of bananas. Reaching the top I grabbed hold of the fronds which came away in my hands and although landing on my feet I jarred both of my knees quite severely, enough for me to visit the sick bay and be relieved of duties in the boiler room for several days.

Following a short stop at Singapore we reached Hong Kong where dozens of ships of every sort, including most of the Royal

Navy's Far Eastern Fleet, filled the harbour. After dropping anchor a tender drew alongside to take a large number of us to our delegated ships, together with kitbags, cases, and hammocks. There were quite a few for H.M.S. Concord, mostly seamen, Horse and I were the only stokers.

After being welcomed aboard by the duty officer we were taken down to the stoker's mess where we were introduced and handed over to Leading Stoker Slatcher who was in charge of No.12 Mess.

Stokers were housed in the forward part of the ship on the lowest deck, and although spanning the ship from side to side this area, accommodating over thirty men for sleeping, eating, and off-duty recreation, was severely limited for space. A circular hatch in its deck-head, reached by a ladder, was the only means of access, both in and out of the two messes located there. No.12 Mess was on the port side and No.6 on the starboard, each having two tables placed end to end. Wide cushioned seating on one side of the tables ran alongside the hull and doubled up as lockers; long stools, also cushioned, were along the other sides.

A hammock storage area between the two messes took up a quarter of the remaining space which was further reduced by the inclusion of free-standing clothes lockers for senior ratings. Everything was firmly screwed to the deck.

Set into the low deckhead were hooks and bars for supporting hammocks, and fixed to the bulkheads were cabinets for the mess cutlery, chinaware, pots and pans, and other utensils; also for staple foods like bread, butter, tea, sugar, and tinned milk.

I was allocated one of the seat lockers for storing my kit, and a hammock billet over one of the tables, fortunately sited next to a porthole.

This messdeck was to be my home for the next two years and being so cramped I soon became familiar with my new surroundings and the men I was sharing it with. Except for a few 'old hands' these were mostly new arrivals like me and within six weeks of my stepping aboard the whole of the ship's company had been replaced.

On getting to know some of the old hands before they left it was apparent that an air of resentment existed concerning political reaction to H.M.S. Concord's involvement in the historically famous 'Yangtze Incident' a few months earlier. This may have had something to do with the changeover of the ship's company.

H.M.S. Amethyst, a frigate, had ventured up the Yangtze River and was subjected to extensive heavy shelling from gun batteries manned by Chinese Communists which resulted in extensive damage and over fifty of the crew being killed or injured.

A rescue mission was attempted by the Royal Naval ships London, Consort, and Black Swan, which unfortunately resulted in further loss of life and the H.M.S.Amethyst remaining captive for one hundred days more, forty miles inside Chinese territorial waters.

It was then that H,M,S.Concord sailed up the Yangtze under cover of darkness past the massive shore artillery, transferred supplies, and 147 tons of fuel to the Amethyst, before escorting it to safety in the morning mist. A daring and successful mission completed.

Unfortunately, it contravened certain international protocols and H.M.S.Concord's part in the whole affair was hushed up. The ship's log book was removed, the crew were warned to stay quiet about it, and the British press was stopped from referring to it.

The upshot of it was that a general service medal was awarded to every crew member manning each of the ships involved in what was to become known as the Yangtze Incident with the exception of those manning H.M.S.Concord. No wonder the crew were bitter.

I was soon to learn that life on board H.M.S.Suvla had been a doddle compared with my new assignment. The messdeck had been three times as roomy and kept ship-shape by a stoker whose sole job was to keep the bathroom, toilets, and living area clean. He also brought our food from the galley - three hot meals a day, prepared and cooked by professional chefs.

That first morning on board H.M.S.Concord I was up early, hammock stowed away, washed, shaved, and looking forward to my breakfast, only to find that the best on offer was buttered bread spread with jam and a mug of tea to wash it down.

"You're on canteen messing now mate!" Someone remarked, whilst at the same time handing me a knife. "Here, help peel some spuds for your dinner."

I joined the others around the table peeling potatoes and learnt just what canteen messing was all about.

Each morning, determined by rota, two members of each mess throughout the ship would be 'cooks-of-the-mess'. In harbour, this duty would be in addition to their other duties, although they would be allowed time off to attend the demands that this made upon them. At sea, it would be arranged to suit watch keeping duties.

Once everyone had left the mess their first job was to scrub the tables and the floor, getting hot water from the galley situated amidships on the upper deck. After this they would prepare the dinner and take that to the galley in trays and fannies (pots) for a professional chef to cook, then at dinner-time collect the food which would be piping hot. In doing all this they would be up and down ladders, through hatches, and along gangways which at any time is an arduous set of tasks, but when the ship is leaping about in rough seas it is not only arduous it is extremely alarming.

Dinners were many and varied and were determined by the meat being issued each day at the meat screen by the ships butcher. This was mostly beef, but could be lamb, or pork, from which a cut of meat was chosen depending on what the cook-of-the-day intended to do with it. Say they chose a joint of meat for roasting; they would then put it in a tray with the potatoes all around, maybe accompanied by onions. Dried peas, soaked over night, were always welcome, together with a further tray of potatoes to make sure everybody was fully sated.

"What about a Yorkshire?" One of the cooks might say to the other. "I'm quite proud of my Yorkshire puddings."

"I should say so, a roast is not the same without Yorkshire pudding, and whilst you're at it, make two, one with sultanas in it for afters," the other might reply.

This was the procedure day by day, each cook of the mess having a particular skill in his culinary repertoire.

When having a potmess (a stew) where anything and everything in the way of vegetables (fresh, tinned, or dried) was put in with the meat, a specialist in dumplings, if not one of the cooks, would be asked to return to the mess and prepare them. The same as when a clacker (rolled out pastry) was needed to cover the meat for a pie. These experts only emerged after a great deal of suffering inedible soggy dumplings, or rock hard pastry, as men who had never even boiled an egg, by necessity, had to try their hand at such culinary procedures.

The cooks would be at it again after tea (e.g. bread and jam) preparing the evening meal. This would be lighter than dinner, such as sausages and beans, kidneys on fried bread, or herrings in tomato sauce. Nevertheless, by the time they had washed up all the dirty dishes it was the end of a hard day.

Their was a limit to how lavish your meals could be as it was limited by the budget allowed, Each man in the mess was given an allowance to use collectively and if at the end of the month it had been under-spent the difference was shared out in cash. If overspent we were required to make up the difference. It was necessary for somebody to manage this and a caterer was elected to do the tricky job of feeding us adequately whilst at the same time keeping us solvent.

I soon got to know all the stokers, also many of the seamen, and with very few exceptions they were a good bunch of blokes. The stokers, with possibly one or two exceptions, proved true to form and liked a drink or two, and those who had been on board long enough to familiarise themselves with Hong Kong soon led Horse and me to the best watering holes.

Of course, there were many other things to do and wonderful sights to see in Hong Kong and during my time there I became familiar with them many times over.

The view from the Peak was breathtaking. Large passenger liners and warships that lay in the harbour, along with dozens of smaller ships, and many, many, more sampans dotted amongst them, all looked no bigger than Dinky toys. The conglomeration of buildings forming the districts of Victoria, Wanchai, and Kowloon, with the distant mountains of the New Territories, and China, were all spread out in a panoramic tableau. The long and strenuous walk up was worth the effort.

We tended however to favour the shorter walks from one bar to another, our favourite being the China Fleet Club. We usually started our spell ashore in the luxury of its cocktail lounge, that being the only time we were sober enough to fit into the sophisticated atmosphere it had to offer. Then after touring the various bars and clubs we would be back there, but this time in the large saloon which by then would be filled to capacity with sailors swamping down San Miguel beer, rumbustious and very merry indeed.

This was the most convenient place for our last port of call because directly above the bars there was a multi-storied establishment which provided a restaurant, and sleeping accommodation, specifically for servicemen. Having booked a bed for a moderate price there were no worries about missing the last liberty boat, or returning to the ship drunk, and waking up your mess-mates when trying to sling your hammock.

None of the moans like. "Keep the bloody noise down, I'm trying to get some sleep – I've got the morning watch in a couple of hours."

No! You could stagger up to the bed you had booked in one of the dormitories, crash out for the night, knowing that you would be woken up in time for a wash, and a full English breakfast, then stroll down fresh and well fed to the jetty in time for the first liberty boat back to the ship.

Nothing better, and that's how it ordinarily was, except for one unfortunate night when very drunk I clambered into my bunk, or what I thought was my bunk, and immediately fell into a deep sleep only to be woken up a short time later by a shadowy figure shaking me vigorously.

"You're in my bunk," he said.

Bleary eyed and barely awake, I queried, "What?"

"Get out. You're in my bunk," he repeated.

"Sod off," I said, "Go and get in my bunk."

"There are no empty bunks, come on get out, that's my bunk."

"I'm not moving mate, so clear off and let me sleep," I said, snuggling down into the sheets.

184

He moved away and within minutes I was back in the land of Nod and sleeping soundly only to be rudely awakened by two navel policemen, easily identified by there white belts and gaiters.

"What's going on?" I demanded.

"You know what's going on, now get out and get dressed."

I was trying to get my head around it, but things were moving too slowly for their liking and I was roughly dragged out of the bunk, fortunately the bottom one of two, and told to get my uniform on, which I did. I was fumbling around for my shoes when one of them produced a pair which I put on, and before further ado they hauled me down to the Manager's office.

Apparently, although I could not remember it, the manager had unsuccessfully tried to sort it out and had called in the navel policemen who were on patrol in the street outside.

"Where's your ticket?" The manager asked, referring to the receipt which I would have received when booking a bed earlier in the day. This would have had my bed number on it.

If I could have found it things may have turned out differently, but after fumbling around in my pocket without success it was concluded that I had made an attempt to secure a bed without payment. This resulted in me spending the rest of the night in cells at H.M.S.Tamar, the naval base in Hong Kong.

The following morning, after being made to scrub out my cell, I was taken under escort back to my ship and put on first lieutenant's report charged with being drunk and disorderly, causing a disturbance ashore, plus one or two more charges thrown in. This resulted in seven days extra duties and stoppage of leave.

I accepted that I only had myself to blame, but was further disappointed, and irritated, when putting on my shoes that morning to find that they were not mine, they were at least three sizes too big. I realised that they belonged to the sailor in the top bunk. Still, it brought a smile to my face when I imagined him with his size ten feet trying to walk back to his ship in my size seven shoes.

Once the ship had a full complement we left for Singapore where a major refit (modifications and maintenance works) was to be carried out, which meant being in dry-dock for a couple of months. During a major refit a ship is not a fit place to be residing in; the boilers are shut down for cleaning; there is no hot water; the toilets cannot be used; and almost every surface inside and out are painted. For this reason, with the exception of a skeleton crew, which changed daily, all the ship's company, were housed in H.M.S.Terror, a naval shore establishment situated nearby.

Its name, H.M.S.Terror, belied the conditions and atmosphere which existed there; it should have been called H.M.S. Welcome because it was the most pleasant of all the British naval bases I encountered. If we resided there without tasks or duties to perform it would have been a holiday camp.

The spacious airy bungalow type buildings which accommodated us had been designed with consideration to the hot, sultry, weather conditions which prevailed in Singapore which is just two degrees north of the equator. Large bladed fans were fitted to the ceiling and there were many wide louvered doors which remained open most of the time. Single beds with lockers were spaced well apart, with showers and toilets at the end of each block.

Everything and everywhere was kept clean by employees from the local population who also provided a cheap laundry service.

Apart from the official dining hall, which served up good and adequate food, there was also a large NAAFI where you could get a tasty meal outside normal meal times. It also had a bar leading on to a terrace which was open every evening until late, and mid-day at week-ends.

The whole establishment was graced with expansive lawns, together with a swimming pool which boasted a set of diving boards up to five metres high. The only thing missing was a golf course.

It was a long bus ride into the town centre of Singapore and visited by us mainly at the weekend. The first stop was the Shackles Club, incongruously sited almost opposite the famous Raffles Hotel. It was run by the NAAFI and very popular with all members of the armed forces stationed on the island. Also, soldiers on leave from fighting terrorists in the Malayan jungle.

As well as overnight accommodation the club offered all the usual facilities, including of course, well stocked bars.

After downing several pints of beer we would make our way to the New World, a large amusement park where there was always various forms of entertainment. Apart from the carousels, fair rides, and games stalls, you could watch boxing, wrestling, or other sideshows. If you wanted local culture there was Malay opera, or Chinese theatre with plenty of cymbal clashing.

More appealing to us were the strip tease artists in a show that was always well attended by sailors, soldiers, and airmen, who were also the main patrons of the large dance hall where taxi dancing allowed you close contact with glamorous girls. The girls, Malay, Chinese, and Eurasian, all sat together in a pen, and when inviting them to dance you were required to present them with a disc which you had purchased from a kiosk - three for a dollar.

No naughty business or hanky-panky was tolerated; these girls were looked after by tough looking chaperones and the whole area patrolled by big burly bouncers.

Having H.M.S.Terror as your posting must have been a dream come true, and fortunately for us there was a particular group of sailors in permanent residence who not only seemed to appreciate this but gave enjoyment to all those spending their evenings in the bar. Judging the time to be right, usually after every one was well oiled with numerous pints of Tiger beer, there was one sailor in particular who would take it upon himself to start the singing, and get us all to join in. He was a born entertainer and a natural master of ceremonies, knowing all the popular drinking songs as well as being able to bring out the talents of others.

As the evening wore on the songs became cruder and sung with more gusto, a mixture of rugby songs and ribald sailor's ditties. One in particular which not only gave amusement but embraced all those in the bar was 'The Wild West Show.' He would sing it in his strong bar-room voice, with all who knew it joining in.

"We're going to the wild west show,
The elephant and kangaroo-oo-oo-oo,
Never mind the weather, as long as we're together,
We're going to the wild west show."

Then he would move to the first table, together with an ensemble of his mates, and addressing the tipsy occupants he would point to one and say in a loud clear voice.

"In this cage we have the Oomigooli bird."

To which everyone would chant in chorus.

"The Oomigooli bird --- Jesus Christ --- Stuff me --- What is it?"

"The Oomigooli bird is extremely rare and lives in the plains of Africa. It is a very large bird with a wingspan of fifteen feet, but with unusually short legs only one inch long. Consequently, it is named after the sound it makes when coming in to land – OOMIGOOLIES!

The chorus would then be repeated with everyone joining in as he proceeded to the next table where he would select someone else to be his next choice of animal, and of these he had many. To tell of just a few:-

The Giraffe – a most generous animal. When entering a cocktail bar the highballs are on him.

The Rhinoceros – the richest animal in the jungle. Rhino meaning money, sore-arse meaning piles; thus - piles of money.

The Polar Bear - has offspring at two different private schools, one to the east of the North Pole, and one to the west, and he is forever sliding between the two keeping his own privates cool.

Invariably at the end of the evening when almost everyone was drunk someone would jump up onto the top of a table, encouraged by all and sundry, and perform 'This Old Hat of Mine'. It always amazed me how frequently somebody would wish to do it, and I have seen it done twice in one evening by two different people, The routine went like this.

Standing on top of the table the foolhardy sailor would sing the following:-

> This old hat of mine,
> The inside looks quite new,
> The outside has seen some stormy weather.
> I cast this hat aside,
> Though travelled far and wide,
> Through countries old and new.

He would then toss his hat into the audience before continuing with the next verse which was exactly the same as the first except that it referred to his shirt; this would then follow his hat.

Each item of his clothing would be taken off and discarded in this fashion until he was down to his underpants. At this point a crowd would gather around, and on removal of these throw any beer that was left in their glass all over him.

The swimming pool was a big attraction and we swam in it most days. It closed at dusk but we occasionally sneaked in after the bar closed, which was not difficult as it was nearby and only surrounded by a low fence. It was against all the rules; drunk and with no attendant present the dangers were obvious. A small group of us had been getting away with it for some time but had become not only careless, by not keeping the noise down, but on one occasion foolhardy, by leaving the postman's bike at the bottom of the pool.

We found his bike, which was usually kept close to the mailroom, parked on the path leading to the pool. On spotting it one of the lads threw out a challenge.

"I'll buy a pint for the first one to ride that off the top board."

There were several takers and we hauled the bike up the ladder to the large concrete platform which hung over the pool five metres below. I cannot recall who went first and won the pint, but I do know that we all took delight in performing this stunt several times over.

The following night, after the bar closed, we were back there again but had hardly stripped off when an officer and a number of naval policemen popped out of some bushes which surrounded the pool.

Gathering us together the officer asked each of us our names then told us to adorn dress of the day and report to the police office. He could see that the clothes strewn about the ground were casual civvies which we were allowed to wear when off duty.

After he had gone, and as we were wandering back to our billets to get into our tropical white uniforms, a thought occurred to me which I put to the others.

"Look, he's taken all six of our names without writing them down; by the time he gets back to his office, unless he's Mr

Memory Man he won't recall one of them, and if he does we'll say that we thought he meant us to report in the morning."

Everyone was in agreement so we all got turned in.

About half an hour later I was woken up by somebody shaking my shoulder vigorously and shining the light from a torch in my face.

"Are you Wellard?" A voice demanded.

Even in my dozy state I did not have to think twice to know that he was a naval policeman.

"Yes," I replied.

"Well get dressed and report to the master at arms office now."

I got out of bed and saw him going to the bunk of someone else, others were already dressing.

We all walked along to the block where the naval police had their offices and which also held the prison cells.

It was not long before my name was called and I was marched into a room by the duty petty officer who gave the order "Off Caps" and read out the various charges associated with my misdemeanours. It was a surprisingly odd situation as the officer-of-the-watch was lying in bed and propping himself up on one elbow during the process of the interrogation.

"I don't take kindly to having my orders disobeyed, or losing sleep over toe-rags like you, so I'm not wasting any more of my time -- Captains Report," he said.

The captain was none too pleased and together with the other miscreants I was awarded seven days No.11s.

Men under punishment had to remain on board the ship in dry dock undertaking the extra duties imposed upon them. We were not alone; there were also half-a-dozen seamen, four of whom who had driven away a lorry delivering Carlsberg Lager and found later still in the back of the vehicle blind drunk. They had already served fourteen days in the police cells, and received a fine.

Also on board were a duty petty officer, and the officer-of-the-watch, a sub-lieutenant.

Without a regular crew living on board the heart of the ship was missing. The messes were bare; no clothing in the lockers or on the coat hooks, no hammocks in the hammock rack, and all food and utensils removed. The smell of paint permeated throughout the ship, with dirt and oil being evident from engineering works such as boiler and bilge cleaning. It was a desolate place to be confined to.

Each meal time it was necessary for a small party to collect food from the canteen in H.M.S.Terror, a jeep ferrying it there and back. On our first evening Horse won 'a cut of the cards' to join two of the seamen to form this group, it being a lucky draw because there was time to slip into the bar for a quick pint or two before collecting the food.

The food was brought back in an insulated container together with a large kettle holding soup, and another holding coffee. We were quite pleased when Horse produced two bottles of beer he had smuggled back inside the food container, but our pleasure turned to envy when he told us that the seamen had taken up an extra kettle which they filled to capacity with Tiger beer.

The next day with an old rusty kettle unearthed from somewhere and thoroughly cleaned with wire-wool, I joined the supper party. After a trip to the bar, a couple of pints, and the kettle filled with beer, I was happy to carry that, and a kettle of soup, when returning to the jeep. The two seamen each held a handle on the food container and carried a kettle apiece.

On the return journey it was noticed that the floor of the jeep was becoming wet, and getting a lot wetter. On investigation it was found that my kettle was severely leaking with nothing I could do to remedy it.

The seaman responsible for the two kettles could see the problem this could cause when we got back to the ship.

"Look," he said. "You'd better tip that out the back before we reach the boat. The duty officer will be on the gangway and he'll cop one look at that rusty old kettle leaking and be suspicious."

"You must be joking," I said "I'm not going to do that, the lads will kill me."

"Are you stupid?" He said. "If we get caught taking beer on board we're for the high jump. You know as well as I do that smuggling alcohol onto a ship is a serious offence. Now I don't want to end up in choky even if you do."

He could see that I was loath to get rid of it, and put forward a solution which would reduce risk to him and his messmate.

"Taking a chance with that old kettle you're the one who should be most at risk, so I suggest that you lag behind and allow us to get right cross the deck before coming aboard."

I could see the fairness, and the logic of this, and agreed.

When the jeep arrived back to the ship I made apologises to the driver for all the beer in the back of his truck and held a short conversation with him to allow the seamen a good lead before venturing up the gangway.

On boarding the ship the trail of beer across the quarterdeck stood out like a sore thumb and the officer-of-the-watch would have had to be blind not to have spotted it.

"You've got a leak," he said.

"It's only lime juice," I answered over my shoulder. Fearful that he would investigate further, I added, "I can't stop Sir, the soup's getting cold."

I deposited the soup in the seamen's mess, where we all dined together, before taking the kettle of beer down to the stoker's mess. My messmates were waiting for me to come back before joining the seamen for supper and as I came down the ladder they could see the ale dripping from the kettle.

"Quick! Find me something that I can put the beer into, this is leaking like a sieve. I've already lost a couple of pints."

"Like what? There's nothing here we can use."

Balancing the kettle on the edge of the table and putting my finger over the hole I desperately scanned the empty compartment. Spotting a fire extinguisher which had been lifted off its bracket in preparation for the wall to be painted, I shouted, "The fire extinguisher - We'll put the beer in that."

A few moans followed that suggestion, but with no alternative on offer it was agreed and the extinguisher was swiftly taken up to the bathroom and rinsed out.

Around the table at supper time the seamen let us know that they were not happy with our cavalier approach to smuggling beer on board. They pointed out that it was not just that the leak had been observed, which we were lucky to get away with, but also the smell of the beer once it was on board. They had theirs well stashed away in the paint locker.

I assured them that although beer had dripped from the kettle when carried aboard, none was dripping from it now.

Obviously these seamen were old hands at the game and advised us not to drink the beer until after the officer-of-the-watch had done his rounds. This happened at nine o'clock, when accompanied by the duty P.O. he visited all deck areas and living quarters. During his rounds men under punishment were required to line up for inspection to be accounted for.

The seaman clarified his advice. "This officer is a bit naïve, but the duty P.O. isn't, and he's a bastard. He'll put his face right up to yours and if he smells any beer on your breath he'll have you."

Taking heed of his words of wisdom all went well, and the officer, having noticed the leaking kettle, gave the seamen a chit to take to the stores for a new one. Every night after that, when rounds were completed, we all got to know each other better over a few beers.

Shortly after this, together with many of the ship's company, I was given a temporary draft onto the frigate H.M.S.Jaseur. At that time Guerrilla warfare was being raged in Malaya by communist infiltrators and a large allied force was committed to bring about a peaceful solution. Thousands of troops from different battalions were involved in jungle warfare throughout the country. Our role was to patrol the east coast.

Apart from putting armed parties ashore on numerous occasions, which incidentally never fired a shot in anger, I never understood our reason for being there - or why we warranted the campaign medal which was awarded to each of us.

Back in H.M.S.Terror an opportunity arose to take leave at one of two rest camps set up for the armed forces, one at Penang, and the other in the Cameron Highlands, a beautiful area in the mountain region of Malaysia. Although the cost of the package; fares, accommodation, food, and facilities, was reasonable, it was still a big chunk out of our money and none of my close friends fancied it.

"Look," Horse said." After you've paid for it you won't have hardly any spending money. A few beers and you'll be skint."

I knew that I would have to take it steady, but I quite fancied laying about on an exotic beach for a couple of weeks, so I signed up for the trip to Penang. Another stoker, Ginger Largent was also going and although I never knew him very well (he was in the opposite mess) I was pleased to have his company.

The 425 mile train journey from Singapore to Penang went from one end of Malaya to the other with a stop-over at Kuala-Lumpur; our tickets included sleeping arrangements and meals. The scenery was fantastic but even so it seemed to take forever.

The camp was next to the sea, just behind a long white sandy beach edged with palm trees. There were recreational facilities for various pastimes and sports, with loungers and kayaks casually placed on the beach ready for use.

This suited me down to the ground, but unfortunately Ginger did not have much going for him. He played very little sport, could not swim, and his white body did not allow him to lie, or sit in the sun, without being covered up. All in all, apart from enjoying a glass or two of beer we had very little in common.

Horse's prediction turned out to be right. After the first night in the bar we knew that if we wanted our funds to last the fortnight, drinking had to be a low priority. In fact, I realised, even at that stage, we would be pushed to make our money last without cutting out drink altogether; perhaps the occasional pint.

I settled for this and was quite happy enjoying the various sporting activities arranged. Swimming in the warm sea was a delight, but what I liked best was paddling up and down the shoreline in a kayak.

Soon after learning how to handle one, without turning it upside down every few minutes, I paddled out to a very large rock a few hundred yards offshore. I pulled the kayak onto the rock, clambered up to the highest point, and looked back toward the shore to admire the picture postcard view of the camp nestled amongst the palms.

Something drew my attention to the seaward side of the rock and I got the fright of my life. Sitting there warming itself in the sun was a crocodile – or so I thought. It was most scary with its long snout, scaly body, and long tail. It had not perceived my presence, and I had no idea how it would react when it did, so I crept back down the rock, into the kayak, and paddled back to the beach as fast as I could.

I was told later that it was a Malayan Water Monitor and probably would have scurried into the sea if it had seen me. Although, apparently they can deliver a nasty bite, but only do so if cornered, or threatened.

The very next day, and back in the kayak again, I went off to explore a small island a short distance down the coast. It was not very far from the shore but approaching it from the south, which I did, there seemed to be no way of getting onto it, rocky banks, and dense undergrowth, barring my way. However, I persevered and paddled my way around it until I happened upon a small inlet with a mooring facility and steps cut into the rocks leading to a single storey building.

After tying the kayak up, I mounted the steps which led directly to a small open lobby, its concrete walls and floor bare except for brackets in which incense sticks were burning. It led to a large room, again without a door, and like the lobby it had no adornments except for more incense sticks. On stepping into it I was shocked to see the dead body of a Chinese man lying on a raised concrete slab about the height and size of a large table.

In panic, and without a second look, I quickly stepped outside to flee the island as quickly as I could, but halfway down the steps I thought, 'Hold on, he can't hurt me, he's dead.' So I went back to investigate further.

There was not much more to see, no more rooms, no more embellishments, except for the finery that the corpse was arrayed in; a colourful satin robe of blue and yellow, embroidered with dragons in gold lace. Looking at his lined and wrinkled face I recalled seeing it before.

The first day after our arrival Ginger and I had taken a ride into the town centre of Penang and whilst there we were privileged to observe the funeral procession of a personage whom I assumed to be of some importance. The procession had the semblance of a carnival. It was preceded by a band playing lively, but raucous music, on a variety of instruments, followed by dozens of people all in a colourful form of dress. With long ropes, many of them were pulling a hearse covered in flowers, whilst taking up the rear was a giant paper dragon. On the front of the hearse a large picture of the deceased was displayed - this was the dead man I was now looking at.

I was later to find out that the body remained on the island for five days before being removed and taken away for cremation. This period gave sufficient time for the soul to leave the body for its final destination.

Back at the camp, Ginger had made friends with two soldiers who had just arrived and had arranged for us both to meet them in the bar that evening. He told me that he had been drinking with them that lunch time, and knowing that he was lower in funds than me, I was surprised. "But you've hardly any money," I said.

"They wouldn't let me buy a round," he boasted. "They're loaded."

"Well, loaded or not," I said. "I'm not happy for somebody to shout me drinks all night without putting my hand in my pocket."

"I told them we're almost out of cash but they said not to worry. They'll be disappointed if we don't turn up." Ginger was obviously not bothered about sponging off them.

"Alright, I'll come along," I said "But I'm only having a couple of pints."

The two squaddies turned out to be decent blokes and understood our predicament. They were privates in the Yorkshire Light Infantry and had been in the Malayan jungle rooting out terrorists for months with little to spend their money on, even so, I was uncomfortable sitting in the bar with them buying us drinks without being able buy one back. I probably had enough money to get a round in, possibly two, but with over a week of our holiday to go the thought of having no money at all in my pocket induced me to swallow my pride and accept their generosity.

With jokey conversation, and quite a few laughs, my resolve to have no more than two pints was broken down, partly by my weakness in being unable to refuse more drinks, but mainly by their persistence in buying them. A firm friendship had developed by the end of the evening and they told us how much they enjoyed our company and said that they would see us alright.

Whilst I could see that they benefited from our company, and we, from theirs, I could not go on accepting their charity without recompensing them, and Ginger felt the same. So I said, "Look lads. Thanks for the evening, it was bloody good of you, but it's not easy for us to have someone buying us drinks all evening without paying our way. I'm not saying it should end because with our lack of cash it has resolved a problem, but you can be assured that we'll make a point of settling up with you. When we get back to our ship we'll raise the money to cover what you spend on us and send it to you."

They both pooh-poohed the mention of it, but I had said it with intent and it made me feel better. However, if I had known what was to occur the following day I could have saved myself all the soul searching.

A picnic at a local beauty spot was arranged and a party of us was taken there in a small coach. The focal point was a waterfall set in a tropical paradise of luxuriant flowers, foliage, and exotic trees.

Beneath the fall was an inviting pool of clear cool water and it was not long before we were all in swimming attire splashing about and having a good time. After a while someone suggested that we explore the river above the waterfall and the more adventurous amongst us climbed the rocky cliff to the plateau above.

The river at this level was a rip-roaring torrent, fighting with itself to reach the drop. Ginger and I were with the two soldiers, one of them sporting a camera and eager to get a shot of the four of us together.

The waterfall was somewhat unique insomuch that the river, just before it plunged over the top, split into two, caused by a column of hard rock in the centre. Subsequently, a pinnacle of rock had resulted at the bottom of the fall.

To get a photograph of the full glory of the waterfall disappearing through a gouge in the plateau, together with the column in the centre and the distant scenery behind, he asked us to get as close to the river as possible.

Being the nearest I put my left foot onto a wet rock, very slippery as it turned out, for the next second my face hit the stony bank at the side of the river and I was being swept along at a hurtling pace towards the fall.

Instead of shooting over the waterfall, by a freak of chance my right foot got caught in a crevice a few feet below the surface. Somehow, this left me facing upriver wedged in a V made by the column and the bank. Stuck like this, the river rushed over my head with my face under a deluge of water. It was like having a fireman's hose blasted in my face and the only way I could breathe was to turn my head to the left as far as my neck would stretch.

Stuck at the top of the waterfall, I could not imagine how on earth anyone could help me. With my head turned as it was I could see the people who had remained in the pool below staring up, not knowing what to do.

Hearing a voice above me I managed to turn my head slightly to see that one of the soldiers had crawled through the dense foliage growing on the cliff edge. Being about five feet below him there was little he could do and he held his hands up indicating this.

I had no alternative. I had to free my foot and take my chances with the outcome. Falling one way I would hit the pinnacle of rock, which with its pointed top looked ominous. The other way offered shallow water which was not deep enough to break my fall.

I had no problem freeing my body, in fact I was having a job keeping myself from being washed over the edge, but I had to release my foot first otherwise I would have been suspended in the waterfall by it, the consequence of which I did not like to think about. The difficulty in dislodging my foot was having the strength to thrust it downwards against the strong current that was holding it there.

Whilst I was thinking about this the soldier on the ridge above produced a long thin branch which had been passed to him and which he dangled down to within my reach. He had his arm fully outstretched and the end he was holding was no thicker than my thumb. The leafy end that he offered me, flapping about in the water, had nothing substantial to hold on to.

"Grab hold of that, "he said, "and I'll try to pull you up."

I could see that he was doing his best, but it was a futile gesture and I declined.

I tried again to release my foot, this time using my other one to push it down; even so, I still found it difficult to apply enough pressure. The water cascading over my shoulders and face was making me anxious and I could feel myself panicking. In desperation I twisted my body to the right and stood on my trapped foot with my free one. It became dislodged, but so did my body. Whoosh! I shot over the waterfall and fortunately missed the pointed rock, landing on my back in the shallow water.

The wind was knocked out of my body and for several minutes I was unable to re-gain my breath. People around the pool rushed in, dragged me to the side, and wrapped me in towels, but I was frantic in not being able to breathe. I could not speak to tell them my problem and I could see that they were concerned not knowing what was wrong with me as I thrashed about hoping that this might help. Whether it did or not I will never know, but just as it seemed like I was doomed to die through lack of oxygen my lungs found a way of functioning and I drew in a gigantic breath of fresh air.

Surprisingly, apart from my jaw, some broken teeth, and a very sore foot (lacerated and bleeding) I was in fairly good order.

I never knew how it was arranged but eventually an ambulance arrived and took me to a Military Hospital on the outskirts of Taiping, roughly fifty miles away. There, an examination, together with X-Rays, determined that my jaw and ankle both had slight fractures and I was found a bed on one of the wards.

Other than me, the patients were all soldiers who had sustained injuries, or picked up diseases whilst fighting in the jungle. They were hardened campaigners with interesting tales to tell, and in the main, good company.

The ward I was in bordered onto the jungle and the squaddies found it great fun to get spiders, lizards, beetles, and other creepy-crawlies that abounded there, and put them into my bed. By familiarity, having no fear of these things themselves, they delighted in my horror and reaction to their pranks.

The first time this happened was after I had been up and about. Getting back into bed and tucking the mosquito netting in, I laid down full length placing my feet on top of a red blanket folded neatly across the bottom. The moment my feet touched the blanket a loud buzzing noise occurred. On taking my feet away it stopped. Touching the blanket again – BZZZZ.

Tentatively, I crawled down the bed and eased back the blanket to have the biggest and blackest of flying insects hit me in the face. Shocked, I tried to flee the bed but was thwarted by the mosquito netting in which I became completely tangled up, bringing it and the framework which supported it, down and all around me.

The laughter this received suggested that the jokers got a better response than they had anticipated. I joined them after I got over the shock.

This incident led to another incident some weeks later in Singapore. I was working in a boat-house with some of my messmates and there eating away large holes in the rafters were flying beetles which looked similar to the one under my blanket.

Pointing to the beetles, I said, "When I was in Taiping, the squaddies I met up there held them in their hand."

"Never!" One of them exclaimed. "Look at those holes they're making. They'd bore right through your hand." The rest all agreed.

"It probably lies dormant when it's in your hand," I ventured. "I'll try to grab one."

I awaited my chance, and as one flew near I snatched it, but before I had hardly closed my fist it had drawn blood from the palm of my hand, and it liked it so much I had a job to shake it off.....Another laugh at my expense.

Leaving the hospital in Taiping, it was procedure to get the final nod from the top man. Colonel? Brigadier? Army ranks eluded me, but he was sitting in an office behind a desk all dressed up and presiding with full pomp and ceremony. A sergeant was in attendance to introduce each patient being discharged.

Several soldiers were in front of me smartly dressed in their best uniforms; buttons and buckles shining brightly, caps square on their heads, with boots boned and polished to a bright shine. In

200

extreme contrast I stood there last in line looking exceedingly scruffy in summer-weight trousers, shirt, and plimsolls, which I had been wearing at the time I fell over the waterfall.

The door to the office was left ajar as each soldier was called in one at a time, and from where I was standing I could observe the procedure. When called, it was one-two-one-two-one-two, as they quickly marched to a spot in front of the desk and on the last step lifted their right knee high in the air before driving it into the floor with a crash, whilst saluting at the same time.

When my name was called, I marched in making hardly any noise, and stood in front of the officer's desk. He was looking down at some paperwork at the time waiting for the sound of heavy marching feet, and on raising his head and seeing me, he became almost apoplectic.

He looked at the sergeant beseechingly, obviously looking for a plausible explanation.

"Royal Navy, Sir!" The sergeant exclaimed by way of clarification. "Accident whilst on leave in Penang."

A look of relief spread over the officer's face and his expression gave suggestion to his thoughts. 'Thank God for that.'

He asked me about the incident and whether I was satisfied with my treatment and stay at the hospital before discharging me.

The sergeant arranged transport for me back to the holiday camp in Penang, where I was expecting to collect my clothes, and reimbursement of money for the days of my holiday not taken.

I should have anticipated what the outcome would be – Ginger had collected any money that was due to me as soon as it was established that I would not be coming back, and he had also taken my clothes with him when he left. There was also no sign of my return railway ticket, and I was now penniless. I was given a meal, and a railway-pass back to Singapore but they were unwilling to advance me any money.

It was late in the day when I caught the train, and most surprised, to be told that the pass I held did not include sleeping accommodation when I asked the night-berth attendant which bunk I was in. He could see that I was downcast and kindly let me have a bunk, but without sheets or a pillowcase. That was no problem – I slept like a baby.

The rest of the journey dragged. I had nothing to read, nothing to eat, nothing to drink, and I was feeling queasy. In the morning at the station in Kuala Lumpur, having no money I could not buy food or drink from vendors on the station, so to slake my thirst I drank water from a stand-pipe located on the platform.

Although I was unaware of it, a Malayan lady had been observing me and when the train resumed its journey she sent her young son over with half of a large citrus fruit the size of a grapefruit. It was very juicy but unlike grapefruit the flesh inside was white and slightly sweet. I found out later that it was called a pomelo, or chaddock.

The boy spoke English and sat talking with me for a while. When he went back to sit with his mother I joined them and thanked her for her kindness and explained the reason for my predicament. I remained in their company until we reached Singapore sharing their food and drink. I was lucky to meet such nice people.

On returning to H.M.S. Terror I was told to report directly to the sick bay before returning to my billet. The doctor there took one look at me and asked, "Are you feeling alright?"

I replied, "No Sir. I feel sick and tired, I just want to get back to my mess and crash out."

He pulled my bottom eyelids down. "You're going straight to hospital, you've got jaundice."

"I'll just go to the mess Sir, change, and get some things."

"You're going nowhere. You'll stay here in the sick bay until I get an ambulance to take you to the hospital."

I was to spend the next six weeks in the British Military Hospital in Singapore. I was treated for a severe strain of hepatitis and lost a lot of weight. When I returned to H.M.S. Terror I weighed less than eight stone.

Not long after I was back aboard H.M.S.Concord and on my way to Hong Kong. The war in Korea had started and we were destined to play a role in the activities there. We were delayed however, for when passing close to the Chinese mainland a gun battery fired upon us. Most of the shells missed the ship but one caused some damage to the stern which meant a stay in Hong

Kong for repairs to be carried out. We had one minor casualty, a seaman who was in the team manning our rear gun at the time – he took a splinter of metal in his shoulder.

Whilst all this was taking place I was party to an unexpected act of sabotage.

Reporting for duties when 'Action Stations' sounded (a rattle of loud and alarming proportions) I was detailed to the magazine in the bowel of the ship which held the shells for the two 4.5 inch forward guns. To ensure that the ship remained water-tight if hit below the waterline, the entry hatch was secured from above once all the required personnel had entered. It could not be opened from below.

There were four of us down there passing the shells from the rack they were stored in to a hoist which took them directly up to the gun turret, and every one of us knew the consequences if the ship received a fatal blow, that compartment could well be our coffin.

One amongst us, a sailor who had seen a lot of action in the war, knew the score, and also knew what he was doing when he grabbed a spanner from a rack on the wall and thrust it into the driving mechanism of the hoist. This dislodged a chain which brought it to a standstill.

A young seaman said in disgust, "What did you do that for?"

He did not answer, but I did, "It's bloody obvious; he doesn't want to be locked in here if the ship goes down."

After a very short time the hatch sprung open and a Petty Officer asked, "What's happened?"

The seaman who had wielded the spanner answered immediately, "The chain driving the hoist has come off."

This resulted in a human chain of about ten ratings being formed to manhandle the shells from the magazine to the gun several decks above. With each shell weighing about sixty pounds there was a lot of moaning about the efficiency of the hoist. "Bloody thing, the first time you use it, it lets you down."

The real reason why the hoist failed remained a secret with the four of us in the magazine.

After a short stay in Hong Kong for repairs to be carried out we sailed for Japan, giving escort to a boat which was to be used as the Royal Navy command offices in Sasebo. It was the most unlikely vessel for the open seas, looking more suited to the Mississippi. Resembling a river boat it was double-decked with windows all along both sides, it looked like a flat barge carrying a tram.

Its top speed was not more than ten knots which was painfully slow, and in the rough seas of the Pacific Ocean, being top-heavy it was very vulnerable and had to be kept under constant observation.

One morning, during the early hours, we were all sharply awakened when 'Action Stations' sounded. Rushing along the upper deck in the dawn light I could just make out the outline of a ship which loomed large on the other side of the river-boat. The captain quickly brought our ship around and positioned it between the two which brought us painfully close to the intruder which turned out to be a cruiser of the Chinese navy. It was truly frightening, the size of it in close proximity was enormous, and its twelve six-inch guns trained on us looked very menacing. We had our guns pointed at the cruiser but it was like a Jack Russell bristling at a Rottweiler.

No messages passed between the ships and we travelled in this way until late morning when the cruiser suddenly veered off and left us. They had accompanied us through the entire length of the Formosa Straits and I think they must have been puzzled by the unusual vessel we were escorting.

On arriving at Sasebo I was amazed at the number of ships there. From the mouth of its large natural harbour, to the berths alongside the harbour wall where the river-boat was to be situated, it was filled with warships of all different sorts and sizes, mostly American, there were hundreds of them. This was a serious war.

At the first opportunity all those not on watch went ashore, I was with Horse and Hatch (Hatton), another stoker who had become a close friend of ours, and as usual we were looking for the first bar as we headed towards the town centre. Conveniently, just outside the dockyard gates the NAAFI had set up business, and almost next door was a P.X.Club (the American equivalent). We were spoilt for choice – well there was no choice really we had to be patriotic and give the NAAFI a try.

It was nothing more than a huge warehouse with a bar at one end, a stage at the other, and a collection of old chairs and tables. At five-o-clock in the evening with no more than a handful of ratings in there it had less appeal than a church fete on a wet Sunday morning. The only redeeming feature was the good Scottish ale on draught, Tenants and McEwans.

After a couple of pints in there we tried the P.X.Club. It was clean and bright, serving food as well as beer, and had a dance floor with at least a dozen Japanese girls sitting in line waiting for partners. Tickets purchased at the bar bought you a dance but again there was no atmosphere, it was more like a tea room than a bar. Nevertheless, the girls were pretty and nice to be close to, so I bought a few tickets.

Later, in the town it was not surprising to find the American navy out in force, they were everywhere. British sailors and those from other nations were in evidence but greatly outnumbered by the yanks. Young ladies seemed to be in short supply and those that were to be seen were hanging on their arms.

That first visit to Sasebo was marred by the unexpected aggression towards me by an American sailor. The three of us were walking along the main drag enjoying the occasion, happy with a few drinks inside us, when out of a small group walking a few yards in front of us a short stocky thug suddenly whisked around and smashed his fist in my face, right between the eyes.

Whilst I was recovering from the blow, dazed, and wondering what I had done to deserve it, the group disappeared through a doorway into a building close by, laughing as they went. This fired me up with anger and without giving a second thought to the consequences, I chased after them, followed closely by Horse and Hatch.

We found ourselves in an enormous beer hall, noisy, dark, and filled to capacity with American servicemen, a Jazz band playing on a stage at the far end. Standing just inside the door getting my bearings I spotted my assailant with his pals settling themselves into chairs at a table ordering drinks. He had obviously not expected me to follow him for I was able to move swiftly through the hall without him seeing me and deal out a measure of retribution - a good punch in the face, followed by another to the side of his head.

All hell broke loose as his friends leaped up to retaliate. Horse, fourteen stone of muscle and bone, waded in with fists flying, as did Hatch, although with less effect. Their table went over, and tables close by were greatly disturbed. This annoyed the occupants who sided with their compatriots, and joined in.

A crowd quickly gathered round, shouting, cheering, and baying for our blood, and although we started the affray with an advantage, things were turning against us just as the U.S. Naval Police arrived on the scene and broke it up.

The three of us were frog-marched from the building and thrown out onto the street with stern warnings not to return.

We continued with our look-see of the town, visiting a few local bars, drinking hot Sake for the first time, and sampling some tasty noodle dishes, before making it back to the dockside bars.

The P.X. Club had warmed up but there was still a reserved air about it, obviously the yanks preferred the club that we had recently been thrown out of, however, the NAAFI was buzzing. The warehouse was packed full of ratings and marines in various stages of inebriation all doing their own thing. There was a band of Japanese instrumentalists playing western music on the stage that no one was listening to; various groups singing but no two groups singing the same song; arguments both friendly and antagonistic were ongoing with some resulting in skirmishes and fights; a cacophony of enormous proportions. It was bedlam, and we made up our minds there and then that that was where we would be doing our drinking from then on.

Not as quick as I would have liked though because before going ashore again our ship had taken stores aboard, refuelled, and set sail for Korea.

The North Korean Army had invaded South Korea and was in occupation of large areas and at the time of our arrival Seoul was under attack. The United Nations forces, although mounting a major counter offensive, were retreating, and had been driven back to the coastal city of Inchon. A major evacuation by sea was taking place and we were directed there to give our support.

At that time, I was responsible for the routine maintenance, and operation, of the engine in the motor boat and formed part of its crew as and when required. We were needed at dusk on the day we arrived as the captain had been summoned to a meeting on board H.M.S. Cossack (leading destroyer of the flotilla) which was lying on the opposite side of the bay from where we were anchored, a distance of about four miles.

An intense battle was raging and Inchon was ablaze, the skyline of the city could not be seen due to the flames and smoke rising from its centre, and all along the adjoining coast. Allied planes were raining bombs down, and ships were firing salvoes at enemy targets. With the North Koreans responding in a similar manner the situation was alarming.

After dropping the captain off we had to circle around until the meeting ended. Not a very pleasant place to be with numerous bloated dead bodies floating among the flotsam and jetsam. He was there for at least two hours but it seemed endless and exposed as we were we felt most vulnerable.

Sitting within the engine housing was where I should have been, keeping my eye on the engine, however, I was standing in the well of the boat with the coxswain, and the bowman, watching all the fireworks, and the movements on the shoreline and around the bay.

In the red and orange glow it was possible to see the landing craft loading men from the beach and taking them to the larger vessels which were there for that purpose. With that and the guns from the ships all around keeping up a constant barrage it was surreal, like being in a scene of a panoramic war movie.

Such engaged, it was not until the captain returned, and the coxswain had given the signal to move forward, that I noticed the needle of the temperature gauge was at its highest point, only stopped from going around the dial again by a little brass stud.

The fault was obviously due to insufficient water circulating around the engine, perhaps the water cooling pump not working, or more likely seaweed clogging the filter fitted in the cooling water intake.

Panicking, my immediate thought was to shut the engine down before it seized up while I sorted it out, so in a loud voice and looking over my shoulder I addressed the coxswain. "The engine is overheating, permission to turn it off while I find the fault?"

Before the coxswain could reply, the captain barked, "Permission not granted, just get us back to the ship."

In making this decision he would have thought that I had been diligently keeping an eye on the gauges and had just noticed the temperature rising, not that I had been gazing in awe at the debacle that was going on all around me while the engine was being starved of water.

This left me no alternative; I had to find out what was causing the problem, and find it pronto. Looking at the weed trap with the engine and the pump running, I knew that the water would flow quickly into the boat once I took the cap off and drew out the filter, which it did. To my surprise the filter was clean and I had it back in a matter of seconds without too much water overflowing into the boat.

This left me in a dilemma; the engine was running at full power, getting hotter and hotter, and I still had no idea why the cooling water was not doing its job. I concluded that there had to be a leak from the casing of the engine so I wormed my way around to the back of the engine compartment not knowing what I could do if that was the case. I was alarmed when I found it to see the copious amount of water being shipped aboard, but relieved to find the fault, and that it could be remedied. A half-inch plug had come out of the engine and a stream of water was filling the bilges to a dangerously high level. The boat must have been six inches lower in the water since the plug came out which would have caused it to be more sluggish and most unusual for the coxswain not to have noticed these changes.

I immediately stopped the flow of water by putting my finger in the plug-hole, while at the same time fishing around in the bilges with my other hand for the plug; unfortunately without success.

The bowman of the boat had been observing my dilemma and I asked him if he could find a piece of wood and furnish me a plug. After finding nothing more suitable he cut off the end of a small broom with his knife and tapered it to a point, I was able to drive this into the plug-hole with a spanner sufficient for it to hold until we reached the ship.

For my sins I spent the rest of the journey back to the ship pumping out the bilges with the hand-pump which delivered about a cupful for every movement of the handle. Still, it took my mind off the warfare raging just a short distance from us, and thinking about what would have happened to us if the engine had seized up.

Ironically, the captain on leaving the boat, having observed the actions I had been taking, said to me, "Well done Wellard, a jolly good effort." How little did he know?

The following six weeks were spent in action patrolling the Yellow Sea off the East Coast of North Korea, a period of intense anguish and monotony. Not knowing what to expect, the captain kept the boat at 'Action Stations' the whole time, with periods for leisure almost non-existent.

The day, involved eight hours normal duties, eight hours at a designated action station, (mine was giving attendance at the rear gun turret), and eight hours off-duty, which was mostly spent in sleep. Lights were dimmed during the hours of darkness so there was little to do after our evening meal by way of amusement.

If you were off-duty in the daylight hours you could not sleep in your hammock because each morning all hammocks had to be taken onto the upper-deck where they would be tied to the guardrails on both port and starboard sides. This was to give protection to any of the crew working on the upper-deck, or passing along it, at a time when enemy aircraft strafed the ship with machine gun fire. Fortunately, that never happened, and after the first period of operations draping the rails with our hammocks was discontinued.

Hammocks are made of thick canvas and although they got wet when exposed to the sea and the rain, as long as they were tightly laced the inside of the mattress and the blanket remained dry. They could also act as a buoyancy aid, a properly laced up hammock would keep you afloat for several hours.

Apart from the occasions when we were directed to shell specific land targets the ship's routine was of monotonous continuity. Our task was to give protection to one or other of the three British aircraft carriers which were constantly sending aircraft to bomb or strafe the enemy. In doing this, paired with another C Class destroyer, we would be circling the aircraft carrier in a figure of eight fashion keeping an eye out for mines, and assisting in protection against enemy aircraft.

Mines, laid down by the North Korean Navy at the beginning of the conflict were frighteningly bobbing about in the area we were patrolling. One evening, after one of our look-outs had spotted a mine we spent a very long time trying to blow it up without success, both with fire from our Oerlikon guns, and pot-shots from our marksman, who was an excellent shot with a rifle.

Most of the ship's crew were on the upper deck watching the spectacle and becoming very familiar with the big round object which we knew could blow us sky high. The shots were on target with the bullets and shells bouncing off the steel casing and we were most surprised when the captain called time on the proceedings.

"That's enough," he said. "We'll leave it until the morning, it will still be here."

Circling the area that night we trusted that he had marked the spot with a good deal of accuracy and would keep the ship well clear of the mine
. The situation was fraught with the men tense and anxious, the atmosphere pumped up by a few doom mongers harping on about how the mine could drift with the currents, with comments made such as, "There is no way of knowing where it will be in a couple of hours from now, we could be blown to smithereens."

Fortunately, the captain, with the help of Asdic and Radar knew better than them, for the next morning he brought the ship back to the mine and the marksman blew it up with just a few shots.

A second tour of duty in Korean waters followed after a short respite in Sasebo and the harsh conditions imposed upon us previously were eased. Attendance at action stations was relaxed, only enforced when there was imminent danger, and hammocks were no longer draped over the guardrails. Off duty times in the mess became more pleasant with a game of darts, cards, or

Uckers (Ludo) to be enjoyed. A film was shown in the seamen's mess at least once a week, with Tombola (Lotto) similarly arranged for all of the ships company.

A ship newly arriving in the war zone would perform the task of circulating much awaited mail to the ships already on duty there, others leaving would take mail off. My parents, and Joan, wrote to me regularly, and it was always a pleasure to hear from them. Their letters were written with wit and humour about everything that was going on; family news; the things they were doing; items of interest back home that would interest me; they had so much to tell, whilst my letters back must have been dull, as each new day was the same as the day before.

Back in Sasebo following this tour of duty, a few weeks before Christmas 1950, found me in serious trouble.

Ashore with some of the lads, I became separated from them late in the evening. I had surprisingly bumped into an old a messmate of mine from H.M.S.Suvla who was now in the Canadian Navy; his name was Spencer.

His parents had migrated to Canada and while on leave waiting for his transfer from the Royal Navy I arranged for him to stay with my mum and dad, so we had a lot to talk about. This was over a few drinks, and a few more too many, in a bar some distance from the dockyard frequented by Canadian sailors.

It was close to midnight when I became aware of the time, and by then I had missed the last liberty boat. With nobody having made a move, I had been lulled into thinking it was earlier.

"What time is your last liberty boat?" I asked Spencer, thinking that there was still a chance of getting a lift back to my ship that night.

"We've got all night leave," he replied. "Haven't you?"

"No, and I've missed the last boat."

He went on to explain that the Canadian Navy had arranged shore accommodation for their ratings which allowed them to stay overnight and even take week-end leave when possible.

"Look. Come back with me and I'll get you a bed," he said. "You can't get a boat until the morning and you don't want to spend a lousy night on the jetty."

The offer seemed attractive to me. "That sounds all right," I said. "But I must be on the jetty first thing in the morning."

"There are boats coming and going from the jetty all day, any one of them will drop you off on your ship. You're going to be eight hours adrift so you might as well be ten and have a good night's sleep in a decent bed and return after a nice breakfast." Spencer sounded convincing.

I got another round in and considered his proposal which had some merit to it bearing in mind that for each three hours adrift the punishment was the loss of a days leave and pay which started from the day it was given. I would not be getting any more shore leave on this visit to Sasebo, nor spending any money in the coming weeks.

Yes, it was worth it, or so I thought, until arriving late at the jetty the next morning just in time to see my ship sailing out of the harbour, the R53 emblazoned on its side clear for me to see.

The jetty was just a landing stage for putting ship's crews ashore and picking them up, and not within the dockyard which was the base for the American Fleet. I had no other recourse than to report there.

As I walked along the road toward the dockyard gates one of the naval sentries shouted at me.

"Get off the road and onto the sidewalk."

Puzzled by his belligerent command, and before I had a chance to respond, he pulled out a pistol and barked again.

"Get on the sidewalk, you gob."

A few quick steps and I gained the pavement. I felt like telling him to keep his hair on but I bit my tongue on that.

Having told him my plight, he marched me down to the Police Block where I was put into a cell after giving the name of my ship and handing over my paybook to the duty petty officer.

After a couple of hours I was called before the master-at-arms, a giant of a man in his mid forties.

"Well young man." He spoke in a friendly manner with a strong American drawl. "We've been in touch with your ship and it's on its way to Hong Kong. Fortunately, it was required to visit Kure before leaving Japan and you will be escorted there to join it."

I nodded, indicating that I understood the situation.

"He continued. "You're facing a serious charge which will probably be AWOL (absent without leave) although it could be desertion; it is how your skipper sees it. You've got to consider yourself lucky, if the ship had been deployed for combat duty the charge would definitely have been desertion, and the maximum penalty for desertion in time of war is death.""

I must have looked shocked because he added. "But only one man has been executed for that since world war one."

Shortly afterwards, two American sailors were detailed to escort me to Kure which turned out to be a train journey of over five hours and they were none too pleased, hardly speaking to me the entire journey.

The American master-at-arms was right, I was charged with being AWOL, my punishment being three months second class leave, together with seven days confinement in cells at H.M.S. Tamar when we reached Hong Kong a week or so later.

The cell I was in measured just over six feet square and was housed in a block of six. There were no windows in the block which was lit by electric light bulbs throughout the twenty-four hours of each day. All the internal walls of the cell, after rising to a couple of feet above head height, had bars to the ceiling, and a heavy wooden door from the cell led to a passageway giving access to an exercise yard. During my confinement all the other cells remained empty.

A concrete slab less than three feet wide spanned one wall which was my bed at night and my seat by day. My hammock, which I had been required to take with me, was all the bedding I had. The wafer thin mattress, although comfortably lining my hammock when swinging between two hooks, was hardly better than nothing when laid out on the slab, and my single blanket did very little to warm me throughout the cold nights. In early December the temperature drops considerably in Hong Kong.

Each morning I was woken at five-thirty when after a cold shower and breakfast I was made to move my bedding into a store room, throw buckets of water around my cell, and wash it out with a long handled scrubber. This left it damp for the rest of the day – all part of a process to make your time in there as miserable as possible.

This regime also included two hours of rifle drill in the morning, and also in the evening. Also, useless onerous tasks such as cleaning up rusty buckets with emery cloth, followed by hard rubbing with metal polish until they shone; well, as much as it was possible for them to shine.

After lunch each day another meaningless task was given to me, this was picking oakum. It entailed stripping lengths of rope into fine strands, which had a use in the olden days for caulking seams in wooden ships. The loose hemp or jute fibres were mixed with tar to repair leaks, a useful outcome of the work undertaken. My product was just thrown away.

Two lengths of rope were given to me each time and a sack to put the strands into. On the third or fourth day, the pieces given to me were much bigger than usual and more tightly woven, and by the time I had shredded one, the sack was full, albeit loosely packed.

This led me to think of hiding the second length of rope and the only place I could see where it would not be readily spotted was on top of the thick wall around my cell, laid lengthways between the bars. So standing on the concrete slab (my bed) I stuffed the length of rope in my tunic, grabbed the bars, and hauled myself up to carry out my plan. Surprise, surprise, every inch of all the walls held pieces of rope deviously planted there by previous occupants.

Not to be outdone, and now hanging on to a bar by my right hand only, I attempted to slot mine in using my left hand which clumsily dislodged and brought down two of the pieces already balanced there. They were obviously put there by more accomplished people than me, because after another attempt I brought down two more.

An hour later, with my arms aching where I had nearly pulled them from their sockets, hanging first with one hand and then the other, I managed to get the four pieces of rope that had become dislodged, back into place.

I gave up trying to hide my piece and spent the next two hours picking it apart, which I should have done in the first place. Although, I did think at one stage of dragging all the pieces of rope from off the top of the walls and strewing them on the floor of the cell just to see the reaction of the guard when he came in to collect my sack. It would have been a laugh, but I knew by instinct that he would not see the funny side of it and I would suffer as a result. Naval policemen are not known to have a sense of humour.

Soon after I returned to the ship it sailed for Kure, which was once one of the major harbours for the defunct Japanese fleet, but now the official naval base for British, Australian, and Canadian navies.

Arriving there, and mooring alongside the jetty, all the lads off duty went ashore to do a tour of the bars and eye up the local talent.

"Have a drink for me," I said enviously.

Being on second class pay and leave meant that I was only allowed to go ashore once a month, and then only if accompanied by a responsible senior rating, so for the next three months my outlook was bleak. However, circumstances changed very quickly and things turned out a little better than expected. The very next day the ship went into dry-dock, and once all the water was pumped out of the dock, toilet procedures had to be carried out in a washroom ashore.

I could see an advantage that this had to offer and quickly took it.

Men under punishment had to parade on the upper deck for inspection by the officer-of-the-day at nine-o-clock each evening whilst he did his evening rounds of the ship. Standing in line with the others I had my towel and washing gear close at hand and as soon as we were dismissed I was over the gangway to the toilet block.

Washing was not on my agenda. I had showered earlier in anticipation of this and had arranged an evening ashore with Horse and Hatch who were meeting me in the first bar outside the dockyard gates where they would have a drink lined up for me. I chose to hide my towel and washing gear in the cabin of an old train, away from the toilet block to ensure nobody found it, and within ten minutes was in the appointed bar drinking an Asahi beer with them.

When the ship was accessible from land (in dry-dock, or alongside the wall) leave was not restricted as long as you were back on board by seven in the morning. We got back about two, along with a number of others who were returning to the ship, so it was easy for me to slip back on board.

We were in dry dock for a few weeks and during this time I went ashore every other day - the days when Horse and Hatch were not on duty - and enjoyed the pleasures that Kure had to offer, that is with the exception of the NAAFI club which was a popular place for chiefs and petty officers.

We were still in dry-dock over Christmas and the notice board was telling everyone that the NAAFI was the place to be on Christmas Eve. The bar had an extended licence with food and entertainment on offer. Only a skeleton crew, which included men under punishment, was required to man the ship.

It was a venue that up to then I had avoided, and should have stayed well clear of that evening, but after the officer of the day had done his rounds I was off to join the party. I reasoned that the large hall would be packed, with everyone drunk, and no one would notice me.

When I arrived a concert was in progress and the act on stage comprised a troupe of marines prancing around as ballet dancers, purposely clumsy in their hobnail boots. I stood at the back until the concert ended before finding my friends.

On the way there I had bought a huge five-litre bottle of sake, thinking it a good idea at the time, and we drank it as a chaser with our beer, but as I got merry I foolishly drew attention to myself by carrying the bottle around wishing shipmates a Merry Christmas and pouring them a tot. Carried away by the occasion and feeling good with myself I took my bottle into the lounge where the chiefs and petty officers were celebrating. By this time they were all in high spirits and joking with me, not one of them seemed to be concerned that I had broke ship; or so I thought.

Back on board the next day the chief stoker sent for me.

"Did you have a good time last night?"

"Yeah, it was a great night; everyone seemed to enjoy themselves?" I replied.

"Yes, but you shouldn't have been there enjoying yourself. The bosun (boatswain) has been in to see me this morning asking me to give him a good reason why he shouldn't put you on a charge. Lucky for you it's Christmas Day and he's feeling benevolent and didn't need much persuading."

"Cheers Snowy," I said. "I owe you one."

"Don't thank me yet, he only wants one person who saw you ashore last night to complain and he'll have to charge you, just keep your fingers crossed."

Fortunately for me the day passed without any more being said, and when I passed the bosun on the upper deck he looked right through me without saying anything.

I should have learnt my lesson but a few days later I was at it again, only this time the routine for getting ashore was much more difficult. The ship had left dry-dock and was tied up alongside a large floating floodlit jetty so leaving by the gangway was out of the question. My means of escape was along the rope which secured the bow of the ship to a bollard on the jetty which required me to manoeuvre down it hanging by hands and feet. This I did quite easily and was in town drinking with my mates soon after nine.

I knew that climbing back up the rope would be more difficult but I was not daunted by this. I also thought it possible that there could be the chance of mingling with a rowdy crowd returning in the early hours after midnight and slipping back across the gangway without being observed. Unfortunately, I had far too much to drink and woke at about six-o-clock the following morning, sharing a bed with a young lady.

Daylight had already arrived and I lay there for a few moments gathering my thoughts. How did I come to be here? My mind was a blank. Any pleasures that I might have enjoyed were lost to me. The last thing I could recall was drinking heavily with the lads in some shady bar.

I jumped out of bed in a blind panic and in a state of utter confusion, worried by thoughts of how on earth I was going to get back on board. I had a job finding my clothes, and in my haste fell over as I tried to put my trousers on. Wrestling with my tight tunic was no better and by now the Japanese girl was sitting up

217

laughing at my predicament, not knowing how serious it was for me. Little did she know that if I was unable to get back on the ship without being seen I would be spending the next three months in a military detention centre?

I fled the house with no idea where I was and what way to go, and precious time was lost going in the wrong direction before I found my bearings. By the time I reached the jetty I could see the seamen already on the upper-deck ready to muster for allocation of duties, this told me that it was nearing seven-o-clock and officially the time when the leader of my mess should report me missing.

I stood behind a stanchion on the quay to which the jetty was attached deciding on what course of action to take. There was no way that I could climb back up the rope, I would have been spotted the moment I climbed onto the forecastle, and to complicate matters there was a sailor patrolling the jetty. I decided therefore to dive in and swim around the ship to where the motor boat was tied to a boom on the stern.

I waited until the patrolman turned around on his beat and was walking some distance away from me towards the stern of the ship before I dived in, but even so he heard the splash and ran back to investigate. When he saw me, I was halfway between the quay and the prow of the ship, and I expected him to cry out and make those on board aware of my presence, but to my surprise, and great relief, he looked up toward the deck of the ship and gave me 'thumbs up' indicating that the coast was clear. Giving him a wave back, as a sign of my appreciation, I noticed that he was in the Australian navy.

On reaching the ship I swam around the seaward side keeping close to its hull where I could only be seen by someone on deck coming close to the guardrail and looking directly down. Swimming in full uniform was heavy going and I had to discard my shoes to give me better propulsion, but I managed to keep hold of my hat throughout. On passing mid-ship I heard the order given, from the gunnery-instructor directly overhead, for the seamen to fall in, upon which lighted cigarette ends rained down upon me. Fortunately, although many ratings must have been close to the guardrail nobody looked over the side.

I eventually reached the stern, clambered onto the motorboat which I knew would be there attached to a boom, and was about to climb up the rope ladder onto the quarterdeck when leading seaman Popplewell appeared above me.

My heart sank. 'The game's up,' I thought.

He was the coxswain of the motor-boat, and although having spent many hours in the boat with him his impassive nature was such that he rarely spoke to me other than to issue orders. Being a long serving man awaiting promotion to Petty Officer I was sure that he would turn me in, but no, he took one look at me, saturated with sea water, and beckoned me to hide under the canopy which shielded the engine.

After a short time under there he called out, "O.K Stokes, it's safe for you to come up now." He even gave me a hand to get on board quickly. I saw him in a different light after that.

I dashed across the quarter deck and into the Seamen's mess located in the aft of the ship. There, I borrowed a pair of overalls, together with a bucket into which I placed my wet clothes, and sauntered forward along the upper deck to my mess. Just in time as it turned out, for Slatcher, the killick of my mess was on the point of reporting me absent.

The ship, now fit for purpose, left the following day for Korea where we were to spend the next six months on active service, with the occasional break in Sasebo. Not as often as we had hoped as arrangements were made to re-fuel, and take on new provisions, at sea. It was during this period that those who suffered with sea-sickness were forced to grow sea-legs.

A destroyer, being a fast moving ship has both 'pitch and roll' simultaneously. The effect of this is that in heavy weather, when riding the waves, the bow rises up while at the same time rolling to one side. It then appears to pause as the bow drops and rolls to the other side with the bow rising again. This motion went on constantly day after day, week after week, with your head in a permanent spin. This makes it very difficult to keep your balance when walking along gangways and on the upper deck, for when you go to put your foot down the deck suddenly drops from under you. To make matters worse the ship was constantly heeling over acutely as it circled the aircraft carrier making it dangerous. I had first hand experience of this.

Whilst at my 'action station' on the aft gun, together with another stoker, Tony Moore, I was given leave to return to my mess for a break and a bite to eat. Walking along the port side, and on nearing mid-ships, an announcement came loud and clear over the Tannoy system to use the starboard gangway – a normal instruction when the ship was making a sharp turn to port. However, it was too late, the turn was already being made and the port side of the ship had dipped into a wave. There was nothing Tony or I could do as a wall of water lifted both of us off our feet and swept us along at an alarming rate until we reached the stern where I was bundled against a metal storage box which I managed to hold on to. I thought that Tony had been swept straight through the wire guard-rails and into the rough sea, but fortunately, when the boat righted itself; there he was hanging overboard from one of its stanchions. I leapt across and pulled him inboard. He was lucky, for the ship would have been a long distance from him before anything could have been done to formulate a rescue. It is doubtful whether he would have been found.

The routine was the same day after day, week after week, very little changed.

When off-watch, apart from tombola, and a film twice a week, we spent a lot of time playing cards.

Gambling is not allowed in the navy but obviously it went on, although stakes were generally kept small on board ship, the killick of the mess made sure of that to avoid problems which could cause friction. However, there was an incident which involved two new arrivals on the mess, leading stoker Raisen, and leading stoker Rice. They were naval reservists who were re-called for the duration of the Korean War, both with a chip on their shoulder at having been called back.

They both joined a number of us in a friendly game of pontoon and all was going well until one of them got dealt an ace, together with a picture card, and became the banker. Immediately, the other one stepped out of the game and acted as his cashier: paying out and drawing in the money. When they lost the bank, they both had hands dealt to them again until one of them won it back; the other acting as cashier once more.

The bank has an advantage in pontoon and it was not long before they were jointly winning the most money. It took a while for it to dawn on the rest of us what was going on, this crafty move was being done in such a subtle manner with one of them slipping out of the game without a word said between them, obviously having been pre-arranged.

We protested at this arrangement and made it clear that we were not willing to play with them unless they stopped their sharp practice, which they refused to do, and the game broke up.

A few days later seven of us were playing 'Chase the Ace', a card game where each of the players start with five lives. We were using a low value coins to represent a life.

The game is played for laughs. All of the players are dealt one card each and try not to be the one left holding the lowest denomination on the completion of each short round. That player forfeits a life.

The procedure is simple. The player to the left of the dealer looks at his card and if he deems it to be low, and thinks he could do better by exchanging it with the next player, he has the right to do so. That player then makes his own assessment and if it is lower than the card he had passed back he would do likewise, if of a higher value he would keep it. A very low card would pass all the way round until it was back with the dealer who has the option of showing that card or taking one from the top of the pack. The ace, being the lowest, would obviously fly around the circle of players, hence the name of the game. Anyone dealt a King (highest card) can turn it over which blocks the progress of a low card being passed around.

Playing our game we were making a lot of noise, shrieking with laughter when someone got stuck with an ace, and generally enjoying the fun, when Raisen came across from the other mess where he had been chatting with Rice.

"Pack that game up," he said. "You know gambling's not allowed on the mess."

This was met with a chorus of indignant and rude replies upon which he put us all on a charge.

"Right, get your caps and come up top with me."

We followed him to the upper deck where he reported us to the officer-of-the-watch who put us on the first lieutenant's list of offenders.

Later that day all seven of us were marched into his office and lined up before him where the charge was read out by the bosun.

Between us we managed to convince him that the object of the game was not to win money, pointing out that the most each player could lose was the paltry sum of a few yen, and that the eventual winner after an hour's entertainment would only be richer by enough to buy a couple of bars of chocolate.

The first lieutenant had no other option than to uphold the charge but let us off with a caution. We had the last laugh however because we heard later that he informed the bosun that such frivolous charges were not good for morale and instructed him to bring this to the attention of the chief stoker who gave Raisen a deservedly good rollicking.

As part of the motor boat crew I was excused watch-keeping duties and carried out various tasks on a day-work basis, usually grotty jobs in the boiler or engine rooms, the work allocated to me each day by the chief stoker.

Entering the mess one morning he said to me.

"What's your handwriting like?"

"Better than most," I said.

"Can you type?"

"Slowly," I replied. "With one finger on each hand."

"That'll do. Report to Dixie Dean in his office – he's broke his right arm and needs someone bright to help him, although on this occasion he's unlucky, he'll have to make do with you."

Dixie Dean was a stoker P.O. who undertook specialised duties as the engineer officer's writer and being his 'right hand' was a doddle. It entailed filling out a daily log of all readings (temperatures and pressures) taken over each twenty-four hour period from the log books in the engine room, boiler room, and gear room. Also, dip oil and water tanks, and type records of remedial works carried out by the E.R.As (engine room artificers).

All good things come to an end. A few weeks into the job, Snowy came up to me, smiling, knowing that I was not going to like what he had in mind for me.

"After breakfast tomorrow you're changing places with Alford."

"Sod off, Snowy!" I exclaimed. "I'd rather go back on watch-keeping.

Alford was mess-man to the stoker P.Os; eight of them. His duties were to keep their mess clean and prepare their food, take it to the galley, and collect it when cooked, and do the washing-up after they had eaten. It was considered by many to be a cushy number, and Alford, who had been the mess-man since before I joined the ship seemed to enjoy the job.

"Look Snowy," I cajoled. "If I had wanted to be in the P.Os mess I would have taken steps to have become a petty officer."

Snowy looked directly at me for a few moments, then, still with a smile on his face, said, "Go and sort out the changeover with Alford."

By mid-morning I was preparing dinner in the P.O.s mess.

The P.O.s were a decent lot and the job was not too onerous, as those off duty and not sleeping between watches usually gave a hand to the various tasks. One of them, Tubby Downey, fancied himself as a 'bit of a chef' and apart from arranging the menus would muscle in when I was making the pastry for pies, or tarts. He also insisted on making the dumplings for the pot-mess, and the mix for Yorkshire puddings. Anyone squeamish would be turned off their food watching him, fortunately that did not apply to me or any of the others in the mess.

He was a large man who liked to wear nothing but a pair of boxer shorts when relaxing off-duty in a manner such that his big fat belly hung over the waistband. He would perspire profusely, and when mixing and rolling pastry used excessive amounts of flour. His arms, chest, and stomach, would become covered in the white powder with rivulets of sweat channelling through it. Absorbed with the task he would subconsciously rub his hands across his torso and in doing so transfer bodily fluids into the dough.

It did not detract from the taste, it may even have improved it, who knows, but one thing is for certain, everybody in the mess enjoyed it, including me.

I settled into my new role of mess-man but never considered it to be my place of residence, returning to the stoker's mess each evening after my tasks for the day had finished. Alford, similarly, and surprisingly, returned to the P.Os mess.

On my ninth day in the job the rum was collected in a bottle at eleven-o-clock as usual by Trader Horne, the senior P.O., and a tot given to each of us assembled there. Before dishing each tot out, using a small copper pot holding exactly one eighth of a pint, he put the same measure of water into the bottle to make an additional tot.

"Whose turn is it for the extra tot?" he asked.

Dickie Dawes answered, "I had it yesterday and Tom follows me, so it must be his turn."

I piped up. "It's not Tom's turn, it's my turn."

There was an uneasy silence for a few moments until Dicky Dawes answered back, "Mess-men don't have an extra tot."

"Well this mess-man does," I replied. "During the past eight days, between you, you have drunk one of my tots. Today it's my turn to get it back."

They all looked a bit stunned, obviously surprised that I was claiming the extra tot. Then Dixie Dean spoke up.

"Fair enough," he said. "But before you have it, I think it's only fair for you to wait for Tom to come up. He's doing the forenoon watch in the boiler- room and he'll be looking forward to that extra tot."

I agreed to this arrangement, and we waited for Tom Bickerton who came into the mess straight from the boiler-room before washing, eager for his double ration of rum.

There were only two tots left in the bottle which he picked up straight away and would have poured it into a glass had Trader Horne not stopped him.

"You've only got one tot to come Tom. Rex has made claim to the extra one."

224

"Mess-men don't get an extra tot."

"I'm not after an extra tot," I said. "I just want my ration, and at the moment I'm owed a tot."

"Well bring back Alford, I say. He didn't take his rum at all." Tom was really put out.

That surprised me; no wonder there was confusion over who was having the extra tot as there had been two of them having an extra tot each day.

I looked at Tom Bickerton standing there in his blue overalls, hangdog face all sweaty and smeared with grease gained from four hours in the boiler-room, and my resolve melted. Addressing him I said, "Alright, you can have the extra tot today, but tomorrow I'll have my tot before any waters added."

Taking the air on the upper deck that evening the chief stoker approached me.

"You can resume your normal duties tomorrow morning; Alford wants his old job back."

In July 1951, after more than nine months patrolling the Korean waters, we returned to Hong Kong for the ship to be decommissioned and the ships crew sent home, and so it was that later that month I was taking passage on the Empire Orwell to Singapore. It was travelling back to Blighty, but for some reason or other we had to vacate it at Singapore to make way for squaddies from the Yorkshire Light Infantry who had been fighting in Malaya.

In a way, I benefited by getting off at Singapore, as I had won a lot of money in a card school and would possibly have lost it back if I had been on the boat for the entire journey.

I had no right to be in the card school really as I had joined the game without a decent entry stake, but standing directly behind the players, mostly soldiers, I got so absorbed that my powers of reasoning were not functioning when unthinkingly I jumped into a chair when one of the participants directly in front of me pushed it back and left after losing a lot of money.

"Deal me in," I said.

Pontoon was the game being played and the stakes were generally high but I was betting the minimum hoping to build on my meagre funds. After just a few hands I was dealt a picture card, and an ace, winning the right to be banker, which I foolishly took.

I dealt each player two cards on which they made their opening bet and their stakes on the table amounted to more than I could cover. Breaking into a sweat I looked around to see if there was anyone I knew who would back me if I lost, but no such luck, I was on my own.

To those who needed it I dealt third and fourth cards, with the cash on the table accumulating. Fortunately, no one had a five card trick, or a pontoon, but nobody had busted. As I turned my cards over my heart was in my mouth, if I had a low total, or I busted, (exceeded a total of twenty-one), at best I would suffer derision, and humiliation, but more likely a good-hiding, as tensions were running high. Fortunately, I had two picture cards and cleaned up.

I went on to win over twelve pounds, which at that time equated to the wage earned over two weeks by the average manual worker.

After several weeks hanging about in H.M.S. Terror we boarded the S.S. Empire Windrush bound for the U.K. This liner was famous for bringing the first migrant workers, after the Second World War, from the Caribbean countries to England. Built in 1930 it was not in the best condition, and a poor relative to the Empire Orwell.

On the morning of the second day out, one of the first class passengers, a master-at-arms who had been heading the police office in H.M.S. Tamar, drew me to one side whilst I was lounging about with friends on the upper deck.

"I think that you may be able to help me," he said. "There's no laundry on board the ship and the naval officers have asked me to find someone to set up a dhobi firm. Your name came up as a likely lad who could organise one."

I was surprised at this, and stood there a few moments thinking about it. "I'll have a word with a couple of my mates," I said.

He then led me to a washroom which he opened up with a key. It was bare except for four large zinc-lined sinks set along one of the bulkheads and a couple of galvanised buckets in the corner.

"I've spoken to the ship's purser and obtained sole use of this washroom."

I nodded, indicating that it was suitable, after which he took me to a space below decks which held a table tennis table. Pointing to it he said, "You'll have to use that as your ironing board, it's the best I can do. I'll get a couple of irons when you're ready for them." He handed me the keys to both areas obviously having taken it for granted that I would accept his proposal.

On leaving him I put the proposal to Horse and Hatch, who were both interested, and we drew up a price list.

On taking it to the master-at-arms in his cabin he took a look at it.

"Wash and iron a shirt for three-pence?" He queried. I was about to protest thinking that he thought the price too much, when he added, "Make it sixpence." He went on. "Shorts for two-pence, make it four-pence." Looking down the list, which included underwear, and socks, he said, "Double all your prices."

He then gave me a stack of his own personal items. "Start with these."

Using OMO washing powder purchased from the onboard shop we soon had our arms deep in suds kneading the dirty linen of both naval and army officers.

We scrounged rope from the ship's chandler with which we rigged up clothes lines on the upper deck directly outside the washroom, and with the tropical sun beating down the first load was dry and ironed by the end of the day - a job well done, and money in our pockets for a few beers that evening.

If only it could have remained that way. It did for a few days while we were dealing with officers only, but we got greedy. The intake from this source slowed down so we opened it up to anyone who wished to take advantage of our facility, and boy, did they, we were inundated with so much dirty washing from the hundreds of soldiers on board that the three of us were unable to handle it.

We soon found three more hands willing to join the firm, but even so, the mountain of dirty washing which confronted us was daunting. Washing each item by hand presented us with an impossible task so we changed our tactics. We separated the whites from the coloureds (mostly khaki) and dumped them separately in manageable loads into the four sinks which we had half-filled with soapy water. Then removing our shoes and socks, two of us clambered into a sink each where we stomped up and down on the washing for several minutes (as if treading grapes) before stepping into an adjacent sink and repeating the process. The others turned the washing over in the departed sink and this method was carried out numerous times. - Stomp around in one sink, turn the washing in the other; change sinks; stomp around again, turn the washing in the other; and so it went on. The washing was done in half the time by this procedure; probably not quite as clean, but a lot more fun as we laughed and splashed about, loudly singing songs to accompany our antics. Each new wash we would change places, those paddling in the sink would then turn the washing while the others stomped. We had the cleanest feet on board.

The bulk of the washing from the soldiers was light tropical kit - khaki tunic and shorts. Many of the items looked like they had not been washed since the wearers were crawling through the Malay jungle, which they may well have been just prior to boarding the boat in Singapore. Our rates for these did not include ironing.

Marking the items was not necessary. In the forces all kit is marked with the owner's name; that is with the exception of socks, and there were dozens of those. Looking for an easy solution to this we cut the OMO box into small squares putting a piece of the cardboard into each sock with the appropriate name written on it in Biro hoping that it would still be legible after washing. No chance, the cardboard was a soggy mash with the names obliterated.

Our only option was to bundle them up in pairs and when the clean washing was collected at the end of each day ask the recipient to sort out his own socks from a cardboard box into which we had put them. Of course, all the soldier's socks looked the same, so the 'first come' picked out the best socks, and by the end of the day those left in the box were ones that had seen better days, many with holes in them.

You can imagine the response of those who were at the tail-end when picking up there washing, and our lame excuses when they were shuffling through the pitiful assortment that were left.

"My socks are not in here."

"That's all that's left."

"Mine were bloody good socks, these have all got holes in them."

"Well take the best pair you can find."

"Sod off! I'm not wearing somebody else's socks with bloody holes in them."

"Sorry mate, but that's how it is. Tell you what; we'll dock tuppence off the bill."

Learning from this, socks in the next batch of washing, and further batches, were washed in the pockets of the tunics; or shorts; whichever came with them, drying them that way as well.

We had anticipated theft of items from the line but with few pegs available to us this had resolved itself. The lines were threaded through the arms of shirts and tunics, and through one of the legs of the shorts making it impossible to remove an item without great difficulty.

Ironing caused us all sorts of problems with the worst possible start. It concerned a shirt belonging to one of the merchant navy officers manning the 'Windrush'.

He walked into the washroom on our first day with four white shirts of Saville Row quality, and said, "Here's five shillings, that's more than your price-list but I'm relying on you to do a good job."

His shirts were in the first wash, and favouring him for his generosity, the first to be ironed. Taking one of his shirts, slightly damp, I placed it directly on the table-tennis table. Then making sure that the iron was not too hot I carefully moved it backwards and forwards across the back panel to remove all the creases but was mortified when the shirt turned green, impregnated with the paint from the table.

Needless to say, the paint never washed out and I had the humiliating task of presenting it to the officer when he came to collect his laundry.

I offered him his money back but he refused to take it. He was very gracious and even made light of it, saying, "When I'm wearing it, I'll have to make sure I keep my jacket on."

By the time we reached the Suez Canal the demand for our services had waned and at Port Said we closed the dhobi firm down, all of us glad to see the back of it. A few unclaimed tunics, and socks (all having holes) we threw over the side of the ship.

At Port Said, all the 'bum boats' gathered around the ship peddling their wares; handbags, suit-cases, and such, which they did for the next ten days; the length of time we were there due to a major fault in the engine-room.

With all and sundry eager to get home there were a lot of long faces, but we were lucky compared with those taking the same trip the following year when a large explosion in the boiler-room resulted in the ship catching fire. It was completely burnt out and sank in the Mediterranean Sea just off the Algerian coast with the loss of four engineers. Fortunately, the fifteen hundred soldiers and sailors taking passage were evacuated safely.

It was while in Port Said that I had a close encounter with a shark. A group of us had taken ourselves to a popular resort nearby to enjoy a day on the beach, and having hired a float, a small flat craft about six feet long, Horse and I paddled out to a raft anchored off-shore. A big lad named Joe swam out to join us.

After jumping, diving, and generally messing about on the raft, we decided to paddle the float to deeper waters. The buoyancy of the float was jeopardised with three of us on board, a total of about forty stone, so Joe swam ashore to hire one for himself.

With Horse at the back, and me in the front, we paddled slowly out and were waiting for Joe when a shoal of fish swam past our bow disturbing the water where they broke the surface.

"You know what that means?" Horse said. "They're fleeing from a large fish; a porpoise or a shark."

In response to this I stood up on the float and held my paddle like a spear. "Right," I said. I'll harpoon it." Upon which I projected it into the sea, and lost my balance as I did so.

Retrieving my paddle I found the whole thing amusing, but Horse was agitated.

"Get back on the float. Get back on the float," he cried.

Putting my paddle on the float I clambered up after it, nearly tipping Horse off in the process. Back on board I found myself the wrong way around, now facing Horse.

Having hardly settled myself in this position, he shouted, "I can see it. It's a shark."

Attempting to turn, such that I could look over my shoulder to see for myself, Horse screamed, "Keep still! Keep still!" Which I did, realising that he was deadly serious.

Facing the shore, as I was, I could see Joe on a float approaching us, so I shouted, "Go back Joe, there's a shark."

I must have sounded convincing because he immediately turned the float around and paddled hard toward the shore.

Horse and I dipped our paddles gently in and out of the water making as little noise, and disturbance, as possible, not wanting to draw the shark's attention to us. Although I have heard since that it would have been better to make a lot of noise.

Moving slowly back, aiming to reach the raft without being eaten alive, I observed Joe coming back out again with a large grin on his face, but then, when quite close, the grin was replaced by a look of alarm upon which he high-tailed it back toward the shore.

Eventually, Horse and I reached the raft physically and nervously exhausted. We were greeted by Joe who confirmed Horse's sighting of a shark, and also explained his own actions.

"When I first came out to join you," he said. "You shouted out that there was a shark. My reaction was to get away from there as soon as possible. But then I thought, 'They're pulling my leg.' So I turned around and came out again and that's when I saw a fin gliding through the water about twenty feet from your float. That was real scary, I wasn't going to hang around and paddled like fury until I got back here."

I was always of the opinion that there were no sharks in the Mediterranean, but enquiries made later revealed that many sharks have been seen in an area close to the canal, coming through from the Indian Ocean, but there is no record of shark attacks..

The Windrush docked at Southampton late one day in July and I stepped ashore the following morning with a pass for twenty-one days leave. By mid-day I was standing in Church Lane outside Charlton Station with my kitbag, and a large case, with the daunting prospect of carrying it up the very steep incline which led to my home in The Heights.

Almost opposite was the manager of our local off-licence sitting on a chair outside his store making the most of a warm sunny day – he held the answer; I would borrow his crate barrow. To show goodwill I bought a crate of bottled beers; Watney's brown ale for my dad and me, and Macheson stout for my mum. This I placed on the carrier, and then, with my case and kitbag mounted on top, trundled up the hill.

Seeing the licensee reminded me of a small contretemps my father had with him in the war. It was at a time when beer was in short supply and on passing the off-licence he observed a man leaving with one or two bottles. Seizing the opportunity he went into the shop and asked for a quart of brown ale.

"Sorry, we are out of stock," The manager replied.

"Well that's funny," My dad said. "I just saw someone leaving here and he wasn't empty handed."

"Let me put it this way, I've only got enough beer for my regular customers."

"I am a regular."

"I might have seen you in here now and again."

"Yes, every time I buy beer to consume indoors. What has it come to? Do I have to be an inebriate to be a regular?"

He got his quart of brown ale.

Arriving home I entered the back door, which was always left open, hoping to surprise my mum, but that fell flat. She must have seen me through the bedroom window because coming down the stairs she called out, "We weren't expecting you until later on." It transpired that my dad had been following the progress of the Windrush in the shipping news provided each day by the Daily Herald.

Entering the kitchen she drew me into her clean starched apron and hugged me close for several minutes; she was glad for me to be home, and I was glad to be home.

Standing back she looked me over and said, "Haven't you put on weight? If I passed you in the street I wouldn't have known you."

I was over two stone heavier than the last time she saw me so hearing her say this was not surprising.

Vivian, my sister Jean's daughter, who was little more than a baby when I went away, was hanging on to my mum's apron looking shy. She had probably been told beforehand who I was, and who to expect, but obviously did not remember me. She was a lovely baby and now a beautiful little girl.

My mum fussed over me while I was unpacking, which I did straight away to give Vivian the small Japanese novelty toys I had brought home for her. There were also mementoes for the rest of my family.

Jean came in a short while later, and then my dad, both pleased to see me home. His greeting was less emotional – a big smile, a handshake, and, "It's nice to see you back home."

Over a nice meal, and until late in the evening afterwards, I told them about the places I had been and the things I had seen, whilst they told me all the latest news concerning family, friends, and relatives. I would be meeting most of them soon as a party had been arranged for the following weekend to celebrate my homecoming.

Before that, I met up with Joan. Our letters to each other had brought us very close together, and I was really looking forward to seeing her. I was not disappointed, she was still smart, witty, and fun to be with, and more attractive than ever. I was smitten with her.

It was a pleasant reunion and by the end of it Joan and I had made arrangements to spend some time together, which we did, and by the time my leave expired we had become very close.

On returning back to the Royal Naval Barracks at Portsmouth I was sent, together with most of the stokers from H.M.S.Concord, on a training course to learn the 'ins and outs' of internal combustion engines. This was held on H.M.S.Alaunia which was rigged out with petrol and diesel engines of all types, from outboard motors to large marine engines. This ship, a converted cruiser moored in Plymouth Harbour was to be my birth for the next four months. Not my favourite posting for many reasons but one in particular comes to mind.

Going ashore one very cold evening a short time before Christmas I needed to borrow an overcoat. I had been without one since the day I left H.M.S. Suvla, for having been abroad to hotter climes I had not yet renewed it. The loss of my overcoat was hardly my fault, as on lifting it from a coat hook to pack it in my kitbag I noticed that it was smouldering. Unwittingly, I had hung it over a low wattage bulkhead light where it had been hanging for weeks, gradually reaching the point where it was ready to combust. I immediately took it onto the upper deck whereupon reaching the fresh air it burst into flames and I was lucky not to be burnt before I tossed it into the sea.

With most of the mess going ashore there were not many remaining on board to ask and of those only one was willing to lend me theirs, a leading hand called Ginger Haworth. This presented me with a problem as there was a red anchor sewed to the sleeve indicating his higher rank. Still, it was bloody cold, and I needed an overcoat.

Nearing the end of a good night out with Horse and Joe, pub-crawling along Union Street, I emerged from an infamous pub called The Long Bar with the overcoat across my arm. Because of the pub's reputation there were several naval policemen observing the exit and making their presence felt.

One of them called me over. "Where did you get that coat?" He questioned sharply.

He had obviously seen the anchor on the sleeve of the coat and the absence of one on my tunic.

"I borrowed it," I said.

"You've stolen it from in there," he replied accusingly.

(It was common practice for unscrupulous matelots to enter a busy public house without an overcoat, or raincoat, and come out with one which he would sell on).

"I would never do that, you ask my mates."

Horse and Joe backed me up.

A second, more senior snowdrop, poked his nose in. "Well, you're masquerading as a killick and we're taking you in."

I spent that night in a cell of the prison block in Plymouth Barracks (H.M.S.Drake) and escorted back to the ship the next morning where I was charged with stealing the overcoat and falsely adopting the rank of a leading hand.

By the time I went before the captain as a defaulter the charge of stealing was changed to 'taking an item of clothing without the owner's consent' -- a much lesser charge. Ginger had told them that he did not mind me taking the coat, and wanted to say that he loaned it to me, but I persuaded him against this as he would have been on a charge himself. My punishment was fourteen days No 11s.

Being no stranger to this tedious routine it would normally not have bothered me, but on this occasion it overlapped my annual Christmas leave by five days.

Regarding this I approached the master-at-arms, a twenty-two-year man now on extended service, who had mellowed with age.

"No problem son," he said. "It's just normal procedure. Put in a request for the five days to be deferred until after your annual leave."

Following his advice I was standing in front of the captain the next day anticipating his approval which I now thought would be a formality.

"Not granted," he said. "Loss of leave is loss of leave, whether annual, or shore leave."

Shocked, I went back to see the master-at-arms.

"I'm as surprised as you are," he said. "The trouble is, he's an engineer. The whole ship is run by engineers. He hasn't got a clue on normal administrative procedure. Sorry son, I can't help you."

Leave over the festive season was arranged such that Scotsmen had fourteen days which included the New Year, whilst all others were home for Christmas. I was due to go on leave on the 15th of December and return on the 29th but now found myself painting the officer's wardroom until the 20th before getting away.

On arriving home my mother said, "We expected you home five days ago."

I had already made up my mind that I was not going to lose one day of my annual leave and replied, "That's how it was supposed to be, but a few of us have been allowed home for Christmas and the New Year." Giving her a big hug I added "Lucky me."

The time passed quickly, I spent a lot of time with Joan, and all my family and relatives got together for the usual knees up on Christmas Day. I had the bonus of joining them down the pub to see the New Year in.

It was not until the 2nd of January that my subterfuge was blown. I returned home from an evening out with Joan to find my mum very agitated.

"We've had the Naval Police here looking for you. You should have returned days ago."

"Don't worry," I said, "I'm going back in the morning."

She was concerned for me, as was Joan. "You'll be in a lot of trouble."

"Look mum," I said, in an attempt to allay her, and Joan's, fears, at the same time glancing at my dad who seemed to be amused by it all, "I'll be given a few days extra duties and a couple of days loss of pay; believe me, it was worth it."

As things turned out it was worth it. I got a further fourteen days No.11s (the most severe punishment that can be given by the Captain without him applying to higher authority) and twenty-one days stoppage of pay.

The stoppage of pay was a blow, but fortunately, coincidental with this, gratuities were being paid out to all ratings who had served on ships involved in the Korean War, and surprisingly, as things turned out, this resulted in me not losing any money at all.

We were each paid out the sum of thirteen pounds, but the ship's paymaster had authorised it in error. He had the go-ahead to pay out Plymouth ratings only, not those of Portsmouth and Chatham, so consequently he took the money back by deducting it from the pay-packets of each of the ratings concerned. Having no pay to come I paid nothing back.

A few weeks later, having finished our course, we were back in Portsmouth where I joined the angry crew at the pay office demanding payment of the gratuities which were due to them. Standing in the queue which had formed, I was ready to be given a dressing down for attempting to obtain a payment which I had already received, but fortune favours the brave and I was paid out without any fuss. It was roughly the same as the twenty-one days pay that I had been fined.

The next six months was spent in H.M.S. Hornet, a naval base for motor torpedo boats (M.T.Bs) although it was more like their graveyard, for apart from the half-a-dozen or so moored in a creek alongside purpose-made jetties, there were several times that many moth-balled, and mounted on chocks, in an area called Gun Boat Yard. Used in the war for attacking enemy shipping in the English Channel they had become redundant.

Based in Gosport it was an easy posting which allowed me to get home every other weekend and the workload was minimal as the boats very seldom went to sea. Mind you when they did, it was an experience not to be missed. They were about sixty feet long, heavily armed with torpedo tubes mounted on each side and driven by two huge Packard engines running on high octane petrol. These boats could maintain a speed of fifty knots (57 mph), the fastest craft in the fleet.

When reaching full speed the bow-wave arced high over the prow and the wake left behind the boat was over half a mile long whilst the engines screamed at such a high level of decibels that all personnel in the cramped engine-room compartment were required to wear ear-muffs.

With high octane fuel stored on the base, and its presence in the boats, a small fire station existed which housed a sizeable mobile pump capable of providing a forceful delivery of water through two standard Fire Brigade hoses. I was detailed to be part of the fire fighting team.

The chief stoker, apart from his normal duties overseeing the stoking section of H.M.Hornet, also gave his personal supervision to the fire fighting unit where he had his office. His name was Butcher but was generally known as Butch, and like many of us there had served on a ship in Korea and had only recently taken up the post.

Each year an event took place at a venue near Southampton where fire fighting teams, with their pumps, competed with each other for a trophy which was awarded to the most efficient outfit. Hornet had not yet achieved this honour but Butch was determined to win it and to give us guidance in method, and training, he enlisted the help of a senior officer from the Gosport Fire Brigade.

There were five of us in the team and the routine was simple. We were required to pull the heavy pump about ten yards until alongside an open top tank filled with water. Butch and Sid (a leading stoker) then unclipped a cumbersome four inch diameter suction hose, connected one end to the pump, and threw the other end into the tank. Butch then primed and started the pump.

Simultaneously, I helped Mitch and Dan (stokers like me) connect hoses to the delivery side of the pump, unroll them and attach nozzles to the ends. Finally, when the water arrived, hit a pre-set target.

On the lead up to the competition we practised daily until we had perfected the routine beyond all expectations of the Fire Brigade Officer.

About this time a dance was being held to commemorate H.M.S.Liverpool which was being decommissioned after years of active service. It was exclusive to the recently discharged crew of the ship, and included a free buffet and drinks.

Dan, having served on the ship, and being allowed a guest, took me along to the event which was held at the Embassy Ballroom in Southsea. We met up with his old shipmates, who had cornered a niche near the bar, and joined them in some heavy drinking. Not a lot of dancing was done, with men vastly outnumbering women, so by the time we were chucked out at one o-clock I was plastered. Three sheets to the wind, as they say in nautical terms.

Having got separated from Dan, I was staggering up Clarendon Road, with the long walk to Queen Street in front of me, when the heavens opened up. With the rain stair-rodding down I stood under a tree which unfortunately provided very little shelter and within seconds I was getting soaked. Close-by, standing in the kerb, was a car, and in desperation I tried one of its doors, which happened to be the one giving access to the driver's seat. Surprisingly it opened and I quickly jumped in.

It was snug in the car and I sat there waiting for the rain to stop, or at least die down, but I must have dozed off, for the next thing I knew was my head hitting the side window and becoming aware that the car was on the move.

I sat bolt upright and looking through the windscreen realised that the car was moving quite fast down the slight hill I had previously walked up, and gathering speed all the time. It was now in the middle of the road and angling toward the opposite kerb.

Grabbing the wheel I tried to steer it away but got very little response. I attempted to brake, but never having driven a car before, and not knowing which pedal to press, my effort was unsuccessful and before I knew it the car had mounted the kerb, crossed the pavement, and crashed through a brick wall into someone's front garden.

Sobered up by this, I grabbed my hat from off the floor where it had dropped in the crash, opened the door, and fled the scene. Running wildly down a side street I found myself in Clarence Parade, a line of houses facing the sea. I had hardly turned the corner when a police car came into view and my immediate thought was to hide in the front garden of the house I was passing in the hope that they had not seen me, but I immediately abandoned the idea knowing that it would make me look guilty if they had, so I continued walking, looking as natural as I could.

The car drew up in the kerb alongside me and a policeman got out.

"Hello Jack," he said, in a friendly manner. "Do you mind telling me where you've just come from?"

"No," I said. "I've been to the Liverpool Ship's Dance."

"That finished over an hour ago," he queried.

My brain gave an immediate response and provided my mouth with a feasible lie.

"I took a girl home afterwards."

"Where did she live?"

"I don't know. I didn't actually take her home; we had a snog in the Granada doorway. I think she lived near there."

"What was her name?"

"Joan." That name came to me naturally.

The policeman took a notepad from his pocket and asked me for my paybook from which he copied my name, rank, and number.

"What ship are you on?"

"H.M.S. Hornet," I said, pointing to my hat.

"I can't read it; your hat's on back to front."

I put my hat on straight but this flustered me, I had been careless and wondered if this had registered with him.

Whether it had, or not, he made no comment other than to indicate that the questioning was over, then handed me my paybook before getting back into the car and driving off.

Walking on, my brain was racing and reasoning what would happen next. What would be their next move? Probably to stop and question other people, mainly sailors still in the area, then take fingerprints in the morning and check them against those questioned.

I then knew what I had to do. Return to the car and wipe any surface that I may have touched.

Fortunately, the rain had almost stopped as I kept to the shadows and made my way back, skirting the block until I was in the same street as the house in whose garden I had left the car, but at the other end. I entered a garden on the same side and stealthily worked my way toward it clambering from one garden to the next. The street was tree-lined and the lighting poor, so with the large gardens having plenty of foliage it was dark with good cover.

Eventually, I reached the garden adjacent to that where I had left the car but it had been moved and was now standing on a concrete strip on the other side of the road. Alongside the car were the two policemen who had questioned me earlier talking to two civilians. In the clear night air, crouched down behind a wall, I could hear clearly what was being said, the substance of which was that someone had seen a sailor running from the scene of the crash. Also, one of the men, probably the owner, was saying that the car was not roadworthy, having a faulty steering column.

The intercom sounded in the police car which brought their conversation to an end and the policemen immediately sped off.

The civilians left the scene shortly after.

I waited for a further fifteen minutes to make sure the coast was clear before darting across the road and slipping into the driving seat of the car. Keeping well down I quickly wiped the steering wheel, and anywhere else I may have touched, including the handles of the door both inside and out. This was all done within a few minutes.

Keeping to the back streets, for fear of being picked up again, I arrived back in Portsmouth Town Centre at half-past-three and crashed out on a settee in the lounge of Aggie Weston's Sailor's Club.

The following Monday, a short article appeared in the Portsmouth Evening News giving information about the incident, adding that fingerprints had been taken and that the police would be interviewing a number of sailors who were questioned in the vicinity at the time.

Each day that passed I was on tenterhooks waiting for the tannoy to blast out a request for me to report to the police office. An article in one of the daily papers told of two sailors stationed at Portland being sentenced to six months for taking a car away without the owner's permission. 'What was in store for me,' I wondered. 'Who is going to believe my story?'

Towards the end of the week Butch sent for me.

"Close the door and sit down," he said.

When I was seated he asked, "Have you got something on your mind?"

"No. What makes you say that," I responded.

"I'll tell you what makes me say that. I drink in the Shipwrights Arms which is located close to Portsmouth Central Police Station and the publican lets the coppers drink in there after closing time. Being a regular I enjoy the same privilege, so I am friendly with quite a few of them and consequently the conversation generally revolves around criminal activities, usually very interesting, but particularly so last night. It concerned a stolen car.

Butch paused, looked across his desk and raised his eyebrows questioningly, obviously looking for a response from me. Not getting one he continued.

"They picked up a number of sailors in the area, including you. The various reasons given for being there all proved accountable except yours." He paused. "The police are sure it was you."

"I told them why I was in the area," I said.

"Are you guilty?" Butch asked.

I declined to give him a direct answer. "What do you think Butch?"

"I don't know, but if you are, I've got something to tell you that will put your mind at rest. The police will not be pursuing the case any further."

"Well someone will be pleased about that Butch," I said.

"Go on, off you go, back to work; and make sure you don't let me down in the competition."

I stepped out of his office a stone lighter, the weight removed from my shoulders.

Thinking about the information Butch had imparted to me I wondered why the police had not followed it through......

.....Had Butch been able to persuade them to drop the case, knowing how difficult it would be to replace me at this late stage in the Fire Fighting Competition? No! Even if he bought them drinks all night, that would be most improbable.

.....Could the man who owned the car have persuaded the police to drop the case. Perhaps the insurance payout was worth more to him than the car; most unlikely.

.....Could it be that I was successful in wiping all the fingerprints away and that they had no evidence to charge me; possible.

Having weighed things up I was satisfied that I would hear no more about it.

A few days later, with our pump spruced up, all brass-work polished, and brand new hoses, we took our place in the designated site at Southampton to 'do battle' with the competition.

When the pistol was fired we were off our mark and had the pump alongside the reservoir in record time.

Leaving Butch and the Killick to deal with the suction side of the pump, Mitch, and I, released the four hoses and un-clipped the nozzles. We then placed a hose under each of Dan's large arms and put a nozzle into each of his hands. A heavy load to run with but one that Dan had done many times before.

Mitch and I then connected our hoses to the pump before running toward our targets, reeling out the hoses as we went.

At the point where the hoses expired, Dan was standing with his back towards us holding the hoses in a manner to expedite speedy connections. On making the connections we ran in a similar fashion with the second set of hoses to where Dan was standing in front of the targets with the nozzles which we quickly attached to the hoses.

If everything was going to plan water should have been chasing us down the hose and a moment after we affixed our nozzles it would jet out. This never happened.

We scanned the field of competitors and could see them running there hoses out, not one had yet fitted their nozzles. The three of us stood there looking at our flat hose willing the water to arrive but the body language of Butch and Mike back at the pump told us that we were waiting in vain. We had beaten them all, but we were not going to win.

We found out afterwards that everything had gone well to begin with. Butch and Mike had fitted the suction hose, submerged its end in the reservoir, and started the motor, but then Butch in his eagerness banged the priming handle over with such force that it jammed.

The consequence of this was an airlock which eliminated any chance of drawing up water. We were all gutted, none more so than Butch.

In late summer of 1952 a survey boat, H.M.S. Challenger was commissioned after a major refit and I was detailed to be part of the crew. Unlike other naval vessels which are painted grey, this was white with a yellow funnel.

Its sphere of operations was to be the Atlantic Ocean, ranging from areas around the West coast of Ireland, down to the Azores, and up to the Shetland Islands. Unbeknown to any of us on the lower deck it would also be carrying out scientific work of a secret nature, the ship having been modified to accommodate specialist plant and equipment which had nothing to do with surveying the seabed This was built into a compartment on the upper deck, and a large diesel engine/dynamo providing the electrical energy to operate it was located in a plant-room directly below. Two scientists were on board to instruct and oversee operatives from the engine-room department to run the plant continuously whilst at sea, but never less than three miles from the shore.

It puzzled us for months until somebody claimed that one of the scientists had let slip that it was for the production of heavy water, and to bear this out on each of the two visits back to Portsmouth (one of them when the ship was decommissioned) a security van collected a large number of small pressure vessels from the ship.

It is normal for a survey ship to spend weeks at sea performing its normal task, but due to this special project these trips were extended, with visits ashore few and far between. In the twelve months I was on the ship, apart from the one visit back to Portsmouth, where we were fortunate to be given a fourteen days leave, there were only three other occasions when shore leave was available: Londonderry, in Northern Ireland; Lerwick, on the Shetland Islands; and Corvo the smallest island of the Azores. We stayed about ten days in each, the main purpose being to replenish food-stocks, re-fuel, and undertake minor repairs. By the time we pulled into these places the ship's crew were going stir crazy and a few days ashore did every one a bit of good. That is, except the scientists, who on one such occasion I heard moaning about the break to their continuity of production.

Apparently, when re-starting the plant after it had been idle, it took a long time to reach its level of optimum performance.

Trying to relieve the boredom of the long periods spent at sea the ship's doctor took it upon himself to instigate various amusements and activities. He was a young man with a caring attitude, just a year or two older than me. Recently qualified, and on his first ship, he obviously saw his duties not only concerned the health of the crew, but also their welfare.

His biggest venture, with the aid of the wireless operating department, was setting up a radio service broadcasted through the ship's tannoy system. The ship had a reasonable stash of records and his first undertaking was to copy a popular radio show called 'Down Your Way'. In this programme an interviewer would go around a factory, a hospital, or some other interesting place, and get people to talk about their particular job before choosing a record.

The Doc adopted this pattern going into places like the engine room, the P.Os Mess, and other parts of the ship; even onto the bridge where the Captain was interviewed. This programme helped to integrate the crew, for when interviewing someone he not only asked them about the task they were undertaking but also dug into their background. With a crew of only forty-six we soon became to know each other quite well.

Following this he arranged for letters to be sent to wives, parents, or other close relatives of the crew, together with a copy of the ship's record library, inviting them to select a disc and enclose a message. Joan responded (mum had passed the request on to her) choosing the song 'Too Young' sung by 'Jimmy Young'. With a loving message this was a pleasant surprise.

Apart from playing records he gathered around him a small band of contributors to provide a weekly radio show. I volunteered to take part and amongst other things provided an occasional monologue on things that were familiar or topical.

My first rendering concerned the daily issue of rum, (previously written in full when describing the first time I witnessed this event). The monologues always referred to interesting characters amongst the crew.

Just after Christmas 1953 the civilian manager of the NAAFI shop, himself an old thespian, gave us a radio pantomime script of Cinderella. Although not obscene it was rather blue. Written in verse, it was peppered throughout with words and phrases having a double meaning. The doc had his reservations, but the rest of us involved were eager to do it. The captain had previously given a rendition of the 'Farting Contest' which we felt had given licence to material of a risqué nature, so pressing the Doc on this he caved in and agreed to us doing it.

There was about six main characters and a few minor ones, but only enough room around the microphone in the sick bay for four. We each had at least two roles to play, mine being Cinderella, and Baron Stoneybroke.

Chaos ruled. The four of us around a fixed mike each pushing in to speak as the script demanded, whilst at the same time changing our voices which we had adopted for the various characters we were doing. After a lot of practice we were ready to do the broadcast which had been well publicised.

It was an hilarious well written script and proved a big hit, even though we did make all the errors we had tried to avoid; the wrong voice for the wrong part, dropping the mike, background noises. Nevertheless, the captain, although enjoying it, was of the opinion that we had over-stepped the mark and warned the Doc that he was in danger of letting standards slide.

One of the saucy bits he referred to was delivered by me as Cinderella. I had been asked by one of the courtiers, when the slipper was found to be mine, if I would marry the prince, to which I replied in the most effeminate voice I could manage, "To marry him it is my duty, I've seen his dick, and it's a beauty."

The following week I wrote and delivered a parody of 'Brown Boots', a monologue performed on mainstream radio by Stanley Holloway. It went something like this.

> The captain made his rounds today,
> Decks cleared up, gear stowed away.
> It was a posh affair,
> The first lieutenant was also there.
> The master-at-arms led the way,
> Chest swelled out, it made his day.

We'd scrubbed the tables and cleaned the brass,
But our chief stoker, to show his class.
Turned up and made it all a farce,
In brown boots, I ask you, brown boots,
Fancy standing rounds in brown boots.
I must admit he had a nice black tie,
Black fingernails and a nice black eye,
But you can't stand rounds when the captain
   goes by; in brown boots.
And that's why; we gave him the bird,
Until by accident we overheard,
He'd given his black boots to Jimmy Ball,
A stoker who had no boots at all.
So perhaps the captain doesn't mind,
He does like people who are good and kind.
But brown boots, I ask you brown boots.
Fancy standing rounds in brown boots.
That's why we had to be so rude to him.
That's why we never said "How do," to him.
We didn't know, he didn't say,
He'd give his other boots away.
But some day up at Heavens Gate,
Old Dutchy, all nerves will stand and wait.
Till an angel says, "Come in mate,
Where's your brown boots."

The following day the first lieutenant sent for me, and on reporting to his office I found the captain with him who asked me whether the chief stoker was actually wearing brown boots.

I was surprised that they thought it possible and decided to string them along. "Funny you both missed it," I said

They both looked at each other, but before they could question me further I said, "Of course he didn't. Blimey, you two can spot a speck of dust from ten yards; you'd hardly miss seeing a pair of brown boots on the chief stoker."

They both looked relieved and started laughing, and then the captain said, "Off you go then, get working on your next ditty." Apparently, he listened to every one of our broadcasts.

I had hardly stepped back into the mess when someone told me that the chief stoker wanted to see me.

Popping my head round his office door, I observed him sitting at his desk and said, "Hello Dutchy, (his surname was Holland), did you want to see me."

"I certainly do, come in here." He sounded angry.

I entered and sat down on a chair.

"Who told you to sit down? Stand up. I'm not happy with you."

I stood up.

"Why the bloody hell did you say I was wearing brown boots to stand rounds?"

"It was only a bit of fun. A little piece done tongue in cheek; did you listen to it?"

"No, I found out about it when the subby (sub lieutenant) sounded me out on behalf of the captain, he actually believes that I was wearing brown boots."

"He doesn't now, I put him straight."

"You've spoken to the Captain."

"Yes. He was pleased no end with my little charade and the part you played in it. I think he was disappointed when I told him that you were wearing pusser black shoes."

A few minutes later I was sitting back in the chair chatting amiably to him, and when I told him that I would be characterising someone new each week and that my next victim would be the master-at-arms he became quite enthusiastic.

As promised, the following week I featured the master-at-arms in a parody of the well known comedy piece called 'The Tale of Sonia Snell' written and performed by Cyril Fletcher.

It related to him going to the heads and falling asleep whilst sitting on the toilet. It started like this:

> Of the Master at Arms, I will tell,
> Concerning an accident he befell.
> It happened last Friday when work was done,
> And he felt the need for a number one.
> Unfortunately, he was unaquainted,
> With the toilet seat which was newly painted.

It then followed the pattern of Cyril Fletcher's ode where he gets his bum stuck to the seat, and his cries for help bringing all and sundry to the scene. Numerous methods were used to free him without success until an E.R.A. managed to unbolt the seat. The master-at-arms, now free, albeit with the seat still attached, then bent over to allow the doctor to examine him. With everyone looking on the following few lines finalised the poem:

The captain said, "Upon my word,
Could anything be more absurd?
Have any of you, I implore,
Seen anything like this before?"
"Yes, said the subby, unashamed,
Frequently, but never framed."

Making the master-at-arms the subject of my comedy sketch went down really well with the crew. Responsible for discipline he was held in awe; respect, tinged with fear. However, he was not lacking a sense of humour and took it good spirit.

My relationship with the doctor was generally to do with the recreational side of things but on one occasion it was necessary to seek his professional advice. It was my birthday, an occasion when it is customary for your messmates to give you 'sippers' or even 'gulpers' of their rum ration. I was not around when the grog was being dished out being otherwise occupied in the boiler-room doing the forenoon watch, but when I came into the mess there was a jug waiting for me, half filled with rum.

Being quite popular with the seamen and others on the ship, they also had rum waiting for me, and so did the petty officer I was on watch with. It was quite a lot of rum and I drank it with relish whilst eating my dinner.

In the afternoon, after exchanging pleasantries with all and sundry, and generally enjoying the afterglow that the alcohol had given me, I slung my hammock and climbed into it.

When I woke up a few hours later I was in agony. My back felt like it was broken, and it was only with some difficulty that I managed to clamber from my hammock. Still hung over, and addressing anyone who cared to listen, I said, "My back's killing me."

One of four ratings sitting at the table playing cards replied, "You had better see the Doc."

Staggering through the door to the sick bay a few minutes later the doctor on seeing me in a distressed state said, "How are you feeling?"

"Terrible," I moaned. "I feel like I've been kicked in the back by a horse."

"You're lucky to be alive."

I looked at him quizzically.

"Hasn't anyone told you what happened?"

"No," I said.

"You fell through the hatch into the tiller flat."

I stood there in a post-drunken-trance; the consequences of this piece of information had not really sunk in.

"Well!" The Doctor said. "You've walked in here so I don't think you've broken any bones. The only thing I can give you is pain killers."

"The trouble is, I'm on watch in two hours and I'll never get down that ladder into the boiler room. I was wondering if you could put me on excused duties."

"I can't do it."

"Why not, you can see the state I'm in."

"I can, but it was self-inflicted. Not only that, you were drunk. If I authorise you to be excused duties, which in normal circumstances I would, I have to inform the Captain. I would not lie to him and he would want to know where you got enough alcohol to get in the state you were in. You know that it is against the rules to give away rum or receive it from others and you would be put on a charge, together with anyone else who was known to have given you any. Now, do you still want to be excused duties?"

It was obvious to me that this was out of the question and recognised the favour he was doing me by not reporting the incident, so I thanked him and left.

I was unaware of just how much I owed him until I was back in the mess and heard the full story. Apparently, soon after getting into my hammock I got out again to relieve my bladder, and made my way to the heads. This took me past an open hatch above the tiller control room, a chamber in the bowels of the ship some twelve feet below. Although the hatchway had a heavy security rope attached to stanchions mounted at each corner I managed, in my drunken state, to tumble through it.

The doctor was called to the scene and after examining me for signs of any serious damage, arranged for me to be hauled up in a Robinson Stretcher. Strictly following the rules he should have reported the incidence there and then.

Due on the plates in the boiler-room at six o-clock for the first dog-watch I was in agony just moving about, let alone climbing up and down the steep ladder. How I would get through the coming days was of real concern.

Normally, boiler-room watch-keeping is a doddle, just keeping an eye on the gauges and changing over the burners now and then, with a quick clean in shale oil, but these boilers were a different proposition, they had been converted from coal to oil and needed constant attention due to clinkering-up. The clinker removed had then to be taken up the ladder and onto the upper deck in metal bins and thrown overboard. The thought of doing this filled me with dread.

Within a few minutes of arriving in the boiler-room, Lofty Ball, the petty officer I shared the watch with, could see that I was incapable of any of the tasks expected of me and undertook everything that had to be done. Just a year or two older than me he had been streamlined for rapid promotion, deservedly so, but unlike a lot of those who had been fast forwarded, jumped up and full of their own self-importance, he was a naturally good bloke. He carried me in this way for over a fortnight.

When at sea the boilers provided steam power both to propel the ship and to drive turbines to generate electricity for lighting and other uses. In harbour the boilers were shut down and the electricity generated by a large diesel engine. On one occasion, when the ship was moored for a two week period in Londonderry, I was tending the diesel engine in shifts of 'four hours on, four hours off' over a twenty-four hour period. This was followed by twenty four hours leave. On the alternate shifts was a friend of mine called 'Snoz' Durant who I enjoyed shore leave with when off duty.

Watch-keeping on the diesels was most boring, especially during the night shifts. There was nothing to do except observe and take hourly readings of the few temperature gauges. The engines were maintained efficiently by E.R.As and very rarely went wrong. This led Snoz and me to come up with a plan to cut down on the hours we spent on the night watches and so enable us to feel more refreshed the following day when on our extended shore leave.

It was a simple arrangement, whoever was doing the middle watch (midnight to 4am) would fill the log-book up until the end of his watch, but get turned into his hammock one hour before his watch ended. The other, doing the morning watch, (4am to 8am), would arrange for the duty seaman on the gangway to give his hammock a shake at around five-o-clock. This way, both of us were getting nearly five hours sleep.

Of course, in doing this we were taking a huge risk. If found to be absent from our place of duty, or if found sleeping on watch, we could expect to be punished severely. To be absent from our place of duty and found sleeping in our hammocks we could expect to have the book thrown at us. I shudder now to think what the consequences could have been.

All went well until part-way through the second week. I had the morning watch and as usual had arranged a call for five-o-clock, but at half-past-four I was roughly aroused from my slumbers by an agitated seaman.

"Stokes! Stokes!" He blurted out. "There's loads of smoke coming from the engine room."

Wide awake immediately, I clambered from my hammock and fell onto the table beneath. Slipping into my boots, and donning my overalls on the run, I stumbled to the engine room. On opening the hatch I choked on the thick suffocating smoke which belched out. Without a second thought I slid down the ladder onto the plates to find that the whole side of the large diesel engine was glowing cherry red. I immediately closed it down, which plunged the engine room and all other areas of the ship into darkness.

A quick assessment of the problem led me to examine the cooling water system, which I found difficult to reach in the gloom. On lifting the lid of the supply tank, to check the level of water, I was scalded when wet steam spurted out onto my chest. Not too badly I am glad to say.

With the air-extract system in the engine room now switched off the smoke was taking some time to clear, making it hard for me to breathe, so grabbing the engine room log book I went up and joined the seaman at the gangway.

"Have you sorted it," he said.

"No. I'm in big trouble," I replied. "The diesel's burnt out."

"Is that your fault?" He knew of the arrangement I had with Snoz.

"No. Not all my fault, but at the moment I'm holding the baby."

"What are you going to do; only I've got to enter a time in the log when the power was switched off?"

It was not right to involve him in my problem, so I said, "Time it as now. I'll let the smoke clear them wake the chief artificer."

It was still dark when some time later, after filling in the log book to make it look as favourable towards us as I could, I went to the chief artificer's cabin and woke him up.

Shaking him by the shoulder I said," Chief, I've had to close down the diesel."

Bleary eyed he raised himself on one elbow. "Why?" He asked.

"It was running hot," I replied.

After a short deliberation he said, "Get the duty P.O. and light up number one boiler. I'll be down in the engine room shortly, let me know when you've got steam up and I'll start the generator."

The duty P.O. was not too pleased, but got out of his bunk right away and joined me in the boiler-room, where I had already started the lighting-up procedure.

When we had a sufficient head of steam the P.O. informed the chief artificer using the voice pipe, a tube which ran between the boiler room and engine room.

Not long after, we heard the whirr of the turbo-generator as it started up, quickly followed by the ship's lighting.

"WELLARD!" The voice tube was belled out at the end with a hinged cover into which a whistling device was fitted. Blowing into the open tube the receiver was alerted that a message was coming through. The chief artificer dispensed with this preliminary and bawled my name down the open pipe with enough fury to blow the lid off and be heard from the other side of the boiler-room.

Speaking back into the voice tube, I said, "It's me chief, do you want something."

"Get down here. Immediately."

Reaching the plates in the engine-room he was waiting for me at the bottom of the ladder.

"You're in big trouble. You never relieved Snoz at four-o-clock; the engine was left unattended for some time before that - hours before I should think."

"No chief, you're wrong there. I relieved him at four o'clock on the dot."

"You're a liar, come here." He led me to the desk where the log book was kept and pointed to a blackboard above which was used for notes relating to engineering matters. There in bold letters was written 'Bottle of beer in the desk, compliments of George,' and signed off – 'Snoz'

He opened the lid of the desk and pulled out a pint bottle of light-ale.

"If you had relieved Snoz, he would have no reason to leave that note; another thing, you would have drank that beer and wiped the blackboard clean. Go and get Snoz down here."

Quickly up the ladder and into the mess I shook Snoz and enlightened him of all the facts. We quickly decided to stick to my claim that I relieved him at four o'clock and play it by ear.

Back in the engine-room the chief artificer had been examining the diesel and the log book. Addressing both of us when we stepped on the plates, he said, "This engine's bloody red hot and it didn't get this hot in an hour, yet the log book shows regular temperatures up until four o'clock." Turning to Snoz he continued, "Now you tell me what time you went off watch?"

"Four o'clock," Snoz replied.

"Look, don't take me for a fool, you left before being relieved or you wouldn't have left that message about the beer."

"Well, you know what it's like chief, handing the watch over at four in the morning the last thing on your mind is small talk. All you're thinking about is your hammock."

Shaking his head in a disbelieving manner the chief turned to me and said, "O.K. Why didn't you drink the beer and wipe the message off the board? Surely you look at the board to see if there are any messages, anyway?"

"I don't usually go to the desk until I put in my first hourly readings. Snoz would have told me if anything was wrong." It was a weak answer and I knew it.

"I don't know what's been going on here but one thing I am sure of is that you never relieved Snoz on the plates. That diesel would never have got that hot in your watch alone."

His diatribe continued for several more minutes before he dismissed us with the threat that he would be charging us with dereliction of duties when the engine had been stripped down and the total extent of the damage was known.

Things looked bleak for Snoz and me, until later in the forenoon when I went down the engine-room to see what progress was being made in repairing the damage we had done. The engine was stripped down and working on it was a young artificer.

"You certainly made a mess of this," he moaned. "You let it run so hot that all the white metal bearings ran."

"Sorry for that mate," I said. "But I'm going to be paying for it when the chief tiffy decides to charge me."

"He's not going to put you on a charge."

"Of course he is, he made that quite clear."

"He's changed his mind, because if he charged you, he would have to charge me. It's partly my fault and he wouldn't want to do that. Not to one of his team."

"How's that?" I said

He then explained. "Well, the day before, during the afternoon watch the water pump packed in and I was detailed to repair it, but it was a long job and I had a date with a girl I met ashore....."

He went on to tell me that instead of working on the job until it was completed he connected an auxiliary pump, and hose, to circulate sea water around the engine, a standard emergency routine. Unfortunately, the filter on the suction end of the pipe got blocked up with seaweed.

Early that afternoon, just before we were ready to go ashore, Snoz and I were called into the chief artificer's office.

"You're lucky to be standing here in front of me instead of being before the first lieutenant with your caps off," he said. "I understand that you know what happened, but that doesn't mean you weren't to blame. If you had been on the plates all the time, keeping an eye on the gauges as you were supposed to, you would have noticed the unusual rise in temperatures and shut the engine down before any damage was done. I know what you were up to. You're bloody fools, the pair of you, taking a chance like that, you could have set light to the ship."

Snoz and I stood there like the fools he said we were, tactfully not saying anything.

Continuing, he said, "It didn't go unnoticed, the shut-down was logged by the quartermaster and I've got to explain to the captain what it was all about. For all our sakes I hope he doesn't dig too deep. Whatever happens, I'll be keeping an eye on you two, and so will the chief stoker who knows all about your part in this little escapade. "

On dismissing us his parting shot was, "Oh, by the way, tell George Dunnlowes that he could have been lifting his cap as well, it's a serious offence smuggling drink aboard." He added, with a sardonic smile, "I've confiscated it."

Needless to say we undertook our watch-keeping duties most conscientiously after that.

Apart from this incident I had kept a clean sheet on board the Challenger, although there was an occasion when the doctor had reason to put me on a minor charge, together with George Dunnlowes.

George had been confined to the sick-bay with influenza, and whilst in there had thumbed through a medical book which included pictures of facial disfigurements.

When he was discharged and back on the mess he was telling me about this, and making particular reference to one illustration which showed a man with an extremely large proboscis which he claimed looked the spitting image of the first lieutenant.

"I can't believe that," I said. "I know the first lieutenant's got a big nose but nothing like you're describing."

"When the doc goes up for his lunch, we'll slip into the sick-bay and I'll show you," he said.

Not long after, the doctor left his surgery and we slipped in there.

George was about to lift the book from the shelf when the doctor walked back in, obviously having forgotten something.

Taken aback at finding us in there, he said, "What's this then? What are you doing in here?"

Neither of us answered, not knowing what to say.

"It's not drugs, is it? You're not looking for drugs?"

"No Sir!" We both piped up together.

"Well you had better have a bloody good reason for being in here." He was very angry.

George spoke up, "I was going to show Rex a picture in one of your books."

"Which one?" the doctor asked.

George got the book down from the shelf, opened it up to the picture in question, and showed it to him.

"Is there a reason for showing Rex this?"

George, for obvious reasons, could not say that he thought it looked like the first lieutenant, said, "No, it was just a laugh."

"I don't know whether to take you seriously George," the doctor said. "This business with the book could be a blind, an excuse to distract me from the real reason why you are in here."

"No Sir," I protested. "George is telling the truth."

The doctor stood there for a few seconds looking at us like a couple of naughty schoolboys. "Well. You know that this is a serious matter and I should report it to the captain, but I'll give you the choice of that, or accepting my punishment. Which is it to be?"

Seeing George nod, I said, "We'll take your punishment."

"Alright, come back here at five o'clock."

Back in the mess we conjectured on what our punishment would be. We both came to the conclusion that it must involve soap and water – cleaning the deck, or the heads in the sick bay.

Surprise! Surprise! When we reported back, the doctor had a wry smile upon his face, and a small glass of nasty brown coloured medicine for each of us.

It was vile, leaving a bitter taste in the mouth that was hard to get rid of, probably a mixture of quinine and cascara.

Back in the mess we fell about laughing at the absurdity of it, but we had to agree the doctor had had the last laugh.

H.M.S. Challenger returned to Portsmouth in early October and decommissioned the following month. We were all given extensive leave to compensate for the long periods at sea and during this time Joan and I got married. The date was 10th of October 1953.

My next posting was to H.M.S. Miner 3. It was a very small ship previously used for mine sweeping but now utilised in laying down boom defences. (These are wire nets strung across harbour entrances or mouths of important water ways to make it difficult for enemy ships, or submarines, to enter).

The early months of 1954 were spent on various small jobs along the south coast until June when the captain informed us that the ship was proceeding to Autbea in Scotland where it was to lay a boom defence network at Loch Ewe. In carrying out this operation a motor boat was necessary to assist and I was to be part of its crew with responsibility for control and maintenance of the engine. P.O. (Tubby) Watkins, the coxswain, a man with a lot of sea time under his belt; Johnno, a naval surveyor; and able seaman Blakey; made up the rest of the crew.

Arrangements were made for us to leave the next day and travel by train to Gairloch, the site of a large naval base in Scotland, where we were to pick up a motor boat from a depot ship moored there. Early next morning found us on Portsmouth Dockyard Station with our baggage – hammocks and kit-bags.

Soon after arrival at the depot ship we were shown to our boat. Expecting to find a motor-cutter, or a small launch, we were shocked to see an L.C.A. (Landing Craft Assault) moored there. Over thirty feet long, it is a barge-like boat with a shallow draft and having a drop-down ramp at the front. Its primary purpose was to ferry soldiers from transport ships to enemy held shores. On newsreels showing troops storming the Normandy beaches in 1944 dozens of them could be seen.

The small engine-room at the rear of the boat held two high powered Ford V8 engines driving twin propellers, with a seat centrally placed behind them from which all controls could be easily reached. Access to this space was through a round hatch directly above the seat and also by means of an opening directly in front which led to the hold.

We were assured that the craft was in good working order and after a dummy run we set off on our journey along the Firth of Clyde, aiming for Crinan where we were to meet the Miner 3, but not before a young naval lieutenant had joined us. Chatting to him we found out that he was at a loose end waiting for final instructions before taking up a post as an attaché in Belgium. In the meantime it seemed that he had been given the job of nursemaid to us and the boat.

It was a beautiful sunny day without a cloud in the sky, the water was as still as a millpond and the views all around of breathtaking beauty. I was able to leave the engine on full throttle and join the others sitting on the side of the boat; excepting Tubby who was in the conning tower steering.

The conning tower was at a raised level shielded by armour plating and located at the prow of the boat alongside the ramp. From this he could relay instructions to the engine room.

It was a long, but pleasant, journey through the inland waters around the Isle of Bute and by early evening we reached Airdrishaig.

The officer left us as soon as we moored up to look for hotel accommodation. No such provision was being made for us, so before we went ashore for food and drink, we slung our hammocks across the hold, attaching their cleats to the gunwales. He had however, given Tubby a days victualling allowance for us and we made our way to the nearest bar to make good use of it.

Having fed well and with our bellies full of beer we returned to the boat and were happy to sleep underneath the stars that warm night.

Our next leg of the journey took us through the Crinan canal which cuts through the Kintyre peninsular, and after using the ablutions ashore we set off. The canal was only nine miles long but had fourteen locks to negotiate which gave me some concern,

259

for on the previous evening when approaching the wharf I had found some difficulty when trying to put the engine into reverse gear. The mechanism giving drive to the starboard propeller kept jumping out of gear.

Sure enough, when we reached the first lock this happened, and the only way I could keep it in reverse gear was to physically hold the control lever in position.

The locks came along frequently and on entering each one there was the need to reverse as often as there was the need to go forward. The pointer on the dial in front of me, operated by the coxswain, was constantly moving from the green area (ahead) to the red area (reverse). At the same time a bell would ring with each instruction to draw my attention to it. With separate controls for each engine, and having to operate the gear sticks forward – neutral – reverse each time, and hold the faulty one in manually, I had my work cut out.

It was mid-afternoon by the time we passed through the last of the locks taking us onto the plateau at the top and during the preceding time I had seen each of the others, through the opening directly in front of me, take the opportunity to help themselves to bread and cheese which was laid out on a board in the hold. I was ravenous, and when two 'dings' indicated a change to HALF AHEAD I stood up and looked through the hatch to see a long stretch of canal with not a lock in sight, so after giving it more throttle I nipped into the hold to avow myself of the platter.

I had barely cut two slices off the loaf of bread when I heard 'ding-ding-ding' which indicated full speed. I thought 'Blimey, Tubby's in a hurry.'

Diving back into the engine room I gave both engines full throttle before returning to the task of making myself a sandwich.

I had barely moved out of my seat when 'ding-ding-ding' sounded again. I stood up and looked forward to tell Tubby that I was giving him all I had when I saw that we were approaching a low bridge at a considerable rate of knots.

Ducking back down I looked at the dial, which I should have done before, to see that the pointer was in the red section showing FULL ASTERN.

I immediately cut both throttles, but in my haste, when putting the engines into reverse, the starboard engine cut out, and before I could give full throttle to the port engine we had hit the bridge.

There was an almighty crash with the boat coming to a sudden halt.

I sat there for a few seconds, the realisation of what I had done sinking in, but having no other option than to face the music I climbed out of the hatch.

The small conning tower where the steering wheel was located, and where Tubby would have been standing, was severely buckled. Tubby would have been dead or badly injured if he had been in it at the time, but I could see him on the shore alongside the lieutenant in discussion with a civilian who turned out to be the keeper of the bridge. Blakey told me later, that if he had not seen it with his own eyes he would never have believed that Tubby could have performed the athletic achievement required in getting out of a space which he found difficulty getting into.

I jumped onto the bank to join them and was immediately questioned by Tubby, "What the hell happened? When I rang down for full astern you increased the revs."

"No, I didn't increase the revs," I was lying to save my skin. "I put it into astern but the bloody starboard engine packed in. You know the problems I've been having."

"After I rang down for full astern, we went faster," Tubby insisted.

"No," I said, "What probably happened was that it seemed to go faster as you neared the bridge."

"Don't take me for a bloody fool Rex, I've been driving boats like these around for years, you upped the revs; you know it and I know it."

At that point the Lieutenant butted in. "Leave all that for now and let's sort out this bridge, there will be plenty of time to discuss the whys and wherefores later. Before I hand the boat over I will have to write a full report and for that I want a damn good reason for this debacle from both of you."

It was a swing-bridge, the bottom of which was just above the level of the canal bank, and being of a fabricated steel construction showed little sign of damage. If the swing of the bridge had been going away from us we would merely have knocked it open, but the swing was towards us and the weight of the heavy boat had driven the free end off its concrete base and wedged it deep into the soil beyond.

Using a couple of six foot scaffold poles, we managed, over the next half hour, to get the bridge back on its base, and the metal plate of the conning tower fashioned such that Tubby could get back into it. Of course, to our embarrassment the spectacle brought an audience of a few dozen spectators from the long line of boats now queuing up behind us.

We reached Crinan without further ado and tied up alongside the wall in the basin, a mooring area before passing through the last lock leading to the sea.

The officer and the coxswain went off to find out where the Miner 3 was moored and surprised us when they came back some time later with the news that it was still in Plymouth, holed up there due to bad weather. Bathed in sunshine as we were, and had been since arriving in Scotland, this was hard to believe. Furthermore, they informed us that we no longer had to sleep in the boat whilst we waited as they had arranged accommodation for us all.

The officer was to stay in the ultra-posh Crinan Hotel, whilst billets were found for the rest of us; Tubby in a cottage close by, Blakey, Johnno, and me, in a large house a few hundred yards away on a hill overlooking the sea.

It was early evening by the time we settled in and changed into our best uniforms by which time our host, a pleasant middle aged lady, had prepared us a nice hot meal.

Afterwards, we strolled down to the hotel and into its public bar where Blakey was getting a round in when Tubby arrived. After comparing digs, the subject of our mishap in the canal came up, and Tubby, knowing that I had increased speed before the crash, kept pressing this point trying to make me confess.

He asked Blakey and Johnno but they were non-committal, both saying that they were looking straight ahead and not aware of any change in the speed.

Finally, I said, "Look Tubby, I'm not changing my story, but it makes little difference to you what I say. All the others will

262

agree, including me, that you gave the signals to slow down, and reverse, just as you say you did, so that puts you in the clear with nothing to worry about. The onus is clearly on me so there's no point in you pressing home this business about the boat going faster. Come on, drink up and I'll get another round in."

I was at the bar when the officer came through from the lounge in a jolly mood and paid for the four pints of beer that I had just ordered, including one for himself. He then joined us at our table and stayed long enough to be sociable without overdoing the camaraderie. On parting he said, "We'll chat about that nasty business in the canal tomorrow, let us just relax tonight."

The next morning, after a large fried breakfast the three of us met Tubby at the boat, and what a sorry sight it looked. Apart from the twisted sheet metal around the conning tower the ramp was badly buckled.

We spent the time until noon giving the boat a thorough clean throughout and was just finishing when the lieutenant turned up with a notebook in his hand which he tapped with a finger. "Let's do this in the bar, shall we?"

As usual he bought the first round of drinks, which he did both lunchtime and evening for all of the nine days we were there, then sitting around a table he asked each of us in turn to give a statement which he wrote down verbatim. Tubby, to my relief, just told what he had done, without reference to the increase in speed.

The following seven days waiting for the Miner 3 to arrive was a treat, an unexpected holiday. The sun continued to shine and although we reported to the Coxswain each day at the boat we were immediately dismissed as there was nothing to do.

The food and lodgings were first class; we swam and dived in the lock, sunbathed and played ball games on the beach, climbed a nearby mountain, and just generally enjoyed the break.

Each lunchtime and evening we would drink in the bar and socialize with the regulars, and that was the only time we would see the lieutenant. He would pop in, buy us a drink, have a chat, and then slip back into the resident's lounge. We wondered whether he was claiming for it on expenses, if not, and he was paying for it out of his own pocket, he was not only very generous, but also rich.

There was one black day, or so we first thought. It was on a Sunday; when we went to the bar, although open, the barman would not serve us a drink.

"It's against the law in Scotland," he said. "On the Sabbath I can only serve customers who have travelled at least three miles."

Seeing how brassed-off we looked, he wrote the name of a village pub, on a piece of paper having the hotel crest on it, and told us how to get there.

We had a quandary. The pubs were only open for two hours and the walk there would take us about an hour. Was it worth it? You bet it was, so we set off immediately, unfortunately without Tubby who declined. But as he said, with him setting the pace we would be lucky to get there before closing time.

There was a silver lining though, having travelled the three miles back from the village pub the barman in the Crinan Hotel considered that we qualified to drink in the bar that evening. He gave a nod and a wink to us when he served Tubby.

All good things come to an end and so it was for us when the Miner 3 arrived – holiday over. We thanked the landlady for putting us up, and for putting up with us, and we let the lieutenant buy us another pint before the ship arrived in the afternoon.

The Captain of the Miner 3 was none too pleased when he saw the state of the L.C.A. but he accepted the report from the lieutenant without commenting, more concerned at that moment in time to get underway so that we reached Tobermory before dusk.

Things went fairly smooth at first, as we followed in the wake of our mother-ship. That was until we entered the Sound of Mull when the sea became choppy and water came into the boat through the damaged ramp. With Tubby at the wheel, and me keeping an eye on the engines, it was down to Blakey and Johnno to take turns on the hand-operated bilge pump, but the amount coming in was too much for it to handle and before long the hold was about a foot deep in water. To keep the water level down, two seamen were transferred from the Miner 3 with buckets to assist in baling out. This continued until we reached Tobermory.

During the next two days we continued in a similar fashion up the west coast of Scotland stopping at Oban and Malaig before we reached Autbea and within a few days we were helping the Miner 3 to pinpoint the exact position for the boom; our purpose for being there.

We would put Johnno ashore with his theodolite at fixed points of reference, and in liaison with the ship he would help plot the position where the boom had to be laid. It sometimes proved difficult to find a suitable place due to the spiteful shoreline, and on one occasion when trying to land him on a small island, Tubby, after spotting an inlet which he considered wide enough to enter, went in slowly, and stern first. It was certainly wide enough, but not deep enough, for soon after entry there was a terrible rattling noise, and sitting with my back close to the stern it vibrated up my spine. I knew straight away that the propellers had taken a serious hammering and stopped both engines immediately.

Popping my head out of the hatch above me, I said to Tubby, "I don't think that done the propellers much good."

To my surprise, Tubby seemed little bothered, "It's probably not too bad," he replied.

We did not have to wait too long before we found out just how bad it was.

Drawing alongside the Miner 3 later that day after completing our task, a rope being thrown to secure us inadvertently fell into the water and snagged itself around one of our propellers. With the engine stopped, and the crew of the ship looking on, I volunteered to dive overboard and try to unravel it. This was accepted by the captain, so I stripped to my underpants and plunged in, but the rope was so tightly wound around the shaft of the propeller that after many futile attempts I had to admit defeat.

The captain then gave the order to lift the boat's stern clear of the water using the capstan mounted on the ship, normally used to manoeuvre the boom. Whilst this was happening, Tubby, Johnno, Blakey, and I, stood on the jetty.

When the propellers were fully exposed they were both shown to be badly mutilated.

"Good God!" The captain cried out, "How the hell did they get into that state?"

Tubby replied, not wishing to be held responsible for it, "Probably our mishap in the canal, Sir."

I was about to protest, knowing that this would place more blame on me, when a loud authoritative voice from someone standing on the jetty, bellowed to the captain, "The boat's a wreck. Let's get it up on the ramp and see just what the damage is. Someone's going to answer for this."

I turned around to see a naval officer with three gold rings on his sleeve; a commander. He outranked the captain of the Miner 3, a lieutenant-commander, and it turned out that he was in charge of the shore base there, together with all operations associated with it.

With Johnno, Blakey, and me, back onboard, Tubby drove the boat to the other side of the jetty where a wide concrete ramp sloped into the sea. Its purpose was to haul the boom in when necessary for replacement or repair. The commander was there to oversee the operation.

Tubby gently put the prow of the boat onto the ramp, upon which, I stopped the engine and climbed on top of the engine housing to observe the operation, the others joined me. A cable was attached to cleats on each side of the boat and a ring in the middle linked it to a long single cable attached to a powerful capstan housed in a hanger at the top of the ramp.

The capstan was started and gently turned until the wire was taut, and then taking the load it pulled the boat slowly up the ramp. Being a landing craft it had metal-clad runners on the bottom to bear the brunt when running onto a beach; these were now grating on the concrete, causing sparks, and making an alarming sound.

"That's no good," The commander shouted to some civilian workers, "put rollers underneath." Then pointing to some long wooden logs about a foot in diameter, he added, "They'll do."

The first log was rolled into place and held firm by the workers whilst the capstan was operated once again. The front of the boat lifted onto and over the log which rolled to the centre of the boat as it moved forward. We balanced with some difficulty on top of the engine housing whilst this procedure was going on, when suddenly, a loud noise of splintering wood, and the boat dropping from beneath our feet, drew our eyes into the hold where we saw part of the log burst right through the thick ply-wood, which surprisingly, the bottom of the boat was made of. The steel rim of the runners on the bottom of the boat had cut the log into three parts. It was the middle part that we were now staring at.

The commander, like all the rest of us involved, was temporarily stunned, but like all good leaders of men he quickly regained control of the situation and after ordering us off the boat instructed the base workers to drag it up on its runners regardless of any further damage.

Tubby nudged me and said, "I don't think we'll hear any more." He was right, we did not.

We returned by train the next day to Portsmouth and rejoined the Miner 3 when it returned. In the interim I was found accommodation in H.M.S. Vernon where it was based.

Soon after it returned, the Miner 3 was loaned to Pinewood Studio to be used as a German E- Boat in the film 'Above Us the Waves' which was about the sinking of the Tirpitz, a German battleship.

There were many well known actors in the film with John Mills having the leading role. Michael Medwin and John Gregson played two members of the crew on our boat and proved quite entertaining with their stories, and they could certainly hold their drink when we joined them ashore in the pub.

The Miner 3, in its disguise as a German 'E' Boat, left for Jersey where certain scenes wee being filmed close by in the English Channel. The crew being used as extras were donned out in German uniforms.

Although I would have enjoyed the trip, and possibly a bit-part as an extra in the movie, I had a more pressing and important engagement at the Mother's Hospital in Clapton where Joan had been rushed to give birth to our first child, a beautiful baby boy.

Some scenes relating to the aspects of the film concerning the Royal Navy were shot in H.M.S. Vernon, and on one occasion I was walking through the base when I saw an officer coming

267

toward me with three rings on his arm which told me that he was a commander. On passing, and following normal service procedure, I turned my head towards him and saluted. He saluted back, which was not unexpected until I noticed it was John Mills heading for the film location.

Bloody cheek! At some time or another I was told that you salute the uniform and not the man, even so, I would not have saluted an actor, even one as famous as John Mills. However, I found it amusing, and chuckling to myself, mused about his mindset and concluded that he was so immersed in his role that as he walked through the boatyard he actually thought of himself as a naval commander. Whether the irony of it registered with him I will never know, but a smile, nor a wink, came my way.

I was not the only one to be duped; I had hardly walked twenty yards more when I met another rating who indignantly blurted out, "I've just saluted John Mills!"

Most ratings will cross the road to avoid saluting an officer, but not paying them this respect can result in a reprimand. I had the misfortune to upset an officer when failing to salute him whilst crossing the parade ground of the Royal Naval Barracks in Portsmouth. When crossing the parade ground during working hours it is obligatory to march at the double (moderate jog) and on this occasion an officious gunnery officer was reprimanding a rating for walking across, and seeing him thus engaged I dispensed with a salute when passing.

"You!" He cried. "Come back here."

I knew instinctively that he was addressing me so I turned around, doubled back, and stood directly in front of him.

"Stand there I'll deal with you in a moment," he said, addressing me. Then turning to the other rating he gave him a dressing down and ordered him to double backwards and forwards across the large parade ground ten times.

"Off you go," he finally said to him. "and don't let me catch you strolling across the parade ground again."

Turning to me he asked. "Why didn't you salute me when you doubled past?"

"I could see that you was busy, Sir," I replied.

"I was not too busy to receive a salute, but I will excuse you this time. Now off you go."

I had hardly gone two yards when he brought me to a halt and ordered me back again.

"What do you do when you are dismissed by an officer?"

It took me a few seconds before the penny dropped. "Salute, Sir."

"And what do you do when confronted by an officer?"

"Salute, Sir," I repeated.

"Then why didn't you salute when I dismissed you, and when I brought you back?"

"I forgot, Sir."

"In that case I must take steps to ensure that you don't forget again. Come with me."

He then marched me at the double across the parade ground to the master-at-arms office adjacent to the main gates. I assumed it was to charge me, but no, he placed me in front of a full length mirror fixed to the side of the building which was there for sailors to check their dress before going ashore.

I was made to stand there saluting myself in the mirror for the next half-hour on view to everybody in the barracks, and many passers by in the street.

I looked and felt a prize idiot.

A few weeks before Christmas the crew of the Miner 3, all fifteen of us, were invited to Pinewood Studios where we spent the day being taken around, and shown rushes of the film. I was amazed to see a full sized model of the Tirpitz sinking in a giant tank of water. Obviously, it was a construction of the stern only, but projecting, as it was, forty-five degrees out of the water and rising high into the roof of a large hangar, it was an impressive sight.

To finish the day off they put on a banquet for us in the evening with many of the film stars attending. John Mills was amongst them and I politely asked him if he was comfortable offering up salutes when he was not a bonafide naval officer. He explained to me that he never initiated the procedure, pointing out that he only returned a salute after he was saluted and felt it rude not to do so.

Soon after that in early 1955 I was drafted back into H.M.S. Victory in preparation for my demob, and by mid-March I was in Civvy Street.

Appendix 1

Statues:
Standing on the pavement one child spun each of the other children around in turn such that they were propelled several feet away into the road where they took up an unusual pose and stayed as still as a statue. If and as they moved they would be ruled out by the spinner, the last one in being the winner.

Kerb and Wall:
A running race forwards and backwards across the road. Starting with backs to the wall on one side of the road half of the children ran first to the kerb then back to the wall; then across the road to the wall on the far side and back to the starting point. The other half would reverse this procedure running for the wall on the far side first, and then the kerb. A race would embrace several crossings and the fun would be in the confusion which ensued.

Fairy Steps and Giant Steps:
One child being 'It' would face the wall on one side of the road giving instructions to the other children playing who would be lined up with their backs to the wall on the other side of the road. The instructions would be to take a number of Fairy Steps, or Giant Steps in order of rotation. A Fairy Step would be 'heel to toe' and a stride would be taken for a Giant Step – the first to reach the opposite wall would be the winner and 'It in the next game.

Queenie:
One child being 'It' would throw a ball over his/her head to the other players standing in a random fashion behind, one of which would catch, or gather up the ball and hide it behind their back. The others would stand in a similar fashion with their hands behind their backs and shout 'Ready' at which the thrower of the ball would turn around and guess who held the ball. If wrong he or she would be 'It' again, if correct the ball holder would be 'It'.

Hi Jimmy Knacker:
A game mostly played by boys in two teams. In one team (the horses) the first boy would stoop down with his hands against a wall arching his back as in leap-frog. The next boy would then bend down and place his head between the first boy's legs, and so on until a line of arched backs were formed. The second team would then run and leap-frog in turn onto the arched backs until they were all on board. They would then bounce and jerk up-and-down chanting "Hi Jimmy Knacker. One, Two, Three; Hi Jimmy Knacker, One, Two, Three; Hi Jimmy Knacker, One, Two, Three; All Over! If during this ordeal the 'horses' collapsed the 'riders' would shout, "Weak Horses," and have another go, if not the teams changed places.

Tin Can Copper Man:
A tin-can would be placed on a manhole cover or a circle chalked in the middle of the road (known as the pot) and somebody determined as 'It'-- usually by Ick Ack Ock; otherwise known as Scissors, Rock, and Paper. The can would then be hurled down the street and the player who was 'It' had to collect it, walk backwards and place the can in the pot, during which time the others all scattered and hid. He or she would then try to determine where each was hiding, then run back to the pot and declare the same whilst banging the tin down three times; e.g. "I see John Smith in Mrs Jones doorway, one, two three." When all the players had been brought to the pot the last one found would then be 'It'. However, if someone managed to scramble from his hiding place, grab the can and throw it back down the road, everyone in the pot could run and hide again.

Kingie:
Players formed a circle on a flat surface with their feet spread so that their toes were all touching. A tennis ball was then dropped into the centre of the circle where it rolled to touch someone's foot. That person was then 'It', and after a count of three (to allow the others to run away) hunted them with the ball. Each one hit would join him as a hunter until just one remained.

Releaso:

A robust game played with two teams – the hunters, and the hunted. At the start of the game the hunted ran away to hide within pre-determined boundaries, the hunters then tracked them down, the capture being made by three pats on top of the head. This usually took at least two hunters as resistance was given by the hunted who linked his hands on top of his head which negated the patting, all the time struggling to escape and run away again.

Those captured were then imprisoned in a small open area marked out on the pavement until there were none left to hunt, the teams would then change around; the hunters becoming the hunted. At any time before the last capture was made one of the hunted could run through the area of confinement shouting 'RELEASO!' when all those in there could run away free to hide and evade capture once more.

Cannon:

A ball game played with two teams. A small wicket would be constructed of four pieces of firewood about eight inches long against the bottom of a wall. A member of each team would then take it in turns to throw a ball at the wicket until it totally collapsed. The team responsible for this would then run out and the other team would hunt them with the ball, each one being hit would be eliminated from the game. Simultaneously, the team on the run would be trying to rebuild the wicket to win the game.

Tip-It:

This game was played with two sticks, one about two feet long – such as a child's cricket stump, the other about four inches long/half-inch square tapered at each end with 1, 2, 3, and 4, pencilled on the sides. The small stick was placed half on and half off the edge of the kerb and the large stick then used to hit the overhanging part such that it cart-wheeled through the air landing in the road. You then hit the tip of the small stick which lifted it into the air where you hit it again (if you could) up the street. This you did the as many times as the number faced up on the tapered stick when it first landed. The one hitting it farthest from the starting point was the winner.

Appendix 2

Spotty

Spotty was my chum, he was, a ginger-headed bloke,
An everlasting gas-bag and as stubborn as a moke.
He gave us all the hump he did before it come to war,
By sportin' all 'is bits of French, what no-one asked him for.
He says to me 'old son' he says, 'you won't have 'arf a chance,
When I gets in conversation with them demerselles of France.'
I says to 'im 'you close yer face,' he says 'all right, bong swore,
Don't 'urt yourself mong sher amy,' then 'so long! Oh re-vore!'
When we got our marching orders you can bet we wasn't slow,
A-singing, 'Tipperary! It's a long, long way to go.'

On the transport 'ow he swanked it, with 'is parley vooing airs,
Till I nearly knocked 'is 'ead off when he called me 'mal de
mares'.
When we landed, what a beano, how them Frenchies laughed
and cried,
And I see old Spotty swelling fit to bust 'iself with pride,
He was blowin' of 'em kisses and singing 'Vive la France,'
Till the Sergeant-Major copped 'im, then he says, 'Kel mauvay
chance!'
But we didn't get no waitin', where we went nobody knows,
And it wasn't like the fighting that you sees in picture shows.
We 'ad days of 'ell together, till they told us to retire,
And then Spotty's flow of language set the water-carts on fire.

'Im and me was lucky, for two-thirds of us was dead,
With their greasy 'black Marias' and the shrapnel overhead.
And every time they missed us when the fire was murderous
'ot,
Old Spotty says 'Honcore! Honcore!' that's French for Rotten
shot'.
And then at last there came the time, we got 'em on the go,
And 'im and me was fightin' at a little place called Mo
(Meaux).

A-lying down together in an 'ole dug with our 'ands,
For you gets it quick and sudden if you moves about or stands.
We was sharing 'arf a fag we was, Yus! Turn and turn about,
When I felt 'im move towards me, and he ses, 'Oh mate I'm
out.'
'Is eyes they couldn't see me – they never will no more,
But 'is twisted mouth it muttered, 'So long chum, Oh Revore!'
It's never been the same since then, cos 'im and me was pals,
And if I could 'ave 'im with me now, you could keep your
fancy gals.
'E's spouting French in 'eavan, and it's no good feelin' sore,
But Gawd knows how I miss him, – 'So long Spotty, Oh
Revore!'